Out of
Darkness
Into Light

A SPIRITUAL DIRECTORS INTERNATIONAL BOOK

Out of Darkness Into Light

*Spiritual Guidance in the Quran
with Reflections from Jewish and Christian Sources*

JAMAL RAHMAN,
KATHLEEN SCHMITT ELIAS,
and ANN HOLMES REDDING

Morehouse Publishing

An imprint of Church Publishing Incorporated
HARRISBURG—NEW YORK

Morehouse Publishing, 4775 Linglestown Road, Harrisburg, PA 17112
Morehouse Publishing, 445 Fifth Avenue, New York, NY 10016
Morehouse Publishing is an imprint of Church Publishing Incorporated.

Cover design by Brenda Klinger

Visit the authors at www.spiritualityofquran.com

Library of Congress Cataloging-in-Publication Data

Rahman, Jamal.
    Out of darkness into light : spiritual guidance in the Quran with reflections from Jewish and Christian sources / Jamal Rahman, Kathleen Schmitt Elias, and Ann Holmes Redding.
       p.   cm.
    Includes bibliographical references.
    ISBN-13: 978-0-8192-2338-8 (pbk.)
    ISBN-10: 0-8192-2338-7 (pbk.)
    1. Koran. 2. Islam—Prayers and devotions. I. Elias, Kathleen Schmitt. II. Redding, Ann Holmes. III. Title.
BP130.R34   2009
297.1'2261—dc22

                                           2008047489

Printed in the United States of America

09 10 11 12 13 14   10 9 8 7 6 5 4 3 2 1

In the name of God, All-Merciful and Compassionate

———

To the memory of my beloved parents,
Ataur and Suraiya Rahman

And spread over them humbly the wings of thy tenderness, and say:
O my Sustainer! Bestow Thy grace upon them, even as they cherished
and reared me when I was a child.
(Quran 17:24)

———

To my treasured Torah teachers,
Rabbi Ted Falcon and Olivier BenHaim

Let regard for your teacher be equivalent to your reverence for Heaven.
(Avot 4:12)

———

To all my Ancestors whose lives bore testimony to the one God

You will know the truth, and the truth will make you free.
(John 8:32)

Allah is the One Who sends to His Servant manifest Signs,
that He may lead you from the depths of Darkness into the Light.

(Quran 57:9)

Contents

Acknowledgments

Jamal: I would like to express my deepest gratitude and love to my brother, Kamal, and his wife, Naz; my sister, Aysu; my daughter, Kristina; my nephews, Diran, Neal, Tareq, and Javed; and my nieces, Esha, Emana, Suraiya, and Ummul. I also extend heartfelt thanks to my colleagues and friends Karen Lindquist, Katayoon Naficy, Sally Jo Vargas, Linda Jo Pym, Faren Bachel, and Debra Lajmodiere, my "Interfaith Amigos" Rabbi Ted Falcon and Pastor Don Mackenzie, and the cherished members of Interfaith Community Church.

Kate: I lovingly acknowledge my righteous parents, who first pointed my toes on the spiritual path; my sisters and brother, Barb, Diane, and Mike, who have always inspired me with their inner journeys and supported me in mine; my Sufi teacher and co-author, Jamal Rahman; and my rabbi, Ted Falcon, who welcomed me into the Tribe of Israel. I also thank Lynne Carol, Nancy Green, Jesse Green, Rabbi Ted Falcon, Rabbi Marti Leviel, Olivier BenHaim, and Amy Bearmon for reading portions of my Jewish reflections and enriching them with helpful suggestions. (That said, I take full responsibility for any errors or questionable interpretations.)

Ann: I am fully aware that it takes several villages to keep me on the right path. I am indebted to my beloved family: especially, my sisters, Rupa and Judi; my brothers-in-law, Gunther and Stuart; and my nieces and nephews,

India, Stefan, Sophia, Lucas, and Monika. My godchildren Khuthaza, Mkhululi, Paul, Miles, and David keep me inspired. I get by with (more than a little) help from the friends who have supported me in this project: Ayesha Anderson, Judy Andrews, Grant Burger, Janet Campbell, Rod Cardoza, Colette Casavant, Jalaledin Ebrahim, Laura Foreman, Kevin Higgins, Susan Hutchison and Steve Kiyono, Robin Jensen, Abdul Quddus McCarthy, Ali Altaf Mian, Susan Moran, Susan Nicoll, Sue Reid, Beth Sherman, Doug Thorpe, Jaymes Taylor, and Archbishop Desmond Tutu. My communities at the Al Islam Center of Seattle, St. Clement's Church, St. Mark's Cathedral, the Episcopal Diocese of Olympia, the Episcopal Diocese of Rhode Island, and in the Re-evaluation Counseling movement, the Feelings meeting, and the Women Writers Group have been present for me in innumerable ways. Thank you all.

The three of us gratefully acknowledge Liz Budd Ellmann, Executive Director of Spiritual Directors International, for her abiding support of this project, and Nancy Fitzgerald, Acquisitions Editor at Morehouse Publishing, for her enthusiastic support. Our dear friend Jerry Pettitz graciously provided the author photos for the cover of this book.

Jamal and Ann readily admit that without Kate's patient prodding, brilliant compositional skills, abundant good humor, fabulous lattes, and generous hospitality, this book would never have come out of darkness into light. We thank God for you, Kate!

Last but not least, we thank Kate's computer-savvy sister, Diane Marie Chan, for setting up a blog site where we can continue our interfaith conversations about the Quran and its sibling texts. (Visit us at www.spirituality ofquran.com.)

Introduction

To our honored guests who have opened the cover and ventured into the pages of this book, a sincere welcome to the world of the Quran and its sibling texts, the sacred scriptures of Judaism and Christianity. As the last in a series of revealed scriptures of the three Abrahamic faiths, the Quran has not really been integrated into the cultural literacy of readers in the non-Muslim West, a deficit that we hope to help rectify in these pages. Especially since 9/11, the Quran has been an object of suspicion and sometimes loathing by those who know nothing of its deeply spiritual contents. The truth is that although the Quran, like other scriptures, has unpleasant verses that political zealots seize upon to justify extremism and violence, the Holy Book of Islam is actually a compendium of practical and spiritual advice for anyone who seeks a more meaningful life and a closer connection to the divine Source of all that is. It is, as the title of our book suggests, a guide to lead us out of darkness into light.

Here it should be said that our title, taken from a verse in the Quran, in no way implies that light is superior to darkness. Linguistically and culturally, we are conditioned to see "light" as representing hope and radiance, whereas "darkness" often symbolizes gloom, or worse. In spiritual language, however, darkness and light are equal in value, interdependent, and essential to each other. Just as a seed needs to germinate in the dark before sprouting to its destiny, Muhammad needed the dark womb of a Meccan cave to gestate into a prophet who brought light to the world. The Quran itself has its roots in the womb of silence and darkness: it was in the mystery of the night in the Meccan cave that Muhammad uttered the first verses of the Quran. A Quranic verse says that because God makes the night as a robe and sleep as a repose, it is possible for every day to be a resurrection (25:1).

To preempt any complaints that we are focusing only on the beauty of the Quran and glossing over its unpleasant passages, we quote the revered Gandhi, who said it is essential to acknowledge that every holy book has truths and untruths—especially, he would add with a wink, your own! All scriptural writings, as Gandhi pointed out, are open to interpretation. The Quran does have difficult and awkward verses whose meaning depends on the interpreter's state of consciousness and intention. In the imagery of the Sufi poet Rumi, both bee and wasp drink from the same flower, but one produces nectar and the other, a sting. There are verses in the Quran that, if read literally and in historical isolation, lend themselves to exploitation. For example, the Quran tells us, "Take not the Jews and Christians for your friends and protectors. They are friends and protectors to each other" (5:51). Without knowing the historical context of this verse, one could certainly read it as a condemnation of Jews and Christians, but scholars agree that this verse refers only to a specific historical incident and is certainly not a categorical condemnation. Another verse in the very same chapter affirms the basic goodness of other believers: "Those who believe, those who follow the Jewish scriptures, the Christians, the Sabians, and any who believe in God and the Final Day and do good, all shall have their reward with their Sustainer and they will not come to fear and grief" (5:69).

Detractors often quote another verse—"Religion in the sight of God is Islam"—to "prove" that Muslims militantly believe theirs is the only true religion. In fact, "Islam" refers not to the specific religion of Muslims but to any religion that is characterized by surrender to God. To the squabbling members of the Abrahamic faiths—Jews, Christians, and Muslims—the Quran says, "Our God and your God is one and the same, and it is unto God that we all surrender ourselves" (29:46). In this context we wish to add that this "one and the same" God is the Source and Cherisher of every human on planet Earth: men, women, and children; heterosexual, gay, lesbian, and transgendered people; liberals, conservatives, and "undecideds"; rich, poor, and middle class; saints, sinners, and sincere seekers—all are created by and for the God of infinite compassion and mercy, and all are invited to join us as we explore the path of surrender as it is described in the Holy Quran.

As a source of spiritual guidance, the Quran has dozens of verses that could be considered "foundational"—verses to be consulted again and again as we confront the bewildering paradoxes and mysteries of life. Just to whet your appetite, here are half a dozen that the three of us turn to almost daily:

- "Of knowledge We have given you but a little" (17:85). Every event and circumstance in our lives is part of a larger story, and it is advisable not to be quick to judge.

- "And in everything have We created opposites so that you might bear in mind that God alone is one" (51:49). Polarity is evident in all of creation. Without pain and sorrow, how would we know joy and happiness? Honey is sweet in contrast to vinegar. The poet Rumi says that God turns us from one feeling to another so that we may have not just one but two wings with which to fly.

- "Everywhere you turn is the Face of Allah" (2:115). Everyone and everything, in essence, is animated with God's spirit and all are unimaginably interconnected. If a drop of the wine of Vision could rinse our eyes, says Rumi, everywhere we looked, we would weep with wonder. To illustrate our interwoven connectedness, sages in every age have marveled that one cannot pluck a petal without the troubling of a star.

- "Is it not enough that your Sustainer is a witness?" (41:53). Such awareness will keep us on the "straight path," offer hope in difficult times, and make us realize that the only approval we need to seek is that of our Sustainer and Cherisher.

- "The human being can have nothing but that for which he strives" (53:39). God, the Provider of grace unbounded, bestows that grace on those who work for it. In the imagery of the nineteenth-century Hindu saint Ramakrishna, God's grace is like a breeze always present and available, but we have to raise our sails to catch the wind.

- "All that dwells upon the earth is perishing, yet still abides the Face of your Sustainer, majestic, splendid" (55:26–27). No matter how important our dramas and melodramas may seem, they will pass and only one reality abides. That reality is the Eternal One, and although our physical days are numbered, we will forever be part of that One.

This has been just a sampling of the hundreds of verses of beauty and wisdom in the Quran. Throughout this book we have woven many more verses around a number of themes and supplemented them with sayings of the Prophet Muhammad, the words of Rumi and other Sufi poets, and relevant quotations and insights from Jewish and Christian scriptures. Although our primary focus is on the Quran as a source of spiritual guidance, we hope that the inclusion of passages and commentary from Jewish and Christian sources will make the world of the Quran more accessible to non-Muslim readers and demonstrate to Muslim readers how similar in essence Islamic spirituality is to that of earlier "people of the Book." Our experience has been that by contemplating each other's scriptures with informed minds and open hearts, we have come to see how naturally the three Abrahamic faiths complement each other and how beautifully they enrich our understanding of our own traditions.

Our stories

You perhaps should know from the outset that the book you are about to read does not pretend to be the definitive text on any of the holy scriptures, and as you will learn from our individual stories, we are hardly typical representatives of our three faith traditions. Nevertheless, the information and insights that we present are founded in deep love for our individual traditions, mutual respect for each others' paths, and common regard for the spiritual guidance to be found in the Holy Quran.

Jamal

My spiritual journey began more than half a century ago on the other side of the globe, when I was born into a Sunni Muslim family in what was then East Pakistan, now the independent country of Bangladesh. My paternal ancestors were rural Islamic teachers and healers with an orientation towards

Sufism, the mystical dimension of Islam. A Sufi is a Muslim—that is, a servant of God—who is committed to living the spirit of Islam. The Sufi focus is on essence rather than on form, on compassion and awareness rather than on rigorous attachment to theology. The Sufi sensibilities of my ancestors pervaded the home where I grew up and sowed the seeds of my current life. My parents saw to it that I was firmly grounded in the principles of Islam as well as Sufi spirituality and took me with them on Hajj and numerous visits to the holy cities of Mecca and Medina.

From an early age I have been entranced by the beauty and possibilities offered by two Quranic verses that formed the heart of my family's spirituality. The first verse is about spaciousness: "Allah has spread out the earth as a carpet for you so you may walk therein on spacious paths" (20:53). My paternal grandfather, a rural spiritual teacher and healer of note, used the word "spaciousness" extensively in his conversations, sermons, and teachings. Without inner spaciousness, he insisted, we cannot walk the earth on spacious paths. For love, joy, and peace to flow in us so that we can do what is beautiful, we need to create inner spaciousness by transforming the ego and unclenching the heart. My grandfather constantly taught that it is incumbent on a Muslim to do the inner work, and this insight, which I heard often in our household, struck a chord in my heart.

In the other verse that resonates for me, the Holy Book says that God created diversity in humanity so that we might "get to know one another" (49:13). My father was a professional diplomat, first representing Pakistan and later, as the country split into two nation states, representing Bangladesh. Both my parents taught and lived the teaching that differences in nationalities, politics, and religion are part of the divine design, and the best way to overcome feelings of awkwardness or bias is to get to know the other on a personal level. When there is friendship, even vastly opposing beliefs no longer loom as a threat. Growing up in various countries, my siblings and I enjoyed friendships with people of different nationalities and religions. As a teenager I often pondered on this verse and fantasized about working in a career that would create communities of hope and peace by building on the principle of getting to know one another on a personal level.

Because of my father's diplomatic career, I had many opportunities to study with Muslim teachers in several countries of the Middle East, including

Iran, Turkey, Saudi Arabia, and Egypt. It was in Iran and Turkey that in my formative years I was introduced to the teachings of the thirteenth-century poet and mystic Maulana Jelaluddin Rumi, who, it is commonly said, unlocked the mysteries of the Quran. A vast number of Rumi's utterances revolved around verses from the Quran and the collected sayings of the Prophet known as *hadith*, and indeed he was often heard to say, "I am a slave of the Quran; I am dust on the path of Muhammad." In many circles Rumi is considered a second Muhammad and the collection of his utterances, a second Quran. Because of my fascination with Rumi, whenever my father gave me a Quranic verse to ponder on, he would ask me to supply a Rumi verse that illuminated the Quranic insight. Then my mother, who loved stories, offered a relevant teaching story for all of us to reflect on. It was a delightful way to expand my awareness of Quranic verses. It also became my favorite way of deepening my understanding of the Quran, and today it is my preferred way of teaching the Holy Book.

As I approached adulthood, there was some expectation that I would earn a "useful degree." My studies brought me to the United States and by the time I finished my master's degree at the University of California at Berkeley, I knew what the next step had to be: not to pursue another "useful degree" but to undertake an intensive apprenticeship in Sufi practice under the direction of my beloved parents. My steps were bringing me slowly but surely towards the ministry that is so dear to my heart today.

The sudden and tragic death of my mother and, in the space of twenty days, the death of my broken-hearted father, kindled a yearning in my heart to share my parents' teachings in an authentic community. With some trepidation I began teaching classes in my home on the topic of inner work. To my surprise, a steady number of people began coming to these classes, enough to sustain a modest livelihood. As the numbers grew, it struck me that this group of fellow seekers was the community I had been longing for. With the help of key friends, notably Karen Lindquist, we began to lay the foundations of a lasting community. In the first few years we were meeting in each others' homes, and members were most gracious in accommodating our ever-increasing numbers. Over the course of our first six years we grew to three hundred strong and we urgently needed a bigger place to meet.

In 1998 we experienced a miracle. We were led to an enchanting church building, a classic white frame church built by a community of Lutherans in 1890. The original owners had stipulated in their deed that the building could not be sold, but could be given away to a "like-minded group." The current occupants were indeed like-minded, but their numbers were so small that they were unable to pay the monthly bills for basic utilities. Through an astonishing turn of events the church was "given away" to us, several members of that congregation joined us, and we became the Interfaith Community Church of Seattle. And then I, fulfilling my adolescent dream of helping to create a community of hope and peace, became the Muslim Sufi Minister of the new congregation.

It is a sweet paradox that most of the Christian congregants advocated removal of the word "Church," while some of the Muslims argued persuasively to retain the word in the spirit of the Prophet Muhammad, who famously said of his mosque when he asked delegations of Jews and Christians to do Shabbat and Christian services there, "It is simply a place consecrated to God." There is another paradox, particularly dear to my heart: whereas the congregation is largely from a Christian background, it is willing to have a Muslim minister and is touchingly open to the Muslim message of awareness and compassion for self and for each other in the quest for union with the Eternal. Some congregants remain rooted in their original faith traditions while watering those roots with insights and practices from other faiths. Others do not belong to any specific religion, choosing instead to create their own spiritual path by exploring many different teachings and practices.

In the course of my ministry I had the joy and privilege of meeting Kate Elias, who quickly became a family friend. Kate is a consummate scholar with an artist's heart, and together for a period of two years we explored the beauty and wisdom of selected Quranic verses. A few years ago Kate found her home in Judaism and true to her nature, she has delved deep into the Jewish scriptures. Blessed with a heart-felt knowledge of Christianity and Islam, she is able to appreciate the beauty of Jewish scriptures in a uniquely multifaceted way. Kate has been of invaluable personal support to me and to the interfaith cause.

I first met Ann a few years ago when, in her capacity as director of faith formation at the Episcopal cathedral in Seattle, she invited me to speak on Islam and Rumi. From the beginning I was struck by the depth of her spirituality, or as my grandfather and parents would say, by the spaciousness of her heart. Ann is a scholar of the Christian Testament and her understanding of the Christian Holy Book is both personal and intense. As she studied Islam and allowed it to perfume her heart, her love for Jesus grew sweeter and her understanding of the Christian scriptures even deeper. With courage and grace she has accepted the calling to become a Muslim while remaining rooted in the Christian tradition, thus providing a unique and exciting model of interfaith ways of being. I have delighted in co-teaching classes with Ann, who has become a good friend.

As I look back at the twists and turns that have brought me to my current ministry, I am filled with gratitude for all the people and opportunities that have graced my life. And as I look toward the future I hope, with God's Grace, to continue striving for the ultimate goal that awaits each one of us: "Well pleased is God with them and well pleased are they with God: this is the ultimate success" (Quran 5:119). I take my cue from the delightful words of the Prophet Muhammad: "When you arrived here everyone was smiling and laughing but you were crying. Live such a life that when you leave, everyone is crying but you are smiling and laughing."

Kate

The story of my relationship with the Quran and the path of surrender began, appropriately enough, with a broken heart. Needing to understand what had gone wrong in my relationship with a man who happened to be a Muslim from South Asia, I poured out the sorry tale to a counselor from a similar background, who listened compassionately and assured me that I had made a healthy decision to cut my losses and run. As I thanked him and rose to leave, he said, "We're not done yet. Now we need to see what we can do to heal your heart." To my great good fortune, that counselor was Jamal, and he led me through an exquisite Sufi meditation using many of the spiritual practices included in this book.

That meditation changed my life forever. For the first time in almost sixty years, I heard God calling my name—not the "call" to a religious vocation, which I thought I heard when I was seventeen, or the call to rejoin Christianity after a long period of agnosticism, but a quiet, personal call saying "Kate, I'm here, let's talk." After just one meditation, I was hooked. Eager to learn more about the Sufi way of life, I asked Jamal to be my *sheikh*—my teacher—and we met regularly over the next two years for meditation, *dhikr* (sacred chanting in remembrance of the Beloved), and study of the Quran. As a singer, I delighted in learning Sufi chants and making up my own tunes for several Quranic recitations. As I scanned the Holy Book for likely verses to memorize, I soon discovered why I had been able to hear God call my name: in my favorite verse God says, "I am closer to you than your jugular vein" (50:16). You can't get closer than that!

Much though I treasured my quiet study with Jamal, at a certain point I realized that I wanted a framework for my deepening spirituality, and I also needed a community of fellow seekers. Christianity and mainstream Islam were not a good fit for me, so what was I to do? The truth, I told Jamal, is that for more than thirty years I have felt that I have a Jewish soul. "Well!" he replied, "Have you been to Bet Alef?" I had never heard of Bet Alef—as a newcomer to the world of "alternative" spirituality I knew almost nothing about the religious scene in Seattle despite having lived here all my life. It took some months for me to work up the nerve to crash the party, but eventually a pair of friends took me in tow and brought me to Shabbat services at Bet Alef Meditative Synagogue one Friday night. That was all it took: in a single evening I found my faith home, my spiritual framework, and my community. Over the next two years I learned enough Hebrew and Jewish basics to convince the rabbi and the *beit din* (a small panel of "judges") that I could be a bona fide Jew, whereupon I went to the *mikveh* (ritual bath, the precursor to Christian baptism) and became a Member of the Tribe. There's more about that in chapter 13, "Community." Two years later, having mastered the esoteric art of *trope*, the method of chanting from the Torah, I was privileged to carry our beloved Torah—a little old scroll from Czechoslovakia that miraculously survived the Holocaust—and chant publicly from its hand-lettered pages. In that moment I joined the millennia-long line of women who call themselves Bat Mitzvah, daughter of the commandment.

As necessary and life-affirming as it was for me to formally commit to Judaism, I have not completely foresworn my Christian roots nor have I abandoned my love for the many Quranic verses that guided me along my Sufi path. I still sing vespers every week with a Gregorian chant group—a group that includes three Sufis and four or five other friends from unconventional backgrounds. In a nice interfaith twist, the group enthusiastically adopted a vespers program that I designed for the Jewish month of Elul, the period of preparation for the High Holy Days! (A vespers service consists primarily of psalms, the prayers that Jesus would have said, so it is not really such a stretch to do a Jewish prayer service using Christian psalmody.)

As for continuing attachment to my favorite Quranic verses, I can only say that one of the highlights of my life was the day Jamal persuaded the imam of the mosque in Akko, Israel, to permit someone from our interfaith tour group to chant a verse in that sacred space. As Jamal beckoned to me and I stepped forward to sing, the imam signaled "uh-uh" with his finger and then gestured that I should ascend to the women's balcony. Up I went along a steep stairway inside a narrow tower, pivoting to negotiate the curve with every step and savoring the sensation of adding my footsteps to the deep impressions made in the stone by the feet of countless women over the centuries. Finally I arrived in the balcony and gasped at the beauty of the sanctuary below me. Then I stepped toward the railing, fixed my gaze on the *mihrab* (the niche that indicates the direction of prayer in Islam), took a deep breath, and opened my mouth to sing. Out soared the words of *Ayat-ul-Kursi* (Verse about the Throne), celebrating the God of inexhaustible compassion who sits upon a throne of glory (Quran 2:255). "God neither slumbers nor sleeps," says this ecstatic verse, echoing the words of one of my favorite psalms (121:4) written centuries earlier. Hearing the sound of my own voice declaring those joyful words in that holy place, I was profoundly grateful to have been awakened from my long spiritual slumber, to have heard the voice of the Beloved and been given the grace to follow its call wherever it may lead.

Ann

When Jamal invited me to join this project, I jumped at the chance. For over a year, I had been bursting with enthusiasm over the ways that I kept seeing the Christian scriptures and the Quran illuminate each other. This ongoing multi-textual light show had come as yet one more unexpected gift from the convergence of Islam with my Christian belief and practice.

Had anyone told me at the end of February 2006 that I would be a Muslim before April rolled around, I would have shaken my head in concern for the person's mental health. True, I had invited speakers on Islam to participate in the adult faith formation classes at the church where I had been working for five years. After all, my job there as director of faith formation had started on September 1, 2001, and even prior to 9/11 the church had taken a lead in local interfaith activities. My mind had certainly been engaged by what I was learning about Islam, especially when scholars untangled the contradictions between the core tenets of the faith and the sometimes culturally bound practices of some Muslims. I was moved deeply when one presenter gave us a glimpse of the beauty of Islamic devotion by allowing us to witness him at prayer. However, it wasn't until the session on Islamic approaches to repentance and forgiveness that I recognized two practices as somehow mine. In fact, with their focus on the heart, they seemed so familiar that I thought perhaps they had simply slipped my mind. I went home and repeated on my own what I had learned earlier in the evening. Ten days later, I was confronted with a personal dilemma to which complete surrender to God was the obvious—and only—solution. I knew that the word *Islam* means "self-surrender to God," and I knew I needed to take on the identity of surrender from that point on. So, that night I found myself saying the words of the Islamic testimony of faith, the *Shahada*, and—with God and my own soul as witnesses—became a Muslim.

My current situation in life reflects the consequences of that action. By the time you read this introduction, I may well no longer be permitted to be an Episcopal priest because of my identity as a Muslim. The thought that I was leaving Christianity never entered my mind on that night in March 2006. In fact, it seemed I was following Jesus into the welcoming doors of Islam, which was as much a home for him as the Judaism of his birth and practice. I counter the charges of unfaithfulness to his love and care with a request that my Christian sisters and brothers shift the implied metaphor from that of an unfaithful wife to that of a mother of a second child.

The shift in my ordained status also shapes the tone and content of my contributions to this book. My writing here has become a kind of parting "love song" while I reluctantly relinquish the cherished responsibilities and privileges of priesthood and let God rewire my connections within my

Christian community. Indeed, I am seizing this project as an opportunity to give a fitting introduction of my Muslim kin to my Christian people. The "problem child" in the family feud has for centuries been Jesus, so he gets most of my interpretive attention. I have made a choice to focus on some, by no means all, of the Christian doctrines that have been used to reinforce the obstacles to deeper connections among the Abrahamic traditions. I apologize in advance for the necessary trade-off of relatively few Christian counterparts to the rich array of traditional practices and legends Jamal and Kate have offered.

I gladly sing the Christian part in the trio for this book, but as time goes on I am more and more aware that there is only one Song. This realization came home most powerfully to me the first time I sang one of my mother's favorite spirituals after I had become a Muslim. You will find that this music of my African-American heritage was my earliest soundtrack of the Spirit, my auditory introduction to the Creator, the strongest of the threads that bind my ethnic heritage to my faith. My mother used spirituals as lullabies in the nursery I shared with my two younger sisters and with them painted in my subconscious a host of dark-skinned Biblical characters, including Jesus. Sent as a son by a God of love and justice, he was one of us, the one who "knows the troubles I see." From my scholar uncle I knew that many of these songs were coded messages, on the surface about "pie in the sky by and by," while whispering from their depths plans for escape from physical bondage. We actually continued that tradition in the rural Episcopal parish that became interracial when we and another black family joined it. The choir mistress/organist there was a family friend and, unbeknownst to most of the parishioners, an African American. Julliard training notwithstanding, Mrs. Glover might not have gotten the job had she vocally challenged the assumptions made on the basis of her pale coloring. But along with the Victorian Anglican hymns and anthems so beloved in the Episcopal Church of my childhood, we also sang spirituals at St. John's, Concord. Only as an adult did I learn of the racial tensions in that church—the quiet dissolution of the youth group when I became old enough to join or the cancellation of the Sunday School picnic upon my mother's discovery that it was to be held on a day when black children couldn't swim at the local amusement park. The spirituals that we sang there made it a home place for the God I already knew. So a half century later, when, as a new Muslim, I sang in church the one spiritual that historians most clearly trace specifically to the African *Episcopal* Christian experience, I was overwhelmed by the power of the convergence. "When I fall on my knees," the refrain goes, "with my face to the rising sun, O Lord, have mercy on me." Hours earlier, alone in my apartment, in Muslim prayer I had been doing that very thing—falling on (or in my arthritic condition, toward) my knees with my face to the rising sun. There in church I seemed to hear the echoes of my African Christian-Muslim ancestors saying, "Daughter, welcome home."

As you might infer from these brief snapshots of our spiritual journeys, there is an amazing synergy when the three of us sit around a table sharing a meal and talking about the Quran from our various perspectives. The one constant is Jamal, who is grounded in a lifetime of meditation and contemplation on the beautiful verses of the Quran. Kate and Ann discovered the Holy Book relatively late in life, and have read it through a variety of lenses, though in many ways they can use the same glasses because of their shared background in Christianity and similar grounding in Jewish texts. Both delight in the "Aha!" moments when a Quranic verse supports their own spirituality or offers a fresh insight into themes of their Jewish and Christian traditions, and all three of us hope that you too will experience similar moments as you become acquainted with the sacred text that provides inspiration and spiritual guidance for the world's 1.4 billion Muslims.

A few words about this book

Our goal in organizing the chapters of this book was to lead from the first impulse to seek spiritual direction to the final stage of a soul peacefully surrendered in service to the Holy One by whatever name you wish to use. In part 1 we focus on the desire for guidance and possible sources, especially but not exclusively the Quran. In part 2 we address many of the mysteries of life that cause us to ask ourselves, "What's it all about?" In part 3, we embark on the journey of surrender to the Source of our being. In each chapter, you will hear three distinct voices. Jamal leads off with the Muslim perspective, which is the primary focus of this book, and then Kate and Ann provide reflections from the Jewish and Christian traditions, respectively. Along the way we share inspiration and insights from the three Abrahamic traditions and offer a number of spiritual practices that have worked well in our own lives. Some practices are clearly pegged as such, while others are described in the context of our reflections. At the end of the book is a collection of Quranic verses and sayings of the Prophet Muhammad that you may find useful for guidance and meditation. Our prayer is that this book, by God's Grace, will help seekers from any tradition to evolve into the fullness of being and come to be of authentic service to God's creation.

Before we usher you into the first chapter, we need to say a few words about sources and semantics. This being a book about the spirituality of the Quran, the primary source is, of course, the Holy Book itself. There are numerous translations and interpretations available both online and in print, and we have chosen freely among them. At first we documented our choices, but this soon seemed unmanageable and unnecessary in a book that is intended more for spiritual guidance than for academic erudition. A list of the versions we consulted is provided in the bibliography at the end of the book.

A similar policy governed our treatment of the hadith and the many references to the spiritual imagery of the poet Rumi. Jamal learned both the hadith and Rumi's poetry orally and in a variety of languages from his parents and childhood teachers, and he has so internalized them since childhood that it is not possible to identify specific sources. On the rare occasion when we knowingly used a specific translation of Rumi, it is noted in the text. As we have done for the Quran, we have listed a number of Rumi titles in the bibliography.

The Jewish reflections revolve around three primary sources: the Tanakh, Pirke Avot, and Midrash. "TaNaKh" is an acronym for the Hebrew Bible, which is made up of the Torah (the five Books of Moses), Nevi'im (the books of the prophets), and Kethuvim ("writings" such as the Psalms, Proverbs, and Song of Songs). Most non-Jews probably know the Tanakh by the more familiar term "Old Testament," a label that has the unfortunate effect of suggesting that the sacred scriptures of Judaism have been eclipsed by the "New Testament" of Christianity. In fact, at the same time that the Christian Testament was being compiled, there was an enormous outpouring of Jewish scholarship that resulted in the other two sources used in this book. *Pirke Avot*, which means sayings of the fathers, is a Talmudic text full of advice for living a good Jewish life. Like the Tanakh, it is neatly catalogued by chapter and verse, which makes it easy to cite. Convention is to drop "Pirke" in the citation, so you will see references to, for example, Avot 1:14. Midrash is a vast collection of stories and legends told to explain or expound on events in the Torah. Many of these legends have become so much a part of Jewish lore that they seem to be part of the Torah itself. The most popularly accessible compendium of midrashim is *The Book of Legends (Sefer Ha-Aggadah)* compiled by H. N. Bialik and Y. H. Ravnitzky. Full information is provided in the bibliography. Biblical quotations are from the "New JPS Translation" by the Jewish Publication Society.

For reasons that may be inferred from comments in the preceding paragraph, the scriptures that are specifically Christian—the Gospels, Acts, Epistles, and Revelation—are called Christian Testament rather than New Testament. Scriptural quotations in the Christian reflections are from the New Revised Standard Version.

And finally, we need to say a few words about inclusive language. It seems a cop-out to say that everyone knows the Divine Being transcends gender and so please just ignore all the masculine pronouns in our various scriptures. Wherever we could do so gracefully, we replaced the words "he," "his," or "him" with the words "God," "the Eternal," "Sustainer," "Cherisher," or a similar well-established name for the Divine. In our own texts we have made every effort not to affix a gender either to God or to our gentle readers. Where we were unable to avoid male-gendered pronouns for God in scriptural passages, we beg forgiveness and encourage you to look past the pronoun and see the ineffable, indefinable Holy One, who cannot be contained in human thought or human language, but who *can* be contained in the human heart.

PART I

Spiritual Guidance
in the Abrahamic
Traditions

1

Turning to the Spiritual Path

The Guidance of God—that is the only Guidance.
(Quran 2:120)

Bring a heart turned in devotion to God

In Islam, whose name means surrender to God, the central goal is to live our lives in the spirit of surrender to our Creator. Seekers of any religious tradition have a similar desire to achieve union with Divine Reality. Whether we call it surrender, redemption, union, or quest for inner freedom, the journey is the same. It is a lifelong adventure, and along the way there are many twists and turns, many opportunities to get lost or go astray. There are no maps to guide the human heart, but in every religion there are teachers and basic guidebooks—scriptures and sacred texts that point the way toward Mystery. In Islam, we have the Quran. We also have fourteen centuries of wisdom distilled from the Holy Book by Islamic sages, mystics, and teachers. From the Quran we learn, for instance, of the delights that we will enjoy in the Divine Presence if we have learned to bring our hearts "turned in devotion to God" (50:33), and from the thirteenth-century Sufi mystic Maulana Jelaluddin Rumi we learn what that devotion should look like. When a woman asked her lover if he loved her as much as he loved himself, he replied that his whole being was so full of her that there was nothing left of his own existence except his name. Feel toward God, Rumi says, as that lover felt toward his beloved.

This is the total surrender to the Divine that observant Muslims seek to achieve over the course of their lives, and truly it takes a lifetime. "Die before you die," said the Prophet Muhammad, by which he meant die to your own ego, tear down the walls around your heart, and offer yourself in service to God.

Veils of heath and wealth

To be sure, the path of surrender—of Islam—requires ceaseless attention to what Sufi teachers call "the inner work," and we are not inclined to volunteer for such hard work unless circumstances compel us to do so. Ordinarily we hide behind the twin veils of health and wealth, which protect the illusion that we are sufficient unto ourselves. When our health is good and we feel financially and emotionally secure, any talk about spiritual practices and surrender to God seems irrelevant and inconvenient. But should one of these veils be ripped by ill health, say, or by the loss of a loved one or a dramatic downturn in our sense of security, our restless hearts become desperate for solace. We ask deeper questions. We feel the need for help from a Source higher than personality or human institutions. The beloved fourteenth-century Persian sage Hafiz understood this well. In a tender poem beautifully interpreted by Daniel Ladinsky in his book, *The Subject Tonight is Love*, Hafiz says that "something missing" in his heart makes his need for God "absolutely clear."

Almost without realizing it, as we begin our search for that Higher Power we take our first steps along the spiritual path. "Show us the straight way, the way of those on whom You have bestowed Your Grace," we plead in the words of the Quran (1:6–7). Soon we sense that we don't have all the answers, that we are inadequate to the task. If we are serious about doing our inner work, it is time to find a spiritual guide. Without a guide, says Rumi, we would need two hundred years for a two-day journey. To travel up the mountain, to use a familiar metaphor, it is wise to consult with someone who knows the terrain.

The teacher kindles the light

In the words of the Prophet Muhammad, "The teacher kindles the light; the oil is already in the lamp." The "oil" in this case is the divine essence of every human soul. The Quran says that we are all *fitra*, that is, originally noble and good, created "in the best of molds," but that we are also capable of sinking to the "lowest of the low" (95:4–5). The teacher's role is to guide us as we become more fully connected to our divine essence and evolve into the fullness of our own being. With the teacher's guidance we learn practices and techniques that make us increasingly conscious of the divine breath within and empower us to make good choices based on compassion and higher awareness. Had Adam and Eve had such guidance, some Muslims like to say, they would not have made "slips" in heaven and had to spend time in the lower world learning to make right choices (Quran 2:36–37).

The teacher has a special place in the long tradition of Islamic spirituality because Islam has no official priesthood or ordained ministry. In the Sunni tradition (85% of Muslims), the designation of Imam, Maulana, or Sheikh can be self-appointed or bestowed by a community on an individual who has demonstrated learning and piety. In much of the Shia tradition (15% of Muslims), men can attain a variety of titles, including Imam, Mujtahid, and Ayatollah, after studying in schools of divinity for several years and demonstrating their scholarship by producing an extensive body of writing that is critiqued by learned scholars. Only in the last hundred years have the Shias developed this more formalized structure of religious authority.

Both Sunni and Shia Muslims share the same fundamental articles of faith in Islam. The differences are rooted in historic grievance about the choice of a political leader after the death of Prophet Muhammad in 632 CE. One group said the leader should be chosen by consensus and the other, by blood lineage of the Prophet. The former prevailed and they are called Sunnis (Adherents of the Prophet's Tradition). Those who believed the leadership rightfully belonged to Hazrat Ali (cousin and son-in-law of the Prophet) and his descendants are called Shias, shortened from Shia-l-Ali (Party of Ali). The Shias are also called "People of the Household of the Prophet." These political differences have spawned differences in forms of practices, which, to some, carry spiritual significance.

The religion of Islam has given birth to myriad spiritual teachers and sages in its fourteen hundred years of history. Especially in the first thousand years after the birth of Islam in the seventh century, when Islamic civilization flowered and flourished, there emerged an extraordinary number of spiritual teachers, some of whom were called Sufis. These remarkable teachers, belonging to either Sunni or Shia denominations, were Muslims who emphasized essence over form, substance over appearance. Focusing not on the letter of Islamic law but on the spirit of Islam, they have had an inestimable influence on seekers from many spiritual backgrounds through their schools, their extensive writings, and their wisdom passed on in the oral tradition. It is generally accepted that the spiritual beauty of Sufi teachings is largely responsible for the spread of Islam in South, Southeast, and Central Asia, where the majority of Muslims live, and in China, Russia, Europe, and parts of Africa.

Sadly, as Islam has become more conservative with the political and economic decline of the Muslim world, Sufis have had to keep a low profile. Once prominent in government and in mainstream activities, they are not welcome in the conservative culture of some Muslim regimes. Sufi teachers focus on spiritual growth rather than avoidance of divine punishment, which has become the focus of many conservative teachers. Whereas conservative Islamic teachers might emphasize the importance of prayers, for example, by telling practitioners that they will be punished in the hereafter if they neglect the five-times-a-day body prayer, Sufi teachers liken prayer to attendance at a celestial banquet. If you fail to pray, Sufis would say, you are missing out on the joy of the feast. That loss is your punishment.

Choosing someone who will "counsel with deeds rather than talk"

Just as we in Western societies consult counselors and therapists, people in Islamic societies often turn to spiritual teachers for advice and guidance. In every Muslim village, town, or city there are teachers with varying degrees of personal evolution, knowledge, and fame. In my hometown of Dhaka, the capital city of Bangladesh, every neighborhood has a number of *pirs*, or spiritual guides. Members of my extended family have their own favorite pir whom they consult frequently and in gratitude give a love offering of money or goods. These spiritual guides, it is often said, derive their *barrakka*, or spiritual power, from all-night prayers, because "in watches of the night, impressions are strongest and words most eloquent" (Quran 73:6).

In my own life, my primary spiritual guides have been my parents. As is customary in Islam, they taught their children to recite the Quran and absorb the tenets of the Faith. About the custom of visiting pirs, my parents offered two pieces of advice.

First, avoid teachers who are loud and aggressive, fiery in speech and noisy in action, eager to draw attention to themselves. Rumi describes them as "all fire and no light; all husk and no kernel."

Second, be aware that a genuine teacher is often "hidden," not easily recognized because of his or her humility. Such is the case of the hidden teacher in the story about two famous sheikhs who arrived ostentatiously at a local mosque and prepared to pray. One sheikh took his shoes off and carried them with him as he stepped inside the mosque. The other teacher carefully placed his shoes outside. After prayers, the sheikhs, whose every movement had been watched with intense interest, were asked to explain their actions. The first sheikh said that he took his shoes inside with him so that no one would be tempted to steal them, thus saving that person from wrongdoing. The other said that by keeping his shoes outside he gave someone the opportunity to resist a temptation to steal and thus gain merit in heaven. "How wise and noble," the townsfolk agreed among themselves. To get a better understanding, they went to a sage and asked which of the sheikhs was the "true" teacher. "Neither," replied the sage. "While you all were busy watching and judging, and the two sheikhs were engaged in their calculation of saving and gracing, none of you noticed a poor, shoeless man with a heart of gold who stepped into the mosque with reverence, prayed with deep fervor and devotion, and beseeched Allah to bless everyone. He is the real sheikh. His heart is turned in devotion to God and he simply brings to the moment a heart that can respond to God." Truly, the presence of such a guide in one's life is a precious blessing. This kind of teacher conforms to the description of an evolved being: one who is "humble before the Unseen and brings a heart that can respond" (Quran 50:33).

Thus, it is wise to exercise discernment in the choice of a spiritual guide. Even in the thirteenth century, Rumi observed that many have learnt to do some "birdcalls"—have learned enough Quranic verses to attract unschooled followers—but lack a heart-knowledge of the Holy Book. Choose someone who has some experiential knowledge of the path. Sages say that those who taste, know. In his book *Correct Islamic Doctrine*, the tenth-century master Ibn Khafif advises that we seek someone "the sight of whom reminds you of God and the awe of whom will move your heart, someone who will counsel you with the tongue of deeds, not words."

As helpful and necessary as it is to work with a good teacher, beware the tendency to become dependent on that teacher and to confuse him or her with your own radiant inner teacher. To illustrate this pitfall, a Sufi story tells about an advanced student who had studied with many teachers and presented himself to the fifteenth-century Sufi master Bahauddin, who was seated with his disciples in a great hall. With deep reverence, the student asked, "May I please study under you? My being would feel deeply honored and grateful." Bahauddin arose and ordered the student to leave the hall immediately. "Be off with you!" he shouted. "Leave, and don't ever return!" The dazed student left in a hurry, and in the stunned silence that followed, a couple of senior students asked the master why he was so hard on the poor student. "Very soon you will understand through a demonstration," the master replied.

Within a few minutes, a little bird fluttered into the hall. Confused and dazed, it darted back and forth, hitting this wall and that chair. Exhausted, it finally sat close to the master, unaware of an open window nearby. Bahauddin arose again, suddenly clapped his hands, and shouted loudly. Startled and scared, the bird flew off into freedom through the window.

Turning to his disciples, the master said, "This sound from me must have been rude, even insulting to the bird, wouldn't you say?" The master then explained that the student was close to a spiritual breakthrough but his progress was stalled because he was "teacher-dependent." He needed a push to arrive into a space where he could flap his own wings.

Both teacher and student need to be aware that the purpose of their relationship is not to turn the student into a clone or groupie of the master, but to open the windows of the heart so that the student and the Beloved can fly into each other's arms. The Prophet Muhammad said, "Take one step towards God, and God takes seven steps toward you; walk to God, and God comes running to you."

Jewish Reflections

Lead me along Your righteous path. (Ps. 5:9)

A poor peasant goes to his rabbi and says, "Rabbi, you've got to help me. The Lord has blessed me with a wonderful wife and six beautiful children, but He forgot to bless me with enough money to feed them or keep them in a proper house. We're all together in a single room, the kids are always underfoot, my wife is always scolding, and I am beside myself. What can I do?"

The rabbi thinks for a moment and then says, "I tell you what. Go and get a goat, and bring it inside to live with you and the family. Then come back and see me next week." The peasant is puzzled, but the rabbi has spoken, so he does as the rabbi advises.

A week later he's back in the rabbi's office. "Rabbi!" he cries. "What were you thinking?! My life was miserable before, but now it's impossible! That goat takes up more room than the kids. It stinks. It poops everywhere and it chews on anything in sight. What am I to do?!"

The rabbi nods and strokes his beard, and then he says, "So now get rid of the goat, and next week tell me how things are."

You can guess how the story ends. "Rabbi!" the peasant exults the following week. "You're a genius! Life is beautiful! I feel blessed beyond measure!"

The rabbi is not necessarily a genius, but this story from the rich lore of Eastern European Jewry illustrates the genius of Judaism in recognizing that practical advice can have a powerful influence on our spiritual well-being. The veils of poverty and personal problems can be just as effective as the veils of health and wealth in preventing us from seeing beyond our everyday lives and exploring the blessings of the spiritual journey. Jewish tradition teaches the potential for healing and renewal in our daily circumstances and gives us three millennia of teachers and texts to point the way.

The Hebrew Bible, like the Quran, is replete with admonitions to seek wisdom and guidance. In a typical example, Ecclesiastes tells us that "Wisdom is superior to folly as light is superior to darkness; a wise man has his eyes in his head, whereas a fool walks in darkness" (2:13–14).

"Out of darkness and into light," says the title of this book—but who shall lead us? The Eternal One, dwelling beyond time and space but also in the space of each human heart, is our primary Teacher. "Your word is a lamp to my feet, a light for my path," sings the psalmist (Ps. 119:105). "Guide me in Your true way and teach me, for You are God, my deliverer" (Ps. 25:5). And how does God guide? Sometimes, when we are quiet and open ("surrendered," in the word of Islam), God speaks in the ear of our innermost heart. More often, we hear God in the words of the prophets and rabbis, from Abraham in antiquity to the rabbi in our local shul or synagogue. "Apply your mind to discipline and your ears to wise sayings," says the book of Proverbs (23:12); "The ears of the wise seek out knowledge" (Prov. 18:15).

For a Jew, it is both an obligation and a sacred act to study and learn how to walk in the path of righteousness called Torah. "Get yourself a teacher, find someone to study with," exhorted the ancient rabbis (Avot 1:6). In practical terms, our guides for the past two thousand years have been rabbis—scholars who are ordained to teach and interpret Torah and to guide the faithful in terms of beliefs, customs, and rituals. (The word "rabbi" literally means "teacher" in Hebrew.) In every tradition of Judaism—and there are as many traditions as there are places where Judaism is practiced—communities gather around a rabbi, who serves as teacher, guide, and spiritual director. Where no rabbi is available, Jews often form *havurot* (plural of *havurah*, a fellowship or study group) in their own homes to discuss Torah and worship together. "Let your house be a meeting place for the wise; sit humbly at their feet; and, with thirst, drink in their words" (Avot 1:4). Even without the guidance of rabbis and fellow-seekers, we are expected to study Torah by ourselves and find there the wisdom to walk in the paths of righteousness. "I have gained more insight than all my teachers, for Your decrees are my study" (Ps. 119:99). In the Jewish tradition of *tikkun olam*, repairing the world, each one of us is responsible to study and to teach and learn from our companions, healing ourselves and bridging the gap between wounded ego and divine essence as we journey along the path to spiritual wholeness.

The guidelines for selecting a spiritual teacher are as common-sense in Judaism as they are in Islam. The first step is to recognize what kind of guidance you desire. Do you want to know how to live according to the letter of the law? Or are you drawn to a more meditative, mystical type of Judaism? There are teachers of every kind: Orthodox, Conservative, Reform, Reconstructionist, and Renewal rabbis; rabbis who specialize in Kabbalah; Chasidic rabbis, who combine mysticism with strict orthodoxy; "Bu-Jew" rabbis, who incorporate Buddhist principles in their teachings; "Jew-fi" rabbis, who employ Sufi techniques—the possibilities are endless, and exploring them with an open heart is half the fun.

Once you have ascertained that a teacher is qualified and worthy of respect, it becomes a matter of personal style. Take, for example, the famous story of Rabbis Shammai and Hillel. A man came to Shammai and said, "Teach me as much Torah as I can learn while standing on one foot." Annoyed by what must have seemed a frivolous attitude, Shammai seized a stick and chased the man away. The man then posed the same question to Hillel, and Jews have been quoting his answer for two thousand years: "What is hateful to you, do not do to others. That is all the Torah. The rest is commentary. Now go and study." Some of us may learn well under threat of the stick, but most of us do better with clear guidance and a challenge to study. In the words of a famous Chasidic master, Rabbi Nachman of Bratslav (1771–1810), quoted in *Gates to the New City: A Treasury of Modern Jewish Tales*, "The genuine teacher [must] go down to the level of his people if he wishes to raise them to their proper place."

The words of Rabbi Elazar are as wise today as they were when he spoke in the second century of the Common Era: "Let the honor of your student be as dear to you as your own . . . Let the respect due to your teacher be equivalent to the reverence due to Heaven" (Avot 4:12). In his book *The River of Light*, Rabbi Lawrence Kushner, like the Sufi master Bahauddin, reminds student and teacher alike that the mutual enterprise is to kindle the oil that is already in the lamp. "At the time of teaching," he says, "it is the teacher who—by some word or deed, a question, a blow, or simply through silence—forces the student to hear a voice that comes from within. All genuine learning is thus the self's disclosure to itself."

Christian Reflections

Teach us to pray. (Luke 11:1)

In Christian practice, Jesus is the model of the teacher, one who teaches by the pattern of his life of surrender to God and by his deeds, as much as by his words. In fact, most Christians believe that Jesus' death on the cross and his resurrection are the source of our salvation, freeing us to act as the whole human beings we are created to be. Jesus' actual teachings about spiritual practice itself are few and far between; more often, his teachings are about how to live a full life. In John 10:10b, he says, "I came that they may have life, and have it abundantly." Jesus embodies the Islamic notion of *fitra*, the innate nobility of human life. Over the centuries, his followers—ordained and lay— have taught one another to walk in his way, as that path has been handed down in Christian scriptures and in the life of Christian communities.

Jesus is called teacher many times in the gospel, by his disciples and others. Especially in the Gospel of Matthew, he is presented as a rabbi among rabbis, challenging the teaching of his peers about living a life devoted to God. He says, for example, "You have heard that it was said, 'You shall love your neighbor and hate your enemy.' But I say to you, Love your enemies, and pray for those who persecute you" (Matt. 5:43–44). He also is seen as the embodiment of Divine Wisdom, *Khokhma* in Hebrew or *Sophia* in Greek, the one who says, "Come, eat of my bread and drink of the wine I have mixed. Lay aside immaturity, and live, and walk in the way of insight" (Prov. 9:5–6).

When pressed to identify the most important commandment from the Torah, Rabbi Jesus responds, "'Hear, O Israel: the Lord our God, the Lord is one; you shall love the Lord your God with all your heart, and with all your soul, and with all your mind, and with all your strength.' The second is this, 'You shall love your neighbour as yourself'" (Mark 12:28–31). These are the lessons of surrender and service that he puts into practice in his life. At the outset of his ministry, he passes the test of Satan in the wilderness, showing how repeated submission to God saves him from the perennial temptations of material, social, and spiritual stardom. He tells those who come to him for healing that their own surrender to God's grace through their faith is what makes that healing possible. He goes willingly to his death, his ultimate surrender, and teaches by example that God brings new life to those who give everything to God.

Over the course of his ministry Jesus acts as model, teacher, and coach to his closest followers, sending them out two by two to preach, teach, and heal. On one occasion, when they come to debrief and boast to him of their triumph over evil spirits, he reminds them that the proper motivation is love of and intimacy with God, not kudos from other humans. When they have difficulty with one exorcism, he says, "This kind can be dealt with only through prayer" (Mark 9:29).

Prayer is an essential part of the surrendered life that Jesus teaches, and we have in scripture one prayer that he taught his disciples. Addressed to God as the parent of the community of faith, The Lord's Prayer, found in Matthew 6:9–15 and Luke 11:2–4, begins and ends with praise and submission to God's will. Over the centuries Christian teachers and spiritual guides have built on the foundation of that prayer.

Jesus instructed his intimates to go forth and make disciples of all peoples (Matt. 28:19). Although this directive has most frequently been taken to mean to go out and convert people to the Christian faith, the Greek verb used, *matheteuo*, has connotations of guidance and formation. The work of spiritual nurture has been at the heart of Christian ministry ever since. Early on, deacons and elders were set apart to instruct believers in how to "put on Christ," or to live a Christian life. Preparation for baptism, the rite of initiation into the faith, took three years of intense instruction in a process called the *catechumenate*. Once baptized, believers continued their formation within the ongoing life of the community.

Today, in most Christian traditions, spiritual formation is grounded in community and, especially, in the weekly gatherings of the body for worship. Depending upon the denomination, the ritual of worship—known as the liturgy—includes prayer, readings from scripture, preaching, and the sharing of the sacred meal of Christianity. Beyond the liturgy, Christian spiritual guidance happens in many venues, including formation classes, bible studies, prayer and meditation groups, and healing circles.

Spiritual direction developed in Christianity as one of the practices of monasticism, a movement that began in the late third century. Responding to the call of Jesus to give up their possessions and follow him, Christian men and women retired from the world to devote themselves to disciplined lives of prayer and holiness. They soon realized that total isolation exposed them to grave spiritual danger and that they needed the support of a community both to resist that danger and to encourage them to follow their calling from God. Those with special gifts of discernment and insight emerged as spiritual directors and guides. Of course, spiritual direction occurs outside as well as within monastic communities, especially since the resurgence of this practice in the twentieth century. Believers sometimes seek a spiritual director at times of transition only to find that such guidance so deepens their encounter with the Divine that it becomes a steady beat in the rhythm of their ongoing journey. Spiritual directors usually meet with their clients one-on-one, but they also nurture small groups of students in settings such as quiet days, workshops, and retreats.

Although the earlier monastic model often assumed strict obedience on the part of the one being directed, the sign of a wise and trustworthy director is the frequent acknowledgement that both teacher and student stand on level ground in the company of the Holy One, who is the real guide and goal of the whole endeavor. In a seminary class on Christian spirituality, my professor once told a story from his time as a young, newly professed monk. One of the oldest, best-loved brothers approached him and asked this newcomer to be his spiritual director. Horrified, the young monk asked, "Why me?" The old man replied, with a twinkle in his eye, "So that we both can remember who God is."

PRACTICE

Regardless of your choice of tradition, one essential practice in turning to a spiritual path is showing up, which can be daunting when it means trying to locate fellow travelers or a guide. When I visit a spiritual community for the first time, I usually do so at the suggestion, preferably the invitation, of a member. Even so, I like to go with a friend so that we can compare notes about our impressions. I challenge myself to move past the back of the room and sit where there are other people in fairly close proximity. One visit to a community does not usually give enough information to rule it out as a possible home place. I suggest that you return at least twice, if you feel a connection at all; and let yourself be known as a guest or seeker. The very act of visiting is a significant step on your journey: "Seek and you shall find" (Matt. 7:7).

2

Guidebooks for the Spiritual Journey: the Quran and Other Sources

---

This is the Book; in it is guidance sure.
(Quran 2:2)

At the end of his life, the Prophet Muhammad said to his followers, "I will leave you with two teachers after I am gone—a silent teacher and a speaking teacher." The silent teacher is awareness of our own death. In the process of making difficult choices, mindfulness of our impermanence helps us rearrange priorities and make sound decisions. The speaking teacher is the Quran, the Holy Book of Islam. Mysteriously transmitted in Arabic to Muhammad through the angel Gabriel, the Quran tells us

"It is God who sends Blessings on
you, as do the angels that God may
bring you out from the depths of
darkness into Light . . ." (33:43)

From the outset, the Holy Book cautions that some verses are literal and others are metaphorical, but does not say which ones are which. Each verse is said to have an inner and an outer meaning. According to the Quran, "none understands except those who possess the inner heart" (3:7). In Islam, an authentic spiritual teacher is presumed to have attained, through the process of inner work, a deeper understanding of the Quran. For such a teacher, the Holy Book is a wellspring of guidance, discernment, remembrance, and mercy.

Night of Power

From an early age, the Prophet Muhammad often went into the caves around Mecca to meditate in silence, sometimes for forty days and nights at a time. Seventh-century Arabia was a place of savage warfare and brutal disregard for human life, and the Prophet was in a state of despair for humanity. Worship of money and power had spawned idolatrous practices, women were treated as chattel, and many female infants were killed because they were considered a financial burden with little redeeming social value. These issues weighed heavily on Muhammad and he sought solace in the majestic silence of the mountains.

One fateful evening in the year 610 CE, the Prophet experienced an extraordinary phenomenon during a period of silence in the Meccan caves. A blinding light approached him saying it was the angel Gabriel. "Recite!" commanded the light. "Recite in the name of your Creator . . ." (Quran 96:1). Petrified with fear and certain that he was hallucinating, Muhammad mumbled that he was illiterate and ran down the mountain to the comforting arms of his beloved wife, Khadija. After consoling him, Khadija consulted with a kinsman, a blind seer named Waraqa. Waraqa was familiar with the Jewish and Christian scriptures and recognized that Muhammad, like Moses and Jesus, had been chosen as a Prophet of God. Persuaded to return to the cave, Muhammad once again saw the light and heard the same command. This time he experienced physical pain as if he were being squeezed, and suddenly, from the mysterious depths of his being, he began to utter words of startling beauty. The words were seared into his soul and poured from his lips to family and friends, who wrote them down on parchments, tree bark, and stones. This transmission continued intermittently for twenty-three years, sometimes unexpectedly and sometimes in response to questions. The Prophet said that he typically heard the "reverberating of bells" at the onset of the divine transmission, and he always felt a powerful physical pressure bearing down on him. On one occasion Muhammad was on a camel when a revelation arrived unexpectedly, and community members were astonished to witness the camel being forced to squat because of the weight of the invisible pressure.

The collection of these revelations is the Quran, which means "recitation." During the Prophet's lifetime, his family and intimate companions knew the order and arrangement of the revelations, and after his death in 632, his cousin and son-in-law, Ali, worked with others to collate the revelations in a book form with chapters and verses. Twenty years later a standard version was produced with one hundred fourteen chapters and well over six thousand verses. The earliest copies of the Quran were written in a script called Kufic Arabic, which had no diacritics to indicate vowel sounds. It took another forty years before the Quran with diacritics was produced. By the end of the seventh century, a consistent version, which continues till today, was sent all over the world. In less than a century, Islam had spread to the four corners of the globe.

Even though its words can be read on the printed page, the Quran is a sonoral revelation, meant to be heard. No translation in any language can convey the powerful vibrations of its Arabic words and the impassioned cadence of its verses. It is as if Divinity is expressing itself through the limitations of human language, as if the entire musical scale is being expressed through a single note. The sound of the Arabic verses penetrates the Muslim body and soul even before it reaches the mind. As a child I liked hearing from my parents that God loves to hide in those verses so that as you recite them, God can kiss your lips. Not only is the message sacred, but also the sounds of its recitation, its words written as calligraphy for meditation, and the physical presence of the book itself.

Brimming over with spiritual direction, the Quran also contains rules and regulations for daily life, covering a vast array of subjects: marriage, divorce, inheritance, social conduct, usury, theft, adultery, and murder, to name just a few. It is commonly said that the Quran covers everything from the sun to the moth. Essentially, the Quran challenges each of us to become fully human and remain conscious of God. It recommends a way of life and suggests spiritual practices that put Divine Reality at the center of human consciousness. The Quran is keenly aware of personalities and condition-ings of human nature and insists on "repeating its teaching in various guises" (39:23). It appeals to those who are moved by compassion and awe, to those who are stimulated by reasoning, and to those who need "tough love," a dose of fear and threats mixed with hope.

A shy bride

I usually advise my non-Muslim friends who wish to explore spiritual direc-tion in the Quran not to rush out and buy a copy of the Holy Book. It is better, I tell them, to get a book that contains annotated selections from the Quran. In the first attempt to read the Quran itself, you can easily get con-fused and overwhelmed if you are not familiar with the exuberant and hyperbolic style of its language and with specific events in the Prophet's time. I also recommend that before you begin to read the Holy Book, you become familiar with the words of an Islamic sage of your choice. The bulk of the prose and poetry of Islamic mystics is about the inner meanings of Quranic verses. Listen to an insight by Rumi: "The Quran is like a shy bride. Do not approach her directly. Approach her through her friends." The world of Islam abounds with "friends" of the Quran—mystics and teachers from the seventh century to our own day. Find one who speaks your spiritual language, and prepare gradually to meet the bride.

Stories of prophets

Fully one-fourth of the Quran is devoted to stories of prophets who pre-ceded Muhammad. God sent innumerable prophets who were as impor-tant as Muhammad, says the Quran, and it tells their stories to illustrate spiritual truths. The primary prophets mentioned in the Quran will be familiar to readers from every Abrahamic tradition.

The first of these prophets is our common ancestor, Abraham. As pre-cious to Islam as he is to Judaism, Abraham is called *Khalil'Allah*, "Friend of God." Indeed, because of his unflinching devotion to God and his willing-ness to sacrifice his beloved son, Abraham is considered the first Muslim, the first human to be utterly surrendered to God. For his virtue and piety,

God appointed him "Imam of humankind" (Quran 2:124), that is, the foremost model and teacher of surrender and righteousness.

The prophet Moses, who heeded God's call to lead the ancient Israelites out of slavery in Egypt, occupies as much space in the Quran as does Muhammad. Because he repeatedly confronted the Pharaoh to relay God's message to let the Israelites go, Moses is called *Kalim'Allah,* "Voice of God." Defying Pharaoh's claim to be "the Lord," Moses persisted in his demand that Pharaoh bow to a Higher Authority, and finally was able to prevail. By telling us this story, the Quran seems to be saying that we all have choices in life: shall we listen and act on the voice of the Higher Self, or shall we be enslaved by the commanding ego within?

Christians may be surprised to learn that Jesus is a deeply revered prophet in Islam. Called *Ruhu'Allah,* "Spirit of God," he is accorded "great honor in this life and in the life to come" and is thought to be "in the company of those nearest to God" (Quran 3:45). Describing his virgin birth as akin to the creation of Adam, the Quran says that "The nature of Jesus before Allah is that of Adam; God created him from dust, then said to him 'Be!' and he was" (3:59). The Quran says that Jesus did not die during the crucifixion, but that God made him ascend into heaven in his time of affliction (4:158). Spiritual teachers interpret this to mean that a pure soul can never be killed; it can only ascend into the bosom of God's compassion and love. Jesus, as Spirit of God, represents our divine or higher self. Sufi teachers say that one of the primary purposes of creation is for each of us to give birth to our own "inner Jesus." Only then do we become true human beings.

Mary, the mother of Jesus, is accorded a separate chapter in the Quran and is called the "holiest of the holy." "O Mary!" says the Quran. "God has purified you and chosen you above all women" (3:42). The Quran tells the story of how Mary suffered "birth pangs" and then retired to an isolated place where a withered date tree sprang into life, offering her dates, and a stream appeared magically by her feet (19:22–25). Islamic teachers elaborate on the significance of these verses: the work of giving birth to our higher self involves birth pangs and God graciously provides us with life-giving sustenance in our noble work of transformation. Sages also point out that to give birth to our inner Jesus, we need the receptacle of a Mary: a womb of purity and the feminine qualities of compassion, forbearance, and nurturance.

Muhammad, the prophet chosen to receive the Quran, is called *Rasulu'Al-lah*, "Messenger of God." In him we have "a beautiful model of conduct" (33:21) and he is a "bearer of good tidings and a warner for humankind" (7:188). The Quran says that he is the "seal of the Prophets." Till the Day of Judgment, there will be no more prophets of revelation. Mystics see in this a deep insight: humankind has received sufficient revelations; it is time now to practice and live those revelations. Enough with our excuses that we don't have revelations to guide us!

Other sources of guidance in Islam

Besides the Quran, which is the central source of wisdom and guidance in Islam, Muslims have three other sources for spiritual direction. The first is the wisdom and example of the Prophet Muhammad as expressed in the *hadith* (his collected sayings) and the *Sunnah* (stories about his life and conduct). There are two kinds of hadith: *qudsi* (sacred), which are God's words to Muhammad through direct revelation, and *sharif* (noble), which are the Prophet's own utterances. The hadith are the subject of continual scholarship to ensure that any citations that have crept into the literature are consistent with the spirit of the Quran and the Prophet's known example. The second source of spiritual direction is the vast body of writings and insights of jurists, sages, and mystics, whose authority in matters of scriptural interpretation is analogous to that of rabbis, priests, and ministers. Their work, which prospered for at least a thousand years after the birth of Islam, is a remarkable source of wisdom and inspiration. And finally, an important source of spiritual guidance is individual reasoning. If a question cannot be illuminated by Quran, hadith, or sage, the Prophet encouraged his followers to expand their own understanding of the issue. "Even if the religious judge advises you about worldly affairs," he said, "first consult your heart."

To give an example of how Muslims use the four sources of guidance, consider the debate about organ transplants. When, a few decades ago, it became possible to transplant the human heart, a serious question arose: is it ethical to have someone's heart beating in another person's chest? Consulting the Quran and the hadith and Sunnah, Muslims found nothing about organ transplantations. But when they consulted their elders and their own reasoning, they came to a conclusion that combines the best of common sense and Quranic values. The reasoning went like this: *A*, the purpose of a heart transplant is to allow a person to live longer. *B*, a longer life gives a person more time to do righteous deeds. *C*, the Quran says it is "righteous deeds" that get us into heaven. *Ergo*, the heart transplant that permits those righteous deeds to be performed must be consistent with the Quran! Thus heart transplants (and other organ transplants) are happily acceptable in Islam.

A book of signs

Of itself, the Quran says:

> (Here is) a Book which
> We have sent down
> To you, full of blessings,
> So that they may meditate on its signs
> And that people of insight might take them to heart. (38:29)

The Quran describes itself variously as a book of guidance, discernment, remembrance, and mercy. The "signs" in the Holy Book are the verses themselves. Spiritual guides often assign their aspirants specific Quranic verses, supplemented by hadith and insights from Islamic poets and sages, for meditation and contemplation. Like meditating on a koan, this process has the power to create shifts within the soul. A few examples will illustrate this simple practice.

At a time in my life when I was frustrated and confused about making the right career choices, I took to heart the following Quranic verse:

> Seeking only the Face of thy Sustainer most High,
> that one will know peace of mind. (92:20–21)

I meditated on this verse, along with Rumi's wonderful insight that any occupation that veils the sight of God's face is "the essence of unemployment." Together, these lines from the Quran and my favorite poet gave me remarkable guidance and discernment.

The Quran had powerful words of mercy and guidance for an elderly friend who was suffering from terminal cancer. Daily he meditated on two special verses: "To God we belong and to God we are returning" (2:156) and "Allah is the Lord of Grace unbounded" (2:105). Along with these lines, which gave him the grace to face his death with equanimity, he also took guidance from a hadith of the Prophet: "It is better to blush in this world than in the next." Taking these words to heart, the old man worked tirelessly in the last year of his life to repair relations with his estranged family and to repay all his worldly debts.

In yet another example of the power of a simple Quranic verse, a Sufi friend takes his cue from a few words about nature: "And the Dawn as it breathes away the darkness" (81:18). Reflecting on these words, my friend has mastered the art of gently and patiently shining the light of awareness on himself to dissolve his inner shadows. This constitutes his main spiritual practice, besides daily prayers, and he now teaches it to his students with much enthusiasm.

Another friend, a successful businessman, aspires to keep God continuously in his consciousness, guided by the admonition to be one of those "whom neither business nor striving after gain can turn from the remembrance of God" (24:36–38). Every time he feels he is faltering, he asks himself, "Say, what has seduced you away from your Most Generous Instructor" (82:6) and follows this with another verse:

> If one desires the rewards of this world
> Let him remember that with God are the rewards
> Of both this world and the life to come. (4:134)

Of all the signs (that is, verses) in the Quran, my favorites are the ones that mention water, the symbol of compassion. Divine compassion is the spiritual heart of the Quran, and the quality of compassion is considered by Islamic spiritual teachers to be the most essential provision for this journey called life. In the Quran, as in other traditions, this quality is best symbolized by water in the world of nature. Water in the Quran is life-giving, the source of all that exists. "Wherever water falls," Rumi says, "life flourishes." The sign of compassion in nature is that of parched land that, once showered by the waters of mercy, becomes "clothed in green" (22:63).

In addition to its life-giving qualities, water is authentic strength. In this too, it is a good symbol of compassion. It may appear soft and fluid, but nothing is more powerful than water for overcoming the hardest stone. Likewise, compassion has the power to erode the stone walls around our hearts and soften the soil within, thus preparing a place for the Divine to grow.

> And among Our signs is this: you see
> The earth barren and lifeless,
> but when We pour down
> rain on it, it is stirred
> to life and yields increase. (22:5)

PRACTICE

Choose a verse or two from the list appended at the end of this book. Find those that speak to you on any given day. Select those that splash in your chest! As often as you can in your meditative state or in your waking hours, reflect on them. Turn them over in your consciousness again and again. Allow them to perfume your heart. If you go deep with them, your heart will open up and from within you will flow guidance for right action. You will experience an influx of grace and love. In the words of the Holy Book,

> Truly those who have faith and do righteous deeds
> Will the Most Gracious endow with love. (19:96–97)

Jewish Reflections

The teaching of the Lord is perfect, renewing life; the decrees of the Lord are enduring, making the simple wise. (Ps. 19:8)

"O Children of Israel! Call to mind the grace which I bestowed upon you, and that I preferred you to all others for My Message" (2:47). Thus does the Holy Book of Islam speak to the first People of the Book, the children of Abraham and Sarah, calling them to remember their covenant with the Eternal One and reminding them that if they follow the Jewish scriptures and "work righteousness," they shall have their reward with their Lord: "On them shall be no fear, nor shall they grieve" (2:62). Unfortunately, says the

Quran, too many of us have gone our own defiant way, to our eternal damnation, and thus begins a long history of sibling rivalry over who came first and who is most favored in the eyes of God.

Rivalries aside, there are amazing similarities between the Quran and the Tanakh, starting with the belief that both are the inspired word of God. Both began as oral recitations in Semitic languages that are as alike in sound as they are different in appearance. That God is "One," for example, we know from both scriptures: *Ekhad* in the sturdy letters of Hebrew and *Ahad* in the flowing script of Arabic. Over the years the oral traditions were written down by Jewish and Muslim scribes, codified, and translated into myriad languages. At each step in the process the texts were vulnerable to human error. The Hebrew of Torah scrolls, like the Kufic Arabic of the early Quran, is written without diacritics to mark the vowel sounds, and both languages are so sensitive that the slightest change in a vowel point can change the meaning of a word. This presents enormous difficulties for interpreting the original text, let alone translating it into modern English, and it is easy to see how misunderstandings and misrepresentations occur.

Like the Quran for Islam, the Torah (the first five books of the Tanakh, also known to Christians as the Pentateuch and to all three Abrahamic traditions as the Five Books of Moses) is the foundational scripture of Judaism. "Turn it, and turn it, for everything is in it," said an ancient rabbi. "Reflect on it and grow old and gray with it. Don't turn from it, for nothing is better than it" (Avot 5:22). Beginning with ancient myths about creation and prehistory, the Torah tells the story of humankind's evolving awareness of a single Source of the universe and sets forth rules for living in relationship with the Eternal One and with each other. Involving animal sacrifice and sometimes violent punishment, many of those rules now seem tribal and primitive, as they do in the Quran. Yet even in the mists of time the rules reinforced a fundamental principle that we are still trying to incorporate in our modern lives: God is One, we are all one in God, and whatever we do to another, we do to ourselves.

The rest of the Tanakh consists of prophetic and poetic writings that often find their counterparts in the Quran. There are novellas, jeremiads, lamentations, proverbs, and songs. The narratives are more linear and the materials seem more organized in the Bible than in the Quran, but the figurative language is the same in both traditions: God is loving and compassionate (and, admittedly, sometimes angry and vengeful) and will reward us with verdant gardens beside flowing streams (Num. 24:6–7; Ps. 1:3; Quran 2:25) if we live righteously. And on this theme too, the Tanakh and the Quran are astonishingly similar. Righteousness, says the Tanakh, is

> to unlock fetters of wickedness
> and untie the cords of the yoke
> to let the oppressed go free . . .
> It is to share your bread with the hungry,
> and to take the wretched poor into your home;
> when you see the naked, to clothe him,
> and not to ignore your own kin. (Isa. 58:6–7)

And, says the Quran,

> It is righteousness
> to believe in God . . .
> to spend of your substance
> out of love for God
> for your kin,
> for orphans,
> for the needy,
> for the wayfarer,
> for those who ask,
> and for the ransom of slaves. (2:177)

To a Jew, parts of the Quran read like early Midrash, the legends and commentaries written over the centuries to explain and enlarge upon events in the Torah. Perhaps the most familiar example is the story about Abraham smashing the idols in his father's shop. Jews are astounded to find this story in the Quran (21:51–67), for to us it is part of Torah—not literally Torah, as it turns out, but a second-century midrash about the futility of idol worship. In the story, Abraham's family used to make idols and sell them in the market. One day Abraham's father had to go out of town and left Abraham in charge of the shop. As one foolish customer after another came in search of the most powerful idol, Abraham became increasingly scornful, for he knew that the idols had no power at all. Then a woman came with a bowl of fine flour, which she wanted him to offer to the gods. For Abraham, that was the last straw. Seizing a stick, he smashed the idols and then put the stick in the hand of the biggest one. When his father came home, he was astounded at the scene and demanded to know what had happened. So Abraham told him that the idols had argued about who would eat first from the bowl of flour and that the biggest idol had risen up and smashed all the others. Enraged, his father said, "Are you making fun of me? These idols can't do anything!" To which Abraham replied, "You say they cannot. Let your ears hear what your mouth is saying."

To find this story of explicitly human origin repeated five hundred years later in the Quran does raise questions about the inerrancy and divine source of the Holy Book, but the same questions can be asked about all of Holy Scripture. The point of scripture, it seems to me, is not its authorship but its message, and in this regard Torah and Quran speak in unison: The only reality is God, and all of humanity is a cherished part of that Reality.

If I were to create a midrash on the themes in this chapter, I would imagine Abraham entertaining visitors in his tent at Mamre. The desert sun is blazing overhead, but they are cool inside the goatskin tent. Sarah and Hagar have just served them a lavish meal and they are relaxing with dark, honey-sweetened tea. Abraham brings out what seems to be a large deck of cards and the guests lean forward eagerly as he shuffles the deck. Then he begins to deal. One by one he lays out the cards face up, and the guests are astonished to see that the cards are leaves from our holy texts. Card by card, a message begins to appear:

> O Children of Israel and Children of Ishmael! O you People of the Book!

> Have we not all one Father? Did not one God create us? Why do we break faith with one another? (Mal. 2:10)

> All of you: Choose life! Love the Eternal your God, and heed God's commandments. (Deut. 30:20)

> Love one another as I have loved you. (John 13:34)

Do justice, love goodness, and walk humbly with your God.
(Mic. 6:8)

Be steadfast in prayer, practice regular charity; and bow
down your heads with those who bow down in worship.
(Quran 2:43)

As the deer longs for the waterbrooks, so longs my heart
for you, O God. (Ps. 42:1)

Truly, in the remembrance of God do hearts find rest.
(Quran 13:28)

Practice

How often have you promised yourself that this is the year you will read
the entire Torah or all of the scriptures of your tradition, only to be
defeated by the size of the project? In the case of the Torah, the project is
not so daunting if you use an edition that is broken into weekly readings
with commentaries. Many of these editions (e.g., *Etz Hayim* and Plaut's *The
Torah: A Modern Commentary*) are further broken into daily segments, so that
all you need is a few minutes a day. Commit yourself to spending those few
minutes at a certain time each day, and by the end of the year you will have
a new sense of ownership and understanding of this fascinating scripture,
which is the basis not only of Judaism but also of Christianity and Islam.

Christian Reflections

*In the beginning was the Word, and the Word was with God, and the Word
was God."* (John 1:1)

"For each period is a Book (revealed). God doth blot out or confirm what
He pleaseth: with Him is the Mother of the Book" (Quran 13:38–39).
Standing side by side with the Quran and the Torah in "the Mother [of
the] Book" are the scriptures of the Christian Testament: the Gospels of
Matthew, Mark, Luke and John; the Acts of the Apostles; the Epistles; and
the Book of Revelation. The unity of the revealed books is a reflection of

the unity of their one Source. However, for all the thematic recapitulations, reverberations, and parallels among the sibling volumes, their differences are striking. The most obvious distinction of the Christian scriptures is their focus on the person, life, and significance of Jesus. Nevertheless, for this Christian, reading the Quran has been a practice that has illuminated my understanding of the Christian witness to God's truth. It has, to use an expression familiar to many Christians, "broken open" the Word found in the Christian Testament.

"Whether ye believe in it [the Quran] or not, it is true that those who were given knowledge beforehand, when it is recited to them, fall down on their faces in humble prostration. And they say: 'Glory to our Lord! Truly has the promise of our Lord been fulfilled!'" (17:107–108). There are many ways in which familiarity with Christian scriptures can pave the way for understanding the Quran, just as it enabled Waraqa, a Christian, to affirm Muhammad's prophethood. In the gospels, the coming of Jesus is seen in the same way as that of Muhammad in the Quran, as the fulfillment of ancient prophecies. Jesus says, "Do not think that I have come to abolish the law or the prophets; I have come not to abolish but to fulfill" (Matt. 5:17). A similar testimony from the Quran says: "And before this, was the Book of Moses as a guide and a mercy: and this Book confirms (it) in the Arabic tongue; to admonish the unjust, and as Glad Tidings to those who do right" (46:12). Christian scripture also gives due warning that true prophets always face resistance: "Blessed are you when people revile you and persecute you and utter all kinds of evil against you . . . for in the same way they persecuted the prophets who were before you" (Matt. 5: 11, 12b). The Quran picks up on and uses this message as yet another confirmation of the legitimacy of Muhammad. "Then if they reject you, so were rejected Messengers before you, who came with Clear Signs, books of dark prophecies, and the Book of Enlightenment" (3:184).

The family resemblance among the Abrahamic scriptures is obvious in the consistent themes of their teachings about who God is and how humans are to relate to the Divine. Take, for example, the passage in the Torah known as the Sh'ma and the V'Ahavta: "Hear, O Israel: The Lord is our God, the Lord alone. You shall love the Lord your God with all your heart, and with all your soul, and with all your might" (Deut. 6:4–5). The Torah goes on to emphasize this clear proclamation of God as the only One worthy of our total devotion by instructing Jews to keep these words in their hearts and on their lips and in their sight always. It is, therefore, no surprise that Jesus identifies this passage as one of the two most important commandments, along with loving our neighbors (Mark 12:30). In the Quran, the declaration of one God is a constant refrain, and the urgency to love is expressed in the repeated exhortations to remember God and do righteous and compassionate deeds (e.g., 6:161–162).

Even so, hand-in-hand with the consistent messages at the core of the revelation in the different holy books are obvious differences between the Christian scriptures and one or both of its Abrahamic siblings. As in the Jewish writings, continuous, developed narratives are central to the structure and function of the gospels in a way they are not in the Quran. Scholars study even the epistles in light of their "back stories," the historical situations from which they arose. Furthermore, the Christian scriptures revolve around only one fundamental story, the story without which neither the scriptures nor the faith that rests upon them would even exist: that is, the story of Jesus. The holy books of Judaism and Islam agree that there are many prophets, and the Quran is explicit in saying that Muhammad and his followers "make no distinction" (4:152) among them. But in the gospels, Jesus is a prophet and more; the chief messenger of the gospels *becomes the message*. As the Gospel of John says, "And the Word became flesh and lived among us" (John 1:14).

It is at this point that the Quran takes Christian scriptures—and even more, the interpretation of Christian scriptures—to task. The Quran responds in a lively way to the claims about Jesus, somewhat like a younger sibling who has learned from the missteps of an older child. The Quran argues repeatedly against the total identification of Jesus with God and of Mary as God's partner in Jesus' birth: "In blasphemy indeed are those that say that God is Christ the son of Mary. Say: 'Who then hath the least power against God, if His Will were to destroy Christ the son of Mary, his mother, and all, every one that is on the earth? For to God belongeth the dominion of the heavens and the earth, and all that is between'" (5:17). The Quran charges Christians with distorting Jesus' own message and aims to strike a note of clarification and correction.

What is fascinating to me in reading about Jesus in the Quran is not what it denies, but what it proclaims. In both the gospels and the Quran, Jesus comes into existence in a singular way, without the agency of a human father. This miracle is underscored in both the Gospel of Luke and the Quran by Mary's question to the angel who announces that she is to bear a very special child: "How can this be, since I am a virgin?" (Luke 1:34), and "How shall I have a son, seeing that no man has touched me, and I am not unchaste?" (Quran 19:20). In both texts, Jesus is a miracle-worker, even to the point of raising the dead. In the Quran Jesus declares, "I heal those born blind, and the lepers, and I quicken the dead, by God's leave . . ." (3:49). Although the Quran does seem to deny Jesus' crucifixion, there is a measure of ambiguity about this. The point seems to be much more that Jesus' foes were somehow thwarted and did not succeed in their mission to destroy him; in other words, God stepped in and took charge of Jesus' death (see Quran 4:157–158). In the end, the way God delivers Jesus from the trouble any prophet worthy of the title gets into is by bringing him up to heaven, an outcome not so different from the gospel scenes of Jesus' ascension. "God said: 'O Jesus! I will take thee and raise thee to Myself and clear thee (of the falsehoods) of those who blaspheme'" (Quran 3:55).

It is important to note that the Quran interprets Jesus' miraculous deeds and God's rescue of him not as signs of his superhuman or divine identity, but as his God-given means to get people to pay attention to his prophetic message. Furthermore, the Quranic passage about God taking Jesus into heaven continues by saying that on Judgment Day, God will "judge between you of the matters wherein ye dispute" (3:55). In the meantime, believers in God, through the messages of the prophets, are known by the lives they live.

After reading about Jesus through the lens of the Quran, I return to him in the gospels with a more acute awareness that his purpose is to show us what we *all* are meant to do and be. In Matthew 5:3–10 (with a parallel version in Luke) Jesus says,

> Blessed are the poor in spirit for theirs is the kingdom
>   of heaven.
> Blessed are those who mourn, for they will be comforted.

Blessed are the meek, for they will inherit the earth.

Blessed are those who hunger and thirst for righteousness,
for they will be filled.

Blessed are the merciful, for they will receive mercy.

Blessed are the pure in heart, for they will see God.

Blessed are the peacemakers, for they will be called children
of God.

Blessed are those who are persecuted for the righteousness'
sake, for theirs is the kingdom of heaven.

The Quranic perspective helps me appropriate my Christian scriptures as guides to spiritual practice that teach me how to shape my life around Jesus' example. It reorients me and points to Jesus' astonishing words: "Very truly, I tell you, the one who believes in me will also do the works that I do and, in fact, will do greater works than these, because I am going to the Father" (John 14:12).

PRACTICE

A prayer in my Christian tradition asks that we may come to "inwardly digest" our scriptures. One of my favorite ways of doing so is to memorize particularly compelling passages—not to be able to spout them out on command, but to internalize them and let them meet up with the Divine already dwelling in me. Writing out the passage repeatedly is for me an important first step that somehow makes the words mine more completely. The model provided in Judaism and Islam of reading the holy books in their original language is an inspiring challenge for us Christians to expand our horizons and memorize some passages in Greek!

PART II

Mysteries of Life

3

The Mystery of God

God! There is no god but God—the Living, the Self-sustaining, Eternal.
(Quran 2:255)

The very name of God in Islam implies a sacred mystery. That name, Allah, is derived from the Canaanite *Allat* or *Elat*, the Hebrew *El*, and the Aramaic *Alaha*. There are two root words involved: *Al* or *El*, meaning Sacred Everything, and *La*, meaning Sacred Nothing. This fusion of everything and nothing is Allah. Indeed, God is the Ultimate Mystery! "Even if all the trees on earth were pens, and the oceans ink, backed up by seven more oceans," says the Quran, "the Words of God would not be exhausted" (31:27). The phrase "Words of God" has been interpreted to mean divine signs, commandments, and mysteries. The message of this famous verse is clear: God is ineffable and all attempts to talk about our Creator are pitifully inadequate to the task. As the Prophet said, "Whoever knows God, his tongue falters."

Yet the human tongue longs to talk about God. Our entire reason for existing is to know God and arrive at union with our Beloved Creator. "I was a secret Treasure," God said to Muhammad in a hadith qudsi, "and I longed to be known. So I created the worlds visible and invisible." But how do we denizens of the visible world come to know our Invisible God? "No vision can grasp God," says the Quran, "but God's grasp is over all vision: God is above all comprehension, yet is acquainted with all things" (6:103).

35

"The lover visible and the Beloved invisible," says Rumi, "whose crazy idea was this?" Before Rumi, the saint Rabia had her own bafflements about finding words for God. In effect, she said that it is impossible to understand something when, in its presence, we are absent; in its existence, we are dissolved; in its contemplation, we are undone; in its purity, we are intoxicated; in our surrender, we are fulfilled; in our joy, we are parted from ourselves.

If the famous mystics have such difficulty knowing and describing the Divine, how can we lesser mortals hope to know God? The answer, according to the Quran, is that we experience God without knowing it every moment of our lives: "Everywhere you turn is the face of Allah" (2:115). God is the only Reality, as Muslims attest every day when they recite the Quranic text called "Pure Truth," known in Arabic as the *Sura Ikhlas* (112:1–4):

> Say,
> "It is God, Unique,
> God the Ultimate.
> God does not reproduce and is not reproduced.
> And there is nothing at all equivalent to God."

Whether we look for God in the material universe (*Zahir*) or deep within our own souls (*Batin*), God is there to be found. We feel the touch of our Creator every time we experience love or compassion or any other of God's divine attributes in our lives.

In Islamic tradition, Allah has ninety-nine of these attributes, each expressed by a "Beautiful Name" in the Quran. In truth, of course, God has countless attributes and names. Tradition says that Allah has three thousand names: one thousand known only to the angels; one thousand revealed to the prophets; three hundred in the psalms of David; three hundred in the Torah; three hundred in the Gospels; and ninety-nine in the Holy Qur'an. The astute reader will see that this adds up to 2,999. The three thousandth name is known to God alone. Of the names mentioned in the Quran, the best known are *Ar-Rahman* (the All Merciful) and *Ar-Rahim* (the All Beneficent), followed perhaps by *Al-Quddus* (the Pure One), *As-Salam* (Source of Peace), *As-Sabur* (the Patient One), and *Al-Khabir* (the All Aware). The most important of the divine names, and the ones most frequently used, are the first two, Ar-Rahman and Ar-Rahim. Together—and they are almost always used in tandem—they mean the Compassionate One. Derived from an old Middle Eastern word, *rhm*, meaning "womb," *rahman* and *rahim* suggest that compassion emanates from a deep interior and, as such, that divine compassion is as intrinsic as the primordial bond between mother and child. *Rahman*, with an active "-an" ending, is the creative aspect of this womb-like compassion, while *rahim*, with its passive "-im" ending, is the receptive aspect. In mystical language, Rahman is the Sun of Compassion and Rahim, the Moon of Compassion.

God is compassion

Islamic sages teach that compassion, with its many synonyms and interpretations (mercy, tenderness, forbearance, benevolence, and empathy, to name just a few), is the mother of all divine attributes. More than a divine attribute, compassion is the very essence of God and the building block of creation. Without God's compassionate longing to share the treasure of divine life, and to see divinity mirrored in all creation, none of us would exist. The compassion that led to our creation also sustains us, guides us, and redeems us when we fall. *Allah Ir-Rahman Ir-Rahim* is the Ever-Forgiving, All-Forgiving Effacer of Sins. "My mercy encompasseth all things," God tells us in the Quran (7:156). Whether we sin occasionally, habitually, or exceedingly, in every case Allah forgives:

> O my servants who
> Have transgressed against your own souls!
> Despair not of the Mercy
> Of God: for God forgives
> All sins: for God is
> Oft-Forgiving, Most Merciful. (Quran 39:53)

This does not mean that we can breeze through life without regard for the spiritual consequences of our acts and intentions. Numerous passages in the Quran give notice that divine forgiveness of our misdeeds is predicated on our intention to walk the straight path—doing what is good, avoiding what is wrong, and repenting sincerely when we go astray. And what is sincere repentance? It is a heartfelt act of contrition to God and a firm intention to mend our ways. "As milk returns not to the udder," says the Prophet, we must resolve not to return to our sinful ways.

It is often tempting to question the idea of a tenderly compassionate and beneficent God when we see the daily news. Why does God allow natural disasters to occur? Why does the Almighty allow cruel despots to abide, causing untold suffering to innocent people? To these questions there is no answer that will satisfy. The truth is steeped in mystery. Rumi's wisdom comes to mind: "Sell your cleverness and buy bewilderment!" When dealing with such insoluble issues, it is helpful to reflect back on two of the foundational verses mentioned in the Introduction to this book: "Of knowledge We have given you but a little" (17:85) and "In everything have We created opposites that you might bear in mind that God alone is One" (51:49).

Regarding the problem of natural disasters, I heard a story in Bangladesh several years ago that helped me maintain some equanimity in the face of widespread suffering and destruction caused by a tidal wave in the beloved land of my birth. A widow was deeply distressed by the tragic and senseless loss of her two children and had lost her faith in God. "Where is your compassion?" she screamed out to God day and night. Then one night she was graced by a dream in which she had died and angels were escorting her to heaven. She was thrilled as the angels bore her higher and higher into paradise, and then suddenly she beheld the greatest joy of all: her two children, radiant and exuberant, came rushing to greet her! In ecstasy she cried out, "O Allah, my children were lost to me but they were not lost to you! Thank you, my Creator!"

About tyrants and despots who seem to be permitted to abide for much too long, the Quran says this is because God is patient. Out of perfect compassion and knowledge beyond our capacity to understand, God gives evildoers time and opportunities to mend their ways. Why millions of innocents should pay the price of God's compassion to a few malefactors is one of those mysteries that we humans, with our limited knowledge, cannot begin to fathom. According to the Quran, God's mercy veils the wrongdoer many times until divine justice can no longer be withheld. When God's justice does descend, the despot's might and vanity crumble into the dustbin of history.

Be conscious of God

The mystery of God may seem somewhat less impenetrable when we learn to be conscious of the Divine Presence all around us. What this means in practical terms is that we need to focus our energies not on "understanding" God but on living in a manner that reflects our awareness that everything and everyone is part of God. With our focus on God, we are able to resist the temptation to worship our own ego and the false idols of personalities and institutions. In the imagery of the Quran, God comes between us and the desires of our selfish hearts (8:24). The Quran advises us to clothe ourselves in righteousness (e.g., 7:26) and let our conscience be guided by the consciousness of God. The reward is beautiful and immediate: "Paradise will be brought near to the God-conscious, no longer will it be distant" (50:31). The peace and joy of living in a state of God-consciousness is a kind of heaven on earth.

To experience this heaven on earth, we have to learn the art of being present moment by moment. Every single moment has a depth of beauty and insight, if we could only train ourselves to pay attention. Don't dwell on past regrets and future anxieties: focus on the present moment! That is where divine blessings are flowing right now! One of the best ways to sustain the practice of being in the present moment is to be conscious of God as often as possible. That consciousness brings what is called "the Glow of Presence" into the moment and illuminates it. We become a little more aware of the mystery of each moment and the potential it holds. Take a cue from this spiritual tale from Asia: a certain monk had a terrible toothache and went around thinking that if only the toothache would go away, he would be so happy. Then, in the midst of his pain, he had a wonderful insight. Turning to his friends and colleagues, he asked them if they also had a toothache. "No," they all said. "Well then, why aren't you happy?" he asked. "Why aren't you conscious that this very moment is a non-toothache moment? "

To honor the present doesn't mean that we shouldn't delve into the past or the future. We learn from the past and we need to plan for the future. The problem arises when we unconsciously allow our thoughts to flit back and forth from past to present to future. This lack of mental discipline drains us both physically and spiritually. A more productive practice is to give yourself permission to be really "present" with a past or future situation for a few minutes, invoking the presence of God to shine light on those periods of concern, and then bring your ruminations to a close and consciously return to the present moment. Thus in my life whenever I catch myself worrying repeatedly about something, I intervene immediately. I invoke the mercy and help of God and consciously allow myself to ponder about the situation for a limited period of time, say, ten minutes. Then I release the problem to my Sustainer and bring myself back to the present. Whenever I remember this simple practice (simple, but not always easy!), by grace of God the situation always unfolds in my highest interest—hindsight always shows that it was the best possible outcome, whether I realized it at that moment or not.

The power of living in the present moment means that you never have to travel to find God. God is "there" wherever you are. "I am closer to you than your jugular vein," God says in the Quran (50:16). In the words of Tagore, "God sighed and complained, 'Why does my servant wander to seek Me, forsaking Me?'" The art of being present is the art of finding God in the mystery of the moment.

A stretcher from Grace

We all have our moments when life seems impossible and God seems hopelessly distant and invisible. But keep the eyes of your heart open, for as Rumi says, miracles dwell in the Invisible. "A stretcher will come from Grace" to pick you up, heal you, and empower you. "For the one who remains conscious of God, God always prepares a way of emergence" in unimaginable ways (Quran 65:2–3). When things are dark—when, in the imagery of Rumi, a crow sits on a blackened limb and talks about what's gone—look back to a time when God's light was more evident and know the divine graciousness that blessed you then is still sustaining you and will bear you on a stretcher into a time of more visible light and grace. Once again, Rumi assures us, you will enjoy "spring, moisture, intelligence, the smell of hyacinth." Only stay conscious of God. "Do not say we have no entrance to that King," advises Rumi. "Dealings with the Generous are not difficult."

PRACTICES

- A simple way to remind yourself that everything is dependent on God is to say *"Inshallah,"* which means "God willing," whenever you speak of future events or intentions. This practice is based on the Quranic passage, "Do not say of anything, 'I shall be sure to do so and so tomorrow' without adding 'If God wills'" (18:23–24). Take care, if you adopt this practice, not to let the word become an unconscious habit or a hedge against personal responsibility to live up to your word.

- Practice the art of being in the present moment by sitting quietly and focusing on your breath. Follow your breath gently as you breathe in and out. If you are a visual person, see your breath in color. Invoke your favorite name for God and allow each inhalation and exhalation to connect you to the breath of God—to the Breath within the breath.

- Another way to strengthen awareness of the moment is to be mindful of your physical heart. As often as you can, focus on your heart and intend to breathe through it. This practice will help you stay centered and has the added benefit of opening the passageway between human heart and divine heart.

- A practice that comes directly from the Quran is that "In times of affliction," we should recite the words, "To God we belong, and to God we shall return" (2:156). You can personalize it by saying "To God *I* belong . . ." or you can draw comfort from the company of the collective "we." For optimal results, recite this verse like a mantra while focusing on your heart or on your breath. In the latter case, say "To God I belong" as you breathe in, and "To God I shall return" as you breathe out. This can have a very calming effect in just a few cycles of the breath.

Jewish Reflections

Ehyeh-Asher-Ehyeh—I Am as I Am. (Exod. 3:13)

When God spoke to Moses and commissioned him to free the Israelites from Egypt, Moses asked a perfectly reasonable question: "What shall I say when they ask who has sent me? Who shall I say you are?" The answer has been an enigma for at least two millenia: *"Ehyeh-Asher-Ehyeh."*

What does that mean? Some translations of the Torah don't even try to put it in the vernacular—you're reading along, and all of a sudden you bump up against this foreign expression adorned with a footnote. "I am who I am," says the footnote in one edition. "I am *what* I am," says another. "I will be what I will be," says a third, although strictly speaking there is no future tense in biblical Hebrew. All action happens in the present, which is why you will often hear Jews talking about biblical events as if we are there today: we are making a covenant with God this very moment at Sinai. Thus the translation of choice in my synagogue is "I am *as* I am," reflecting the idea that God is a dynamic Being who is constantly becoming "as I am" at any given moment. There are persuasive arguments for every interpretation, and, of course, numerous stories on the subject.

In a midrash that both supports my rabbi's translation and reminds me of the "Beautiful Names" in the Quran, the Holy One said to Moses,

> You wish to know My Name. I am variously called, in keeping with My divers deeds, El Shaddai, Tzevaot, Elohim, Adonai. When I judge created beings, I am called Elohim, 'God.' When I wage war against the wicked, I am called Tzevaot, 'Hosts.' When [while waiting for a man to repent] I suspend [judgment of] a man's sins, I am called El Shaddai. And when I have mercy on My world, I am called Adonai. Hence, 'I am what [from time to time] I may be—I am called in keeping with My divers deeds.'"
> (*Sefer Ha-Aggadah*, p. 505:22)

However Ehyeh-Asher-Ehyeh is translated, it is thought to be a form of the most sacred Hebrew name for God, the Tetragrammaton composed of the Hebrew letters transliterated *yod-hey-vav-hey,* usually printed YHVH and often pronounced "Yahweh." According to Jewish scholars, this is almost certainly not the correct pronunciation—the reasons are beyond the scope of this book—and in any case, Jews do not pronounce the word at all. In our tradition it seems almost blasphemous to say the actual name of God, for a name places limits on a Reality that is utterly limitless. Instead, when we see YHVH in the Torah we substitute the word Adonai, which means literally "My Lord." This is, in fact, a woefully inadequate substitution, for the word it replaces expresses something infinitely greater. Like Ehyeh-Asher-Ehyeh, YHVH represents a continuous form of the verb "to be," and its true meaning is something like "The One Who Is Being Eternally" or "The One Who Is the Source of All Being."

Thus it has become a theological truism that "God is a verb, not a noun," but aside from that, what do we really know about this enigmatic God? Reading the Quran, I recognize the same divine attributes and behaviors that fill the pages of Torah. I see a God of infinite majesty, Creator of the universe—and a God who would destroy it all in a fit of rage; a God of humor and compassion, intimately involved with the affairs of humankind—and a God prone to jealousy and spite; a God of limitless generosity—and a God who would take it all back in an instant. What I really see is a God described by human beings, who have no other way of knowing God than through human filters, no way of describing God except through human language. To me, the mystery is how anyone could respond to such a God with anything but ambivalence.

But then there is the God of the mystics—of the Psalmists and the Kabbalists of Judaism, the Rabias and Rumis of Islam, the Meister Eckharts and Hildegard von Bingens of Christianity. This is a God who created the universe in such a way that all of humanity is surrounded by and infused with divinity, a God who dwells in each human heart and relies on each one of us to complete the work of creation. This is a God who calls us to our higher selves, who invites us to conscious union with the Divine. "I am as I am," says this God, and what that God will be in each moment is up to you and me.

In a teaching story, a Chasidic *rebbe* (teacher) asks his followers, "Where does God exist?" Surprised by such a question, they reply that surely God is everywhere. "Wrong," says the rebbe. "God exists only where we humans let God in." I love this story, for it speaks to the Jewish sense of responsibility for "partnering" with God, but of course the more conventional belief in both Judaism and Islam is the one repeated by the rebbe's students: God is omnipresent and omniscient. Just as Allah is "whithersoever ye turn" in the Quran (2:115), Adonai is known as *Ha-Makom*, literally "the place," in Judaism. One of the earliest Jewish euphemisms used to avoid the blasphemy of uttering the Sacred Name, "Ha-Makom" means that not only is

God present in every place, God *is* the Place. "To God belong the East and the West," says the Quran (2:115), echoing the words of the Psalmist centuries earlier: "The earth is the Lord's and all that it holds" (Ps. 24:1). Even in times of spiritual darkness, when it feels as if we are languishing in a wilderness where God does not exist, "If you search there, you will find the Eternal your God, if only you seek with all your heart and soul . . . for the Eternal your God is a compassionate God, who will not fail you nor let you perish (Deut. 4:29 and 31). In yet another example of parallel concepts of the Holy One in both Judaism and Islam, God "sees well" all that we do (Quran 3:163) and is "familiar with all [our] ways" (Ps. 139:3).

In addition to the omnipresence and omniscience ascribed to the Eternal in the Abrahamic faiths is the attribute of omnipotence, a quality that causes problems for anyone who takes it literally. Does God actually *cause* everything that happens to us? Does God *cause* cyclones, tidal waves, hurricanes, earthquakes, drought, and wild fires? Did God *cause* the murder of six million Jews in the Shoah? No thinking person could lay that at God's feet, and yet that has to be the logical conclusion if you believe literally that God is the prime cause of everything. Similarly, if you believe that God can do anything God wants, then why, as Jamal asks earlier in this chapter, doesn't a compassionate God prevent the horrors and disasters that humans and nature visit on this planet? And—let's follow this logically to another question—why is it incumbent upon us to bless God for the good in our lives and yet blasphemous to curse God for the ill that befalls us? If God is truly omnipotent as we humans understand it, shouldn't God get the blame as well as the credit? These are hard questions to which there is no answer as long as we insist on believing in that kind of God. But this is a God that we humans have created in our own image, a puppet-master who rewards and punishes as we would do if we were running the show.

In Jewish spirituality, God is not running that kind of show—God is not running the show at all. In the case of natural events, stuff simply happens: nature takes its course. Sometimes human activity affects natural events—nuclear weapons and global warming are terrifying examples of the power we humans can have over nature—and that can hardly be blamed on God. In terms of human evil, that also is a matter of nature taking its course. When God created us with free will, the jig was up: God ceded power over our individual choices and behaviors, and it is up to us to learn how to transform our ego-driven tendencies so that we manifest our higher nature, the love and compassion of our Creator. To the extent that we fail in this task, the whole world suffers—and that is something that we cannot blame on God.

This brings us back to that quintessentially Jewish concept of sharing responsibility with God. In the mystical metaphor of Isaac Luria, a leading proponent of Kabbalah in the sixteenth century, the Godhead existed everywhere in the eternity before creation, and had to contract itself to make space for creation to occur. But when the stream of Creative Light flowed into the fragile vessel of empty space, it was so intense and powerful that the vessel exploded, scattering the Light into divine sparks in every direction. Our work is to gather up those sparks and reunite them with their Source. Every time we say *Hineini*—"Here I am"—to God, every time we subdue our commanding egos and "let God in," in the words of the Chasidic rebbe, we gather up another sacred spark and increase the presence of God in our lives and in the world.

Practices

- Whenever you find yourself distressed or in any way entrapped by constricting circumstances or attitudes and find yourself wondering where God is in the picture, center yourself with the words my rabbi once said to me when I was nervous about venturing outside my comfort zone: "I am surrounded and supported by the Golden Light of Being."

- To combat the natural tendency to question God's care and compassion when things go wrong, try to cultivate a sense of gratitude "no matter what." As Job was able to say, even when his life was falling apart, "Should we accept only good from God and not accept evil?" (Job 2:10). If, in moments of pain and confusion, I am able to say, "Thank you for this chance to grow, thank you for the gifts you have already given me to deal with this sorrow," the burden usually shifts and I am able to carry it with more grace.

Christian Reflections

Oh, the depth of riches and wisdom and knowledge of God! How unsearchable are his judgments and how inscrutable his ways!" (Rom. 11:33)

I often enjoy reading mystery novels, especially when their solutions are elegant and just. However, as Kate and Jamal have shown and the passage from Paul's letter to the Romans indicates, in our scriptures—Muslim, Jewish, and Christian alike—God is not the kind of mystery that can be solved. Fundamental questions remain: How can God be both transcendent— "Creator and sustainer of all the worlds"—and immanent—"closer than your jugular vein"? How can a just, loving, and omnipotent God permit suffering? As a Christian, I am tempted to see Jesus as an answer to all questions about God, as the solution to the mystery. Looking at the mystery of God through Quranic lenses helps me resist a tendency to reduce God's bewildering magnitude to a neat Jesus formula. Paradoxically, the more of God's image I see in Jesus, the less formulaic and the more mysterious both divinity and humanity appear.

One of the most significant ways that the Quran reminds me of God's limitlessness is the ninety-nine "beautiful names" of God. Also, God often speaks in the first person plural, the equivalent of a divinely royal "we," evoking awe and respect from human subjects. Of the holy books, the Quran is the most insistent and consistent in pushing against our very human tendency to make God into a super-sized human being, usually a very big guy, even more often an ancient, bearded European man. But remember that both Ar-Rahman and Ar-Rahim come from the Arabic word for *womb*, which is quintessentially feminine. The English translations of the Quran cannot convey the extent to which the text restores the concept that divine identity surpasses gender. The Quran, even as it honors both Jesus and Mary and upholds the latter's virginity in motherhood, also challenges a certain kind of Christian domestication of God by repeating over and over that God has no partners, offspring, or associates (e.g., 2:116; 5:72; 6:22–23, 100–101, 136–137, 163). According to the Magnificat, the ecstatic hymn attributed to Mary in Luke 1, Mary certainly does not see herself as God's partner. She says God "has looked with favor on the lowliness of his servant . . . and holy is his name (1:48, 49). Jesus also repeatedly distinguishes himself from the

One who sent him, the One whose will he is carrying out. For example, when the rich man in Mark 10:17–22 (see also Matt 19:16–22 and Luke 18:18–23) flatters him by calling him "good teacher," he throws the term back in the man's face: "Why do you call me good? No one is good but God alone."

This singular goodness of God is portrayed in the pair of words that Jamal refers to as *compassion*. I find it fascinating that some translations of the Quran use terms from the family of words associated with the English word *grace* to render Ar-Rahman and Ar-Rahim. Muhammad Asad, in *The Message of the Qur'an*, for example, translates these terms as "the Most Gracious, the Dispenser of Grace," as in Quran 1:1. In Christianity, grace is one of the most important theological concepts, a very central "God-word." Grace is the kind of positive notice from God that is totally unmerited. God's grace is revealed in the repeated sending of divinely appointed and anointed messengers, the prophets, who are commissioned to stir people to repent and return to God. Of course, for Christians, the most important of these messengers is Jesus. In the Quran, the titles Ar-Rahman and Ar-Rahim are also associated with God's propensity to forgive and embrace those who turn to God, who remember God, who are God-conscious.

The grace of Allah as described in the Quran sheds light on grace as I understand it in Christianity. In both traditions, although grace cannot be earned and is always available, we humans play a part in gaining access to it. It comes to us through the opening of our hearts. So, when I speak as a Christian of the "saving grace" of Jesus, I am not talking simply about a once-in-a-lifetime, dramatic turnaround, where I gave my life to God in Christ—although I have been privileged to have had such an experience. In a letter quoted in Emilie Griffin's book, *Turning*, Catholic monk and spiritual guide Thomas Merton referred to an "endless series of large and small conversions, inner revolutions . . . without which we cannot be free." The longer I live, the more I see that grace continues to invite me to open my heart again and again, drawing me deeper into its mystery and into consciousness of and participation in God.

As Kate said earlier, this consciousness and participation are the antidotes to the paralysis that often threatens when we get bogged down in pondering the tragic and unfair happenings often placed at God's doorstep.

I heard once in a sermon that there are some questions that God simply does not answer. We are not necessarily to stop asking them; we human beings are built to ask questions—more on this topic in the next chapter. Jesus himself asks the prototypical question of this kind on the cross: "My God, my God, why have you forsaken me?" (Matt. 27:46). The answer in that moment is mysterious and deafening silence; and in fact, for centuries, Christians have continued to debate the meaning of the horrifying event of the crucifixion of one so identified with God as to be called God's Son. However, Jesus continues to be conscious of God and to live out the consequences of his intimacy with God and his divine mission. The Quran and the Christian Testament agree that the outcome of this episode, while never "explained," is God's victorious deliverance of Jesus (see, for example, Quran 3:55 and I Cor. 15:54–57).

Rumi's notion of stretchers from grace called to my mind the apostle Paul's three gifts from God, which are both manifestations of God-consciousness and catalysts for continuing participation in God's purposes. They are faith, hope, and love (I Cor. 13:13; I Thess. 1:3). All three of these forces or energies engage our imaginations and permit us to understand that God is the One who holds sway over all of life. However, faith, hope, and love each stands in a particular relationship to the element of time. Faith is the perspective that frees us from imprisonment to our past by revealing God's power over all that we have already experienced. Hope enables us to look into the future with the conviction that God is in charge of what is to come. Love, Paul says, is "the greatest of these," because it is the dynamic that shows God active in the present. Even though we are always in the midst of the mystery—Paul says, "For now we see as in a mirror, dimly" (I Cor. 13:12)—faith, hope, and love empower and sustain us to continue to persevere.

4

The Mystery of
Human Existence

I have prepared you for Myself.
(Quran 20:41)

We humans are creatures of bewildering complexity and astonishing possibility. Islamic mystics long have maintained that of all God's creation, humanity is the most intriguing, complicated, mysterious, and fascinating phenomenon. The Prophet Muhammad says that we are God's secret, just as God is ours. God's words to Moses apply equally to each one of us: "I have prepared you for Myself" (Quran 20:41). In the metaphoric language of the Quran, our Creator molded us "of water and clay," breathed into us "something of His Spirit," and gave us the faculties of hearing, sight, feeling, and understanding" (32:9). At the end of that verse, the Holy Book can't refrain from tweaking us just a bit for our ingratitude for our miraculous creation: "Little thanks do ye give!"

Continuing its theme of human majesty and human imperfection, the Quran tells us that we are *fitra*—inherently good—and created "upon the most beautiful model" (95:4), but that we are subject to the wiles of the "slinking whisperer" (114:4) who tempts us to the lowest sin and folly. We have divine gifts that enable us to rise above the angels, but when we misuse those gifts we sink to "the lowest of the low" (95:5). We are the "honored children of Adam" (17:70), but we can also be impatient, fretful in the face of difficulties, and selfish with our good fortune (70:19–21). For all our imperfections, our Creator has appointed us *Khalifat-Allah fi al-Ard*, literally the representatives of God on earth (2:30; 6:165). God also extended to us *Amanat*, the trust of free will and self-awareness, which we freely accepted (33:72), and entered into *Alastu bi Rabbikum*, a primordial covenant with humanity that was sealed before you and I were born (5:7; 7:172).

No wonder, then, that with all these internal contradictions, privileges, possibilities, and responsibilities, we are, in Rumi's words, "a little tipsy" when we arrive on earth! We have no real idea of who we are or where we are going. We long for reunion with our Creator, but at the same time we are intrigued by the inducements of the slinking whisperer. Torn by conflicting desires and unaware of the divine gifts that could lead us back to God, we are like the bewildered people described by Rumi, begging for a sip of water from every passerby while standing knee-deep in water, knocking at every door for a crust of bread while carrying a basketful of bread on our heads.

But at some point in our lives, many of us start to awaken and remember. In quiet moments, our souls remind us of that primordial covenant between God and unborn humanity, and we begin to realize that, as Rumi put it, "this drunkenness must have started in some other tavern!" Deep within, we hear God asking again, "Am I not your Lord?" (7:172), and we long to repeat those words reported in the Quran, "Yes! I do testify!" We may struggle with the pull between divine love and human ego, but if we allow our souls to say "Yes!" to that primordial pledge we will discover that we have undertaken not a burdensome responsibility but a joyous surrender.

To illuminate the joy of the mysterious covenant, Sufis tell a story of a time when birds were creatures without wings. God came from the mysterious realms, spoke to the birds, and vanished. The hearts of the birds were so exhilarated by the sound of God's voice that they ached to hear it again. So deep was the ache in their hearts that the birds sprouted wings so that they could fly after their vanished God. To this day, birds swoop here and there, following the air currents and flying great distances, in search of the Beloved. The Quran says, "Are you not aware that it is God whose limitless glory all creatures in the heavens and on earth praise, even the birds as they outspread their wings?" (24:41–42).

The message of this story is that all of our desires and pursuits come from a deeper origin than we may suspect. In my village of Mahdipur in Bangladesh, elders tell the story of a famous nineteenth-century mystic named Ramakrishna, who used to burst into the liquor stores in Calcutta and tell the patrons that by seeking alcoholic intoxication, they were actually loving something beautiful in themselves. But then he would beg them not to get stuck on mere alcohol, but to go deeper. "Go ahead and get drunk," he would say, "but get drunk on the Real Wine!" In similar fashion, he would go into perfume stores and urge the customers to enjoy the enchanting fragrance. "Indulge yourselves," he would tell them, but not with mere human concoctions. "Go wild with the Real Perfume!"

Forgetfulness

According to Islam, our primary problem is that we forget our essential sacred nature and the pledge our unborn souls made to God. This is our biggest wrongdoing: we forget the divine beauty and power within us and get stuck in cycles of acquisition, hoarding, and competition. We get distracted from matters of real importance. "The desire to accumulate distracts you all the way to the grave," warns the Quran (102:1), whereas "those saved from the covetousness of their own souls . . . are the ones who achieve prosperity" (59:9). This is not to say we should deprive ourselves of all pleasure and live spartan lives of self-denial. "Enjoy the beautiful things of this life," counsels the Holy Book, "but do not transgress the bounds of what is right" (5:87).

Even as we devote ourselves to the spiritual path, we need to remind ourselves constantly that the real reason for our efforts is not to outshine the angels and cover ourselves with glory, but to follow the encoded desire of our souls to be united with God. One day the beloved saint Rabia and a well-known Sufi teacher, Hasan of Basra, were sitting under a tree just outside a bustling bazaar on the shore of a lake. Hasan, enamored of Rabia's beauty, was eager to impress her, so when the muezzin sounded the call to prayer, Hasan unfurled his prayer rug and placed it on the water. Standing miraculously on the floating rug, Hasan casually invited Rabia to join him. In reply, Rabia perched herself on her own prayer rug, levitated above Hasan, and invited him to join her in the air. "Isn't this what you want," she teased, "for the people in the bazaar to see us and be impressed? Hasan," she continued, "what you did, a fish can do; what I did, a moth can do. You are forgetting that what we are called to do is more difficult but also more important: our task is to do the inner work of transforming our souls."

Jihad

The work of moving from our mask to our real face, from our personality to our authentic person, requires sustained effort and exertion. This is the meaning of *jihad*, a word that is often misunderstood in Western culture. What the word literally means is "exertion," and in Islamic spirituality jihad means to exert ourselves to make right choices regardless of the temptation to honor our lesser selves. It means saying "Yes!" when God asks, "Am I not your Lord?" and not answering, as Pharaoh declared, "No god do I know . . . but myself" (28:38). This concept of jihad is similar to "right effort" in the eightfold path of Buddhism. According to the Quran, we are well advised to undertake this jihad—what the Prophet called the "greater jihad"—for when we come to the end of time, "Each soul will be paid out just what it has earned" (3:25). No one else can do the inner work that is ours alone to do. The All-Compassionate One will not force us to do it. The Quran says that "God does not change the condition of a people unless they change what is in their hearts" (13:11).

In addition to the work on our own hearts and egos, the greater jihad includes the effort on behalf of right relationships with our families, friends, neighbors, schoolmates, fellow workers, the clerk at the grocery store, and the homeless person on the street corner. To each and every person we meet, we are the face of God. Will that face be smiling and kind, or scowling and self-absorbed?

Finally, greater jihad also includes the struggle to transcend our own self-interest and work for a happier, healthier world. Every decision that protects the ecology or advances the cause of social justice is an outgrowth of our personal jihad.

The jihad that is so feared in Western society is known in Islam as the "lesser jihad," and again, the fear is based on misinterpretation not only by non-Muslims but also by Muslim extremists who carry jihad to lengths that were never sanctioned or condoned by the Quran. This lesser jihad is about defending and protecting oneself and others when under attack—and *only* when under attack. "Fight in the way of God those who fight you," says the Quran, "but begin not hostilities, for God loves not the aggressors" (2:190). This verse has also been interpreted to mean "do not transgress limits in the fight." War is permitted only in self-defense, and the limits are well defined: no hostilities toward women, children, and the aged, no destruction of trees and crops, and no continuation of war once the enemy sues for peace. In the brutal world of the seventh century the terms of lesser jihad were remarkably enlightened, but in any age there are those who ignore the words of scriptures and prophets, wreaking havoc on the earth by over-reaching their role as vice-regents of our compassionate and merciful God. Properly understood, the lesser jihad of self-defense is entirely legitimate, but it will always be secondary to the greater jihad of self-realization as a beautiful manifestation of the Divine. In Rumi's metaphor, the lion who breaks the enemy's ranks is a minor hero compared with the lion who overcomes himself.

We cannot do the inner work of the greater jihad alone. In the very first revelation to Muhammad, later recorded in the Quranic chapter called *Iqra* (Recite), the angel Gabriel declared, "Humankind does indeed go too far in considering itself to be self sufficient" (96:6–7). Even if we were able to cover the entire world with snow, Rumi tells us, the sun could melt it with a single glance. Without God we can do nothing, but, says Rumi, a single spark of God's mercy could turn poison into springwater. When we surrender our egos and align ourselves with God, we share in divine power and glory. "I am the Supreme Reality!" shouted the ninth-century Sufi saint Al Hallaj, by which he meant that human essence is divine. This was perhaps not the most prudent declaration, for he was soon executed for heresy by religious purists who didn't realize that Al Hallaj was coming from a place of deep humility and utter surrender. Coming from that same place, the mystic Bayazid al-Bistami (also ninth century) exclaimed, "Glory be to me! How great is my Majesty!"—not because of his personal greatness, but

because he was a leading proponent of the Sufi concept of annihilation of
the self in God. Far different are the declarations of these two saints from
that of the Pharoah, who was coming from a place of untamed ego when
he announced to his minions, "*I* am your Lord" (79:24).

God is the Seeker

Sufi teachers like to point out that if the Almighty had wanted, we humans
could have arrived on earth already perfect in every way. Why did God
choose people like you and me with all our frailties, all our dramas and
melodramas? The answer is steeped in mystery, but sages over the centuries
have concluded that on this journey of life, the seeker is God, and we
humans are the ones being sought. Despite all our weaknesses and frailties—or perhaps even because of them—we are deeply precious to our Creator. Perhaps in all our struggles to recognize the power and beauty of our
divine essence, we are mirroring to God those very attributes. In a moment
of intense awareness, the Prophet Muhammad declared, "I am He and He
is I, except that I am I and He is He." Once we begin to understand this
sublime truth, we will intensify our jihad to identify with the Divine at our
core, making choices that reflect the wonder of God to ourselves, to our
fellow creatures, and back to the God who seeks.

In my work to honor my own divine essence, I was guided by my parents and other teachers who advised me to focus on two Quranic verses:
"Do not sell your bond with God for so paltry a price" (16:95) and
"Everything that dwells upon the earth is perishing, but still abides the Face
of thy Creator, Majestic, Splendid" (55:26–27). My meditations on these
two verses were enriched by the imagery of two Sufi poets, Awhad al Din
Kirmani and Rumi. The former related a vision in which the Beloved
appeared to him with face hidden by a veil. Lifting the veil, the Beloved said
tenderly, "Take a good look at the One you always leave behind." How
could our hearts ignore such a tender plea! On a similar theme, Rumi urges
us to give up our attachment to temporary fame and revolve with him
around the Sun that never sets. Remember God's words to Moses—"I have
prepared you for Myself"—and do the necessary work to prepare yourself
for an eternity with the Beloved.

Practices

- Whenever you are graced with a blessing, express your praise and gratitude to God and then remember to ask for forgiveness. The Arabic word for this is *Estakhfurillah*—Forgive me, Allah. Why seek forgiveness? To counter the manipulations of the ego, which is always eager to boast and take full credit for anything good that comes our way. The source of this practice is the Quranic verse, "When with God's help, victory comes . . . glorify the Lord and ask for His forgiveness" (110:1–3).

- When thinking about your divine essence and the ways you do or don't manifest it in your life, don't take yourself too seriously. Keep a sense of humor. Laughter is sacred. According to the famous Hindu teacher Ramana Maharshi, when we go over to "the other side" and look back at our dramas and melodramas, we will laugh and laugh. So why not laugh right now? Whatever your sense of failure or inadequacy, remind yourself that you are the beloved of the Beloved. Tell yourself, and repeat as necessary, "All is perfectly well."

- In times of sadness or anger, do an exercise called sacred writing. Start with the phrase, "Right now I'm feeling . . ." and allow yourself to express your feelings and fears as fully as possible. After you finish, invoke the mercy of God and make an intention to connect with your higher self. Start by writing, "I have heard your sighs, beloved one, and I want to tell you . . . ," and continue writing, allowing your higher self to express itself fully. You will be amazed at the insights and creativity that pour out of you and you will be filled with inner peace.

Jewish Reflections

And God said, let us make man in our image. (Gen. 1:26)

Every civilization has its myths about the origins of the human species, and the Genesis story is the one most loved by the children of Abraham. In his hauntingly beautiful poem "Creation," the African-American poet James Weldon Johnson wrote that God "stepped out on space," looked around, and said, "I'm lonely—I'll make me a world." With that, God embarked on the six days of creation so powerfully described in the opening pages of Genesis, the first book of the Torah. At each stage of creation, as wonders mounted upon wonders, God surveyed the results and found them good. But after creating the cosmos and the earth and all the creeping things upon the earth, God looked around and, in Johnson's imagery, said, "I'm lonely still." God thought long and hard about what would cure that loneliness, and finally God said, "I'll make me a man!" Thus at the end of the sixth day of creation, God created a human companion: "In the divine image God created him; male and female God created them" (Gen. 1:27). And for the first time in the story, God found it not only good, but "very good" (Gen. 1:31).

And then God rested. It is as if humanity is God's crowning achievement, and if there is to be an ongoing story of creation, it is in large part up to us. But we are not on our own: far from it! Just as Allah continuously promises aid and support in the Quran, God promises the House of Jacob,

> Till you grow old, I will still be the same;
> when you turn gray, it is I who will carry;
> I was the Maker, and I will be the Bearer;
> and I will carry and rescue you. (Isa. 46:4)

God may not be lonely anymore, but it has not been all sweetness and light since the first people walked on earth. Human history has borne out the legitimacy of the angels' concerns expressed in a delightful midrash about the creation of mankind. When God was about to create Adam, the angels debated fiercely about whether that was a good idea. The angel named Love said, "Let him be created for he will perform acts of love," but the angel called Truth said, "Let him not be created for he will be all falsehood." The Angel of Righteousness was in favor of Adam's creation because "he will do righteous deeds," but the Angel of Peace was adamantly opposed because "he will be all strife." While they were disputing among themselves, the Holy One went ahead and created Adam and then said, "What are you arguing about? I have already done the deed."

In another midrash, it is the Holy One who agonizes about the decision to create Adam and Eve. "If I create them, wicked people will issue from them; if I do not create them, how are righteous people to be born?"

Both of these stories are echoed in the Quranic version of the creation of humanity:

> When your Sustainer said to the angels,
> "I am placing a deputy on earth,"
> they said, "Will you put someone
> who will cause trouble there and shed blood?" . . .
> God said, "I know what you do not know." (2:30)

The message in the holy writings of both Judaism and Islam is that we humans are indeed problematic creatures, alternately (or perhaps simultaneously) delightful and disappointing to our Creator. As the story goes in yet another midrash, the Holy One consulted the angels before creating the first man, saying, "Shall we make man?" The angels evidently were a little dubious, for they asked, "What is to be his character?" That is the question for us today: What is to be our character? Shall we follow the devices and desires of our ego-driven hearts, or shall we heed the deeper yearnings of our restless hearts and surrender them to the Eternal One?

Torah offers a simple answer with no room for argument: "You shall be holy, for I, the Eternal your God, am holy" (Lev. 19:2). This is not an impossible goal reserved for the spiritual elite. It is the sole purpose of every person on the planet. Created in God's image, we are inherently holy and our task is simply to become increasingly mindful of our divine nature and live in such a way that we reflect God to the world.

In a moving passage included in *I Asked for Wonder*, a spiritual anthology of the writings of the the twentieth-century rabbi and philosopher Abraham Joshua Heschel, the beloved rabbi says, "In the eyes of the world, I am an average man. But to my heart I am not an average man. To my heart I am of great moment. The challenge I face is how to actualize the quiet eminence of my being." And that is the challenge for each one of us. According to a fifth-century midrash, the Holy One fashions every human being from the same die used to create Adam, and yet not one of us is the same as anyone else. In other words, as products of the same die we all may seem "average," but as individuals enlivened by the breath of our Creator, we are each beings of great moment. Therefore, the midrash continues, each and every one of us should say, "The world was created for my sake." And, I would suggest, vice versa: each and every one of us should say, "I was created for the world's sake, and for God's." The way of Torah is to live as if it were so.

PRACTICE

From the rabbis of the first and second centuries of the Common Era comes this advice for the daily pursuit of holiness: "Reflect on three things and you will not come into the grasp of sin: know where you came from; know where you are going; and know in whose presence you will have to make an accounting" (Avot 3:1).

Christian Reflections

O God, who wonderfully created, and yet more wonderfully restored, the dignity of human nature: Grant that we may share the divine life of him who humbled himself to share our humanity, your Son Jesus Christ. . . ." (The Book of Common Prayer, *p. 214*)

The words of this prayer, which is one of those used in worship during the Christmas season in the Episcopal Church, convey both sides of the mystery that is humanity. Human nature is "wonderfully created" by God; dignity is intrinsic to it. Yet, there is also something about us humans that makes divine restoration of our intrinsic nature necessary. The Quran calls our problem forgetfulness; in Christianity, we have spoken more often in terms of sin. For Christians, Jesus is the means God uses to restore our original dignity. *How* Jesus carries out this mission has been the topic of centuries of theologizing that goes well beyond the scope of this book. Here, putting on Islamic glasses, I see Jesus—the chief prophet of Christianity, "the pioneer and perfecter of our faith" (Heb. 12:2)—as giving us a window and a path to God, who is the common origin and destination of all humanity.

The ebb and flow in the relationship between Divine Being and human being is dynamic and multi-faceted. As Kate and Jamal have shown us, the deep connectedness between divinity and humanity is in the holy books of Judaism and Islam, even as they also make a firm distinction between the

Creator God and human creatures. That line of demarcation is broad and bold—God on one side, humans on the other. But at same time, the human potential for good is always evident. As ominous as the message of the prophets might sound, their very existence speaks to the continuity of God's invitation to live up to the high calling of being human. Throughout our history, human response to divine initiative has varied widely. There are the stupid and the evildoers as well as the wise and the righteous (see, for example, Psalm 92), the believers as well as the rejecters (see Quran 5:54). All human beings are, in fact, prone to forgetting who and whose we are. Fulfilling our God-ordained potential is a feat that requires sustained human effort on our side—jihad, in Islamic terms. Furthermore, no matter how hard we may struggle, we are repeatedly reminded that all aspects of the journey—our creation, calling, destination, and empowerment—are determined by God.

In the Christian Testament, this human-divine drama becomes encapsulated in the story of Jesus. Christianity's prophet becomes an icon of the capacity for the goodness that is true of all humans in Judaism and Islam. Compare, for example, Genesis 1:26 or Quran 2:30–31, where God announces the creation of humankind—in the divine likeness in the former or as God's own vice-regents in the latter—with Colossians 1:15, which zeroes in on Jesus as "the image of the invisible God, the firstborn of all creation." But a passage like this one needs to be placed alongside others that suggest that Jesus' instructions from God were to remind the rest of us forgetful humans of our shared divine origin and destiny. In Ephesians, one of the most ecstatic tributes to the exalted Jesus, the author is very careful to talk about God as the initiator and patron on whose behalf Jesus acts. God works on us "in" and "through" Christ, but it is definitely God who is doing the work. "Blessed be the God and Father of our Lord Jesus Christ, who has blessed *us* in Christ . . . in the heavenly places, just as he chose *us* in Christ before the foundation of the world to be holy and blameless before him in love" (Eph. 1:3–4). Later in the same letter the purpose of human beings is revealed: "For we are what God has made us, created in Christ Jesus for good works, which God prepared beforehand to be our way of life" (Eph. 2:10). In our enthusiasm about Jesus, we Christians have sometimes forgotten that he is the means to a divine end and have tended to separate him from the rest of the humanity he represents. Some of us also have suggested that all of humanity must use this particular means for salvation. The doctrine of original sin, which holds that Adam's disobedience in the story in Genesis 2 became a congenital defect in subsequent humanity, also has played a part in producing a Jesus who stands alone with God on the far side of the line between human and divine.

The Quran's way of leveling all of humanity, even as it honors the prophets and others who have been particularly responsive to God's call, has challenged and inspired me to focus on the fact that by responding to the call of this particular prophet, I am saying "yes" to the ongoing divine invitation. As Paul writes in 2 Corinthians 1:20, God actually says "yes" first: "For in him [Christ] every one of God's promises is a 'Yes.'" All three of the Abrahamic traditions underscore that fully realized human life requires the development of a practice of saying repeated yeses to God's call, doing the inner work of jihad. As I will explore more in the chapter on surrender, the pattern of Jesus' life is a roadmap of jihad, the struggle to "work out your own salvation in fear and trembling" (Phil. 2:12).

My earliest exposure to Jesus, and particularly to his humanity, was in the spirituals my mother sang to my sisters and me at bedtime. I fell asleep in the invoked presence of someone whose inherent nobility and dignity were profound and unshakeable, even though many people of his own time did not recognize them. I understood before I read my first history book why the connection with Jesus was what saved the humanity of so many enslaved Africans. They shared with Jesus a hidden divine connection that enabled them to resist to some extent the poison of the internalized racism that threatened to enslave their souls as well as their bodies. When in my mid-twenties I survived a serious assault, the humanity of Jesus became my link to God's healing and restoring power. The spirituals of my childhood provided a nurturing soundtrack as I reemerged into wholeness of mind, body, and spirit.

5

The Mystery
of the "Other"

O mankind! We created you from a single pair of a male and a female,
and made you into nations and tribes, that you may know each other.
(Quran 49:13)

As dramatic and mysterious as our individual journeys to God may be, we are not walking the path in solitary splendor. We are sharing the earth with more than six billion fellow humans and countless other living entities. Each of our fellow beings is a face of God, each is a soul that is longing to be known and loved. "O God," Rumi exclaimed, "You have created this business of 'I,' 'you,' 'we,' and 'they' to play the game of adoration with Yourself!" In the language of the Quran, I, you, we, and they all come from one Soul, and our purpose is to get to know and adore our Creator by getting to know and love our fellow beings. But in this "game of adoration," we have to deal with the various personalities of that one Soul, and some of those personalities are not easy to relate to. It is not meant to be always easy. The Quran lets us in on God's little secret: "We have made some of you as a trial for others: Will you have patience?" (25:20). In a hadith that anticipates our twenty-first-century understanding of human psychology, the Prophet said, "The faithful are mirrors to each other." Very often, what we dislike in others is something that we need to acknowledge, heal, integrate, and empower in ourselves. This is difficult work. But in this hard work of relating to others, we deepen and expand our own spiritual worth. Each time we make the effort to recognize the Divine in another human being, we take another step toward actualizing the divinity of our own essence.

Even advanced beings need to be reminded of this. In a chapter called *Abasa*, which means "He frowned," the Quran tells about a time when the Prophet was engaged in a deep conversation about Islam with an arrogant tribal chieftain and was interrupted by a question from a blind old man who had been listening. Impatient at being interrupted, Muhammad frowned. (Though the blind man would not have seen the frown, one wonders whether he might have heard a hurtful edge in the Prophet's voice.) Soon afterward, the Prophet had a revelation:

> And the one who regards himself as self sufficient
> to him you pay attention . . .
> but as for the one who came eagerly to you
> and with an inner awe
> him you disregarded. (80:5–10)

The Prophet, who at heart was always sympathetic to the poor and marginalized, was deeply repentant. Ever afterward he treated the old man with honor—and, as the story goes, the old man became a sincere Muslim and lived to become a governor of Medina. The lesson is clear: be wary of the ego, which tends to be humble with the haughty and haughty with the humble. If prophets need reminding, so much the more do we lesser mortals need to pay heed.

True servants of the Merciful

For our work to connect with the Divine in our fellow beings, the standards are high. Justice is a recurring theme in the Quran, doubtless reflecting the need to tame the brutality of seventh-century Arabia. "God commands justice, the doing of good, and liberality to kith and kin" (Quran 26:90). The constant striving for justice is reflected in verse after verse in the Quran and is perhaps best epitomized in the following words: "Be just, for this is closest to God consciousness" (Quran 5:8). "Do not let others' hatred towards you cause you to deviate from justice," says the Quran (5:8) and "Stand firmly for justice as witnesses to God, even as against yourself, or your parents, or your kin, and whether it be against rich or poor" (Quran 4:135). And there's more! On top of all this, the Quran adjures us to turn our enemies into bosom friends:

> Repel the evil deed with the one that is better
> Then lo!
> He with whom you shared enmity
> Will become as though he was a bosom friend. (41:34)

"No one will be granted such goodness," the Quran continues, "except those who exercise patience and self-restraint" (41:35). In addition to patience and self-restraint when dealing with difficult people, the Quran cautions against gossiping about them, likening such gossip to "eating the carrion of your brother" (49:12). The Prophet himself spoke strongly against gossip, saying that God forbids it in the same category as the harming of a person's life or property. One of the arts of turning an enemy into a bosom friend is to avoid backbiting and to sincerely and humbly highlight that person's good qualities. "Veil the faults of others," says Rumi, so that, by Mercy of God, your own faults might be veiled.

What is asked of us humans in relating to and dealing with others is supremely difficult. We would do well to meditate on the wise words of the gentle Buddhist monk Thich Nhat Hanh: "The miracle is not to walk on water; the miracle is to walk on land."

Unity in diversity

In a multiplicity of remarkable verses the Quran explains that among the signs of God is the amazing diversity of human beings. God has purposely created a "diversity of tongues and colors" (30:22) and has designated "for everyone . . . a law and a way of life" (5:48). If God had wished, says the Quran, we could have been created "a single People," but God had other plans. "Strive then with one another in doing good. Your goal is God" (5:48).

Non-Muslims may be surprised to learn about the extraordinary inclusiveness and celebration of diversity in the Quran. Sadly, such spaciousness does not mean that all Muslims follow the inclusive path any more than all non-Muslims do. And it must be said that the Quran also contains awkward verses that, when taken out of historical context, appear to run counter to the message of inclusiveness in the Holy Book. It is a well-known fact that in any religion we focus on some scriptural verses but not on others, and the way we interpret them is a function of our intention and our personal evolution. The spaciousness with which we regard our fellow beings and their beliefs is a reflection of our inner spaciousness. In the case of the Quran, regardless of verses that reflect the enmity of a specific time and place, the Holy Book says that all of humanity is invited to "the Abode of Peace in this world and the next" (10:25), and it summons all of us, no matter what our differences, "to run the race for the good" (5:48). In one of the most beloved and often-quoted verses of the Quran we find an extraordinary spaciousness for people of every faith:

> We believe in God
> And what has been sent down to us
> What has been revealed to Abraham and Ismael
> And Isaac and Jacob and their offspring
> And what was given to Moses and Jesus
> And all other Prophets by the Creator
> And we make no distinction between them. (2:136)

It is important to reiterate here that in the eyes of God, entrance to heaven is not based on gender, color, caste, nationality, or religion. The password, one might say, is "righteous deeds": "Truly, the most highly regarded of you in the sight of God is the one who does the most good" (49:13). To the peoples of seventh-century Arabia, the Quranic revelation about inclusivity was specific and direct:

> Truly, those who attain to faith in this Word
> as well as those who follow the Jewish faith
> and the Sabians, and the Christians—

all those who have faith in God, and the Final Day
and do righteous deeds—
no fear need they have
and neither shall they grieve. (5:69)

Getting to know one another

As we have seen, the Quran makes it very clear that God plans for us humans
to live harmoniously in magnificent diversity. Yet the horrific events of our
time and the violence in the heart of the Middle East show how tragically far
we have come from reaching this ideal. It is not our nature that divides us—
remember that the essence of every human being is divine. Rather it is those
unfortunate manifestations of the untamed ego, tribalism, and conditioning,
that keep us from honoring the Divine in our fellow beings. The tragedy of
9/11 begs us to create paradigm shifts in our ways of thinking and doing.
No longer can we afford the old polarities of conservative versus progressive,
rightwing versus left, red state versus blue, true believer versus infidel.

But how can we get past this dreadful impasse in human relations? The
Quran offers a simple and sacred hint:

O humankind! We created you out of male and female
and made you into nations and tribes
that you might come to know one another. (49:13)

The operative phrase is "that you might come to know one another." The
key to peace and harmony is to get to know "the other" on a personal basis,
especially those with whom we have differences. We need to connect on a
heart-to-heart level. This can happen only if the process of getting to know
the other is done without any agenda in mind. The Quranic insight challenges us to open our hearts and trust that from a shared place of inner spaciousness will arise creative solutions of reconciliation and inclusiveness.
The idea is simple, but its implementation requires the exertion of our
entire being.

In my own ministry, I have long tried to reach out to those who strongly
disagree with my views and fear my religion. To that end I have been

involved in several interfaith projects, and I also have a private commitment to get to know on a deeply personal level two conservative, rightwing evangelical Christians who have been profoundly suspicious of Muslims and anything to do with Islam. My only agenda is to connect with them on a truly personal level. Some years ago I felt called to approach these two persons in sincerity and humility for the sole purpose of our getting to know one another as human beings. I was eager to put that Quranic verse into practice in a heart-felt way.

After several years of sincere work in coming to know each other, I can honestly report that the results have been transformative. Today my two Christian friends have an appreciative understanding of Islam as a spiritual path, and they view terrorism less as a religious issue and more as having roots in a fight over political and economic resources. What is remarkable is that they have studied Islam on their own and come to conclusions by their own research and through their own motivation. They have voluntarily reached out to a few other Muslims. Our religious views I presume remain far apart, but what is significant is that our differences no longer loom as a threat or a cause for suspicion or defensiveness. We are friends and we co-exist easily and playfully. We enjoy fellowship over food and festivities, collaborate in programs for social justice and earth care, and make good-natured comments about praying for each other.

Our friendship would be reward enough, but even more gratifying is the way I have been transformed by this experience. Through these friendships I have become acutely aware of my own prejudices and stereotyping of Christian conservatives. I had considered myself open-minded, but I came to realize that my views were narrow and uninformed. In getting to know these two friends, their families, and members of their religious community, I have discovered an amazing range of variations and nuances in what had seemed to be a monolith of Christian conservatism. I am impressed by their sincerity and sense of community, touched by their personal sweetness, and inspired by their dedication to social justice and care of the earth. This experience has given me a deeper understanding of the Prophet Muhammad's words: "Move from knowledge of the tongue to knowledge of the heart."

Women hold up half the sky

My mother was a gentle feminist and my father, a strong supporter of women's rights. They lamented the unequal status of women in many of the Muslim societies we lived in and meticulously explained that this inequality was rooted not in the Quran and hadith but in male patriarchy and traditions. From early childhood I became aware of this issue and consider this topic crucial to elaborate on whether it is Islamic theology or spirituality we are talking about.

The status of Muslim women is a complex subject and varies from country to country. The major problem facing Islam today is that the Muslim psyche, overall, is half paralyzed because of the restrictions placed on the rights of women. This is bewildering, given that the Quran lists a number of basic rights for every woman and the Prophet instructed his followers to "See that women are maintained in the rights assigned to them." In the tribal society of seventh-century Arabia, where women were utterly disenfranchised, the Quranic revelations that women had the right to divorce and to own and inherit property represented a radical departure from the norm. Ironically, the continuing repression of women in some Muslim countries in the twenty-first century is a radical departure from the norm that the Quran seeks to establish and the Prophet tried to ensure.

How did this come to pass? The answer lies in the unwillingness of patriarchal societies to acknowledge and implement the teachings of the Quran and the Prophet himself, so that today millions of men don't even know the truth of Islamic "tradition" regarding the rights and role of women. Perhaps the following situation will shed some light. On several occasions in the last few years, Muslim women in America have ventured into the main sanctuary of a mosque to perform the "body prayer" that is required of Muslims five times a day. When the men, who are unaccustomed to praying with women in the main sanctuary, have voiced their objections and concerns, the women have asked where in the scriptures it says that women cannot pray alongside men. Confronted squarely with this question and unable to produce any scriptural insight or verse to support the exclusion of women, the men's recourse has been to repeat the refrain: "This is against the Islamic tradition."

But the historical truth is that in the early years of Islam, women had a role in the religious life of the community that was unheard of at that time—or in this. In the seventh century, women helped build the first mosque in Medina. They performed the Call to Prayer, prayed alongside men, and sometimes led the ritual prayer. A woman, Umm Waarqa bint Abdullah, was especially trained by the Prophet himself to act as prayer leader for her whole tribe throughout her life.

What has gone so terribly wrong that in spite of the Quran and the teachings of the Prophet, the status of women overall in many Muslim societies is reduced to that of a distant second class? The sorry truth is that tribal customs overrode the spiritual teachings of Islam almost from the beginning. When the Prophet insisted on implementing the radical rights for women that were mentioned in the Quranic revelations, many men were enraged. Soon after the Prophet's death, male jurists used their religious and political authority to reclaim dominance over women. The tradition of relegating women to separate and sometimes inferior spaces in the mosque was achieved by male consensus in the Middle Ages. As Islam spread to the feudal societies of Arabia, Persia, parts of the Roman Empire, and India, many of the patriarchal traditions of those societies validated the male bias. Some jurists continued their work of misinterpreting Quranic verses that specifically grant advantages to women, and turned those verses to the convenience and advantage of men.

Perhaps the most egregious example of Quran tampering is the troubling issue of Muslim women who, having been raped, find themselves accused of fornication and sentenced to a terrifying punishment while the perpetrator is often untouched by the law. If a woman is accused of adultery, says the Quran, she cannot be prosecuted without testimony from four reliable witnesses who saw the sexual act (4:15). The purpose of this divine revelation is to protect the rights of women who have been falsely accused: no witness, no prosecution. In practice, however, the Quranic injunction has been turned against women who seek justice after a rape or who are impregnated by the rapist. If a woman is unable to produce four eye-witnesses, she is accused of immorality according to the man-made interpretation of Sharia and, in some Muslim countries, subjected to severe punishment according to those laws. (Sharia is the timeless guidance derived primarily from the Quran and prophetic tradition. Interpretation of Sharia constitutes Islamic law.) Gross misinterpretations of Sharia are profoundly unjust and only recently have measures been taken to rescind the unfair interpretation of the rape law.

It is incumbent on the Muslim community to return to the sacred values of the Quran and the teachings of the Prophet Muhammad. "It is [God] Who has created you from one soul," says the Quran, "and out of it brought into being a mate, so that man might incline with love towards woman" (7:189). The message is that relations between men and women should be marked by respect, tenderness, and affection. Let our model be the Prophet, who, by all accounts, was an exemplary husband—and more: blessed with a heart-felt insight into the mysteries and beauty of divine feminine qualities, he was a radical feminist centuries before that term was coined. "When a man gazes at his wife and she gazes at him," Muhammad said, "God looks at them both with a gaze that is compassion and mercy." Only those with an inner understanding can grasp the beauty of the Prophet's utterance in a well-known hadith: "From Your world, I have loved three things: women, perfume and prayers."

The only way for men to heal their broken relationships with women is the same way that we have talked about in other contexts in this book: taming the ego and opening the heart. Untamed egos not only dominate, they tend to become supremely arrogant. The Sufi saint Rabia experienced male arrogance in the eighth century, and she had a ready answer. Several men were boasting that "the crown of Prophethood has been placed on men's head. The belt of nobility has been fastened around men's waists. No woman has ever been a prophet." "Ah," Rabia replied, "but egoism and self-worship and 'I am your Lord most high' have never sprung from a woman's breast. All these have been the specialty of men."

There have always been exceptions to the reduced status of Muslim women. In some communities, women have been educated and have prayed alongside men for centuries. Today, many courageous women are leading the way to heal the dis-ease between men and women in Islam. There is a good deal of ferment and change occurring in Islamic societies with regard to women's rights, led by what is popularly called "women on the move," who are shining a steady stream of light onto the darkness of male privilege and oppression of women. It is important to note that, as a recent Gallup Poll reports, Muslim women in developing countries and traditional Muslim societies cherish their religion and are not interested in becoming "Western-ized." Their priority is the betterment of the quality of life for the community as a whole, and with that will come the gender equality rooted in the Quran. In the last two decades, the enrollment of women in schools and colleges has grown dramatically in many Muslim societies. In increasing numbers women are entering professions, including politics, previously dominated by men. Most important of all, there is emerging a class of female scholars steeped in knowledge of Islam and the Quran. These schol-ars are challenging medieval theological assumptions and re-interpreting verses, assuming a role that had been the exclusive prerogative of men. As a result, more and more women are raising their voices and claiming their rightful status, and increasing numbers of men are awakening to their con-ditionings and rigidities.

Female scholars point out that gender equality is rooted in the Cre-ation story. According to the Quran, it was Satan who "beguiled" Adam and his spouse into making a wrong choice. There is no suggestion in the Quran that "the woman" caused Adam to sin. After they both failed to make right choices, they were sent to a "lower world," the earth. There they sincerely begged forgiveness and God, out of infinite mercy, readily forgave and exalted both of them. The scholars also point out that shortly after Umm Salama, a wife of the Prophet, asked why the Quranic revelations seemed to be talking only about men, the Prophet received a lengthy reve-lation directed to both men and women: "For men and women who sur-render themselves to God . . . and for men and women who remember God unceasingly, for them God has readied forgiveness and a supreme recom-pense" (33:35).

Marriage, children, and parenthood

Some of the greatest teachings of life unfold in the union of marriage. "Marriage is half of religion," declared the Prophet, and for this reason there is no monasticism in Islam. Not only are men and women "protectors of one another" (9:71) and "garments to each other" (2:187), in their sacred union they experience the mystery of divinity: "Among God's Signs is this," says the Quran:

> That God created for you mates
> From among yourselves
> That you may dwell in tranquility with them,
> And God engenders love and compassion between you;
> Truly in that are signs for those who reflect. (30:20–21)

Spiritual teachers use the example of the Prophet's marriage to Khadija to illustrate the sacred bond of marriage. In an era when polygamy and patriarchy were the norm, Muhammad was married for twenty-five years to one woman, his beloved Khadija. His choice of woman would be considered unconventional—even revolutionary—in any age: Khadija was fifteen years his senior and his social superior. As his employer, it was Khadija who taught Muhammad the art of business. As his confidante, it was Khadija who supported the terrified Muhammad when he began receiving Quranic revelations in the caves of Mecca. After Khadija died, Muhammad married several times, by some accounts nine times. What is highly significant is that all of these wives, except for one, were either slaves, divorcees, or widows—women who were considered "discards" in that era. Thus his multiple marriages, which were not unusual for the time and place, point not to an unbridled libido but to a compassionate concern for women who had no other source of protection and support. Teachers also point to these later marriages as examples of the Prophet's ability to transcend cultural and societal barriers. Two of these wives were Jewish, and one was Christian. One of his wives was Aisha, the daughter of his best friend, Abu Bakr, who later became the first Caliph of Islam. Aisha is considered in Islam to be a model of intelligence and piety, and many Muslim women are proud to bear her name.

It is popularly thought that the Quran permits a man to have up to four wives. What is not so well known is that polygamy is permitted only under very limited circumstances, and indeed, monogamy is the norm in Islam. The revelation permitting multiple marriages occurs only once in the

Quran, and this single revelation arose in the context of the need to protect widows and orphans in a time of war. Even under these limited conditions, the revelation clearly states that multiple marriages are permissible
only if the husband is able to treat each of his wives with equal attention
and affection—which, the Quran cautions, is almost impossible to do.
"You will never be able to deal equitably with all your wives, however much
you want" (4:129). Thus, although the Quran permits polygamy in principle, it virtually forbids it in practice. Men who ignore this aspect of the revelation are flouting a sacred text that was meant to help women, and turning
it to their personal convenience.

The divine principle of motherhood permeates Islam. The Quran says,
"Reverence Allah through Whom you demand your mutual rights and reverence the wombs that bore you, for Allah watches over you" (4:1). The
Quran says tenderly that when man embraces woman, a prayer from their
souls rings out: "Bless us with a sound child!" (7:189). Rumi, marveling at
the mystery of marital union and birth, voices a poetic thought that in the
enchantment of the night, father and mother whisper gentle secrets to each
other and the child of the universe takes its first breath. The sage Tagore
joyously notes that because God continues to send to earth so many children from those mysterious realms, it must mean that God has not yet
despaired of humanity!

"Paradise lies at the feet of your mother," said the Prophet, and a
Quranic verse in God's own voice reminds us that our mothers bore us "in
travail upon travail" (31:14). Therefore, the verse continues, "Show gratitude to Me and to your parents." In an earlier verse, the angel Gabriel tells
us, "Your Lord has decreed that you worship none but Him and be kind
to your parents" (17:23). The juxtaposition of God and parents in both
verses seems to suggest that one of the ways to worship God is to treat our
parents with filial care. Significantly, the Quran tells us not to obey our parents if they would lead us into sin, but even so, it tells us to " bear them
company in this life with kindness" (31:15). The Quran especially admonishes us to be kind and compassionate with our parents in their old age.
"Tenderly lower to them the wings of humility" (17:24) and hold them in
your prayers: "O my Sustainer, bestow Your grace upon them, even as they
cherished and nurtured me when I was but a child" (17:24).

Animals and nature

Unimaginably numerous and varied are God's creations in the visible and invisible worlds. We humans are sacred, but we constitute only one of the many handiworks of our Creator. On this glorious sphere of earth, air, and water, we share space and nutrients with other living beings, and as God's "viceroys" we are responsible for the wellbeing of our planet. "Do not sow corruption on earth," God cautions us in the Quran (2:60; 7:85). "On the earth are signs for those of inner certainty" (45:3). We humans are here, living in relationship with each other and with nature, to serve and learn from one another.

The Quran tells us to be mindful that "animals and birds are communities like your own and are a part of the living world," and "in the end, they will also gather before the Protector of all" (6:38). In a chapter titled "The Bee," the Quran teaches us to be aware of how God has inspired the bee to produce honeycombs and honey. "Verily in this is a Sign for those who give thought" (16:69). How do bees know how to collect nectar, build hives, and produce honey? They have tapped into a sacred intelligence that goes beyond book learning.

Islamic mystics rhapsodize about the nature-based imagery that fills the pages of the Quran. A blade of grass, says Rumi, contains the entire teaching in the Quran or any Holy Book: Grass agrees to die and rise up again so it can receive a little of the animal's enthusiasm. Hafiz waxes eloquent about the sun, which teaches us about unconditional love. "Even after all this time," he says, "the Sun never tells the Earth, 'You owe me!'" Instead, like the love of God, it just keeps on shining. In the movement of tree branches in the wind, Rumi finds a beautiful insight: the branches of the tree sway differently in the breeze but are connected at the roots. There is unity in diversity! And about sacred union, Rumi observes that if the mountain and earth were not lovers, grass would never sprout out of their breasts.

The Quran contains two verses to which Sufis turn again and again to explain that humility is the gateway to connecting with the Mysteries in which we humans are immersed. The first verse tells us not to walk upon the earth "with proud self-conceit," for "truly, you can never rend the earth asunder nor can you rival the mountains in stature" (17:37). In a similar vein, the second verse also cautions against human arrogance. God's viceroys we may be, but "assuredly the creation of the heavens and the earth is a greater matter than the creation of humanity, yet most people understand not" (40:57).

PRACTICE

Whenever your relations with another person arouse feelings of awkwardness or discomfort, try to recognize the feelings right away and honor them in your heart. Perhaps just lower your eyelids for a second, take a conscious breath to center yourself, and do your best to remember that God is right there in the middle of the situation. Then, at the earliest opportunity, take time to revisit your unhappy feelings and really be present with them. They are just energy that is begging to be acknowledged, healed, and integrated. Surrender your feelings to the Beloved in your heart and invoke God's help and mercy. Breathe calmly through your heart and remember the hadith qudsi that Allah resides in the space of every human heart. If you practice this regularly, the spirit of God in your heart will heal your feelings and empower you to handle difficult relationships with grace and compassion for yourself and the other person.

Jewish Reflections

Two are better than one. (Eccles. 4:9)

The mystery of the "other" permeates the pages of Torah, beginning with the story of Adam and Eve. In the first version of the story, elegantly told in two short sentences (Gen. 1:26 and 27), God creates *adam*, a collective Hebrew noun that means human beings, male and female together. In the second version, which is more detailed and fanciful (Gen. 2:4–25), God first creates *ha-adam* ("the" man) and then sees it's not good for him to be alone. The solitary man needs a mate. So God creates a woman, and the man, now called Adam, names this woman Khava (Eve), a Hebrew word meaning "life." And then the drama begins. Mistakes are made, fingers get pointed, and the big happy family of humanity is on its way to dysfunction and divorce.

It's not good for ha-adam to be alone, but neither is it easy to live with our fellow human beings. Untamed egos and self-interest, in both ourselves and other people, create problems wherever we go. They beget heartache at the least, violence and destruction at their worst. It seems ironic in the context of this book that the first murder recorded in the Bible (Gen. 4:8) was committed because of rivalry for God's attention and approval. Some things haven't changed since the beginning of time. After Cain slew Abel, the story goes, he "left the Presence of God" and wandered away from the place of his birth (Gen. 4:16). The truth is that Cain could never leave the presence of God—"Whithersoever you shall turn is the Face of Allah" (Quran 2:115)—but he failed to recognize God's presence either in himself or in his brother. This is the root of all our interpersonal traumas and tragedies: we forget that all are made in the likeness of God. If only we could cultivate an awareness of the divine essence of every human being, how could we possibly allow the Divine in our own hearts to lash out at the Divine in someone else? In one of my favorite metaphors from Hafiz, we are all honored guests at a party thrown by the Beloved. If you realize your fellow guests are personal friends of the Host, asks Hafiz, are you going to be rude to them? "I think not," he says.

In a sense, all the dramas of history are caused by our perception of the "otherness" of our fellow humans. The untamed ego sees other persons and wants what they have, or fears what they look like, or suspects what they may be up to. Perhaps more than any other people in history, Jews know the danger and pain of that "otherness." From the time of the Babylonians in the sixth century BCE to the present day, Jews have been oppressed in their own land, driven into exile, crowded into ghettoes, and herded into gas chambers, all because their so-called otherness was perceived as a threat or an insult to the ones in power. So it seems fitting that the remedy for the terrible social disease of otherness should reside almost literally in the middle of the Torah: "Love your fellow as yourself: I am the Eternal" (Lev. 19:18). Actually, this well-known commandment to love our neighbor is preceded by an equally powerful injunction: "You shall not hate your kinsfolk in your heart" (Lev. 19:17). Taken together, these central lines of Torah mean that we must do the hard inner work of shining divine light on the dark places in our hearts, rooting out our jealousies and our grudges, and expanding our hearts to embrace all the "others" in our immediate circle and in the wider world. The cynical and literal-minded may take "kinsfolk" to mean only our own family or tribe, but in Jewish spirituality, as in the Quran (5:69), all human beings are "kin" in the family of God.

There are two important lessons to be drawn from these paradigmatic verses in Leviticus. First, the command to love our neighbor (*V'ahavta l'reakha*) is not a wimpy, feel-good proposition. Scholars point out that the verb *ahav* speaks to love as an action, not just a feeling, and the "*l'*" before *reakha* (your fellow) is a preposition meaning "to," thus implying that we should actively "do love" to our neighbor. At a minimum this means that we must treat each other with justice and loving-kindness, a theme that we will explore in the final chapter of this book. Second, the juxtaposition of the command to love and the statement "I am the Eternal," like the Quranic apposition of commands to worship God and honor parents mentioned a few pages ago, inescapably suggests that if we wish to honor God, we have to honor our fellow sojourners on this planet. In the context of this Torah portion, which is a compendium of instructions called *K'doshim* ([you shall be] holy), loving our neighbor and forming good relationships with others is a primary way of fulfilling the command to be holy as our Creator is holy (Lev. 19:2). This is why I chose to title these Jewish reflections on our fellow beings with the line from Ecclesiastes, "Two are better than one." How are we to fulfill this sacred commandment if ours is the only face we see in the mirror? And how are we to strengthen the moral muscles needed to tame our egos and desires if we don't exercise them by meeting the challenges of sharing the world and its resources with our fellows?

Jamal's remarks about the status of women in Islam call for a few thoughts about their sisters in the Tribe of Israel. In both traditions, women know only too well what it means to be "other" in terms of visibility and personal empowerment within the society, though that has changed markedly for Jewish women in the last hundred years. True to the tribal ways of the ancient Middle East, women did not fare any better in the Torah than they did in seventh-century Arabia. Few are the women who appear by name in the Torah, and almost always they are in subordinate roles. When they challenge authority, as Miriam does when she thinks her brother Moses is getting too full of himself (Num. 12:1ff), they are quickly put down and told to stay in their place. A notable exception is the story of five sisters named Mahlah, Noah, Hoglah, Milcah, and Tirzah (Num. 27:1–11). When their father dies without a male heir, they challenge the traditional inheritance laws, which favor only men, and demand a more equitable settlement. It is important to note that they don't just say "pretty please," they state their case in the strongest possible language. The Eternal hears them and instructs Moses to amend the law, thus making legal protection for disenfranchised women part of Torah. Later books of the Tanakh shed the spotlight on other impressive women: Ruth, a "Jew by choice" who, as an ancestor of David, was a forebear of Jesus; Esther, who risked her marriage and her life to save her people; and Deborah, a judge and prophet—almost-unheard-of roles for a woman in Biblical times—who led her troops in a successful battle against a foreign oppressor.

Perhaps without intending to, the early stories of the Torah also shed some interesting light on the role of women in humanity's unfolding awareness of, and relationship with, a divine Being. Eve, the first woman according to the Creation story, is the first human to engage in any kind of conversation. (Wags will say that women have never stopped talking since.) She is also the first human to speak of God: in Genesis 3:3, when "the serpent" (aka the "slinking whisperer") tempts her to eat the forbidden fruit of the "Tree of All Knowledge," she at first objects, "But God says we mustn't. . . ." And it is Eve who dares to pursue knowledge even at a terrible cost. When she sees "how desirable the insight [is] that the tree would bring," she takes a bite and takes the consequences. Where is Adam in this picture? He doesn't engage, he doesn't question, he merely eats the fruit and then lets Eve take the rap for his disobedience. He shows no consciousness of the Eternal, and no personal conscience, until it's too late. In that first mention of God, Eve uses the word *Elohim*, a kind of generic word for God. A few lines later, she is also the first human to use God's more personal name, the Tetragrammaton YHVH described in chapter 3. Furthermore, Eve is the first human to speak in terms of co-creation with God: having borne her first son, Cain, she says, according to at least two translations (Plaut, *A Modern Commentary*; Friedman, *Commentary on the Torah*), "Both I and YHVH have made a man." Again, where is Adam? I like this woman, Eve; she is one powerful human being!

Another woman with amazing spiritual insight is Sarah's slave, Hagar. Unable to conceive a child and desperate to please her husband, Abraham (then named Abram), Sarah tells him to lie with her slave. If Hagar conceives, it will be as if it were Sarah's own child. But of course it isn't. Hagar, who has languished in slavery under a demanding mistress, finds herself in the advantaged position of having something that Sarah wants: a pregnancy with Abraham's child. She looks with contempt at Sarah, and Sarah comes down on her hard. Hagar runs away and is intercepted by an angel, who tells her that the child she carries will be a powerful man and progenitor of a multitude. That child, of course, is Ishmael, forefather of our Muslim sisters and brothers. Then, according to the story, the "angel" turns out to be YHVH, and Hagar turns to the Eternal and says, "You are *El Ro'i*," which means "the one who sees me" (Gen. 16:13). This is the only name given to God by a woman in Torah, and what a beautiful name it is! The human longing for union with God is a longing for relationship, a longing to be known to the depths of our being. "Lord, You have searched me out and known me," says the Psalmist many generations later (Ps. 139:1), but it was a woman who first knew and expressed that sacred truth in the pages of Torah.

I find it striking that the biblical passages containing the myths of human origins are able to credit women with the first human knowledge of, and co-creation with, the Eternal One, but by the time of the earliest Hebrews women have slipped into the same place of subordination and semi-visibility as their Muslim sisters. It is not at all certain that women had a place at Sinai—Torah talks only about the men being summoned to hear and ratify our covenant with the Eternal. For the better part of three thousand years, women were kept in the home or hidden behind a screen in synagogue and forbidden to raise their voices in worship with men. Originally they were exempt from the rigors of worship so that they could concentrate on rearing children and providing a good home, but that exemption soon became a proscription. It didn't last. Today, in the spirit of the present tense described in the Jewish Reflections in chapter 3, we women are claiming our place as full members of the Tribe at Sinai—and not only at Sinai, but on the bimah as rabbis and cantors in all but the most staunchly orthodox synagogues. We are no longer content to be "other" within the Jewish family, and the long, painful history has perhaps made us more sensitive to our sisters in Islam and the marginalized in all societies. It is long past time for all of us—women and men, Jews, Christians, Muslims, humans of every nation and persuasion—to look beyond ourselves and see in each other the loving eyes of *El Ro'enu*, the God who sees us all.

PRACTICES

I have two practices that, when I remember them, help me through difficult encounters with my fellow beings.

The first practice is most useful for those brief moments of aggravation when someone cuts me off on the freeway, jumps a line, makes a hurtful comment—the little things that raise the blood pressure much higher than warranted. The moment I catch myself thinking what a jerk that person is, I sing silently (or aloud, if the situation permits) the first line of the priestly blessing in the Torah: *Y'varekh'kha Adonai v'yish'm'rekha*—May the Eternal One bless you and protect you! (Num. 6:24). Though it is called a "priestly" blessing, there is nothing that says we ordinary folk can't wish the same goodness for each other. The magic is not in priesthood or even in the words. The magic is in the effect it has on my own being the moment I say the words: I have let go of my anger and my mind is back in synagogue on Yom Kippur, savoring the moment when we have confessed our shortcomings and shared the peace of that beautiful blessing. While my mind is thus occupied, the culprit has time to make a clean getaway, and I am free to get on with the day without giving the encounter another thought.

My other practice helps with chronic difficulties of the type we all like to complain and gossip about: a relative or friend who is always getting on our nerves, a family responsibility that is getting us down—the kind of thing that has us already narrating the story to a confidante in our heads while we're still actually with the person we're complaining about. When I catch myself doing this, I stop the inner narration, gaze consciously at the person I'm with, and in my heart I say *Hineini*, here I am—and here *you* are, and here *God* is. The effect is miraculous. I relax, the other person relaxes, and the difficult moment passes. Try it—you will like it!

Christian Reflections

So then you are no longer strangers and aliens, but you are citizens with the saints and also members of the household of God. (Eph. 2:19)

According to this passage, in Christ there is a new unity that embraces diverse groups that were formerly at odds. Jesus himself shows an openness, sometimes alarming to his followers, to the "other." Those who represent that category—women, Roman officials and their cronies, Samaritans and other foreigners, the ritually impure, "sinners" —sometimes reciprocate by recognizing and embracing his God-given power to heal and transform. In several cases they provide a bracing and exemplary contrast to the myopia of the insiders.

For Paul and other early Jewish followers of the Christian way, God's apparent move to expand the bounds of divine preference from their native tribe to include the *goyim*, the quintessential "others," was confounding and disturbing. Like most other human groups, Christians since then have all too often tried to redraw the lines of chosenness, in this case by making allegiance to Jesus the new test of admittance to privileged status. However, at the core of the Christian message is the lesson that in God there is no "other," an insight Peter shares in Acts 10:34–35: "I truly understand that God shows no partiality, but in every nation anyone who fears [God] and does what is right is acceptable to [God]." This perspective supports followers of Jesus in imitating him by engaging with—and perhaps even learning more about God from—those whom he could have rejected out-of-hand as being strangers to the divine.

"There is no longer Jew or Greek, no longer slave or free, no longer male and female; for all of you are one in Christ Jesus" (Gal. 3:28). Rather than affirming difference as a reality intentionally created by God, this passage and others like it seem to see diversity as something that has been overcome in light of God's revelation in Jesus. I have some empathy for this attitude when I consider Paul's words in Romans. "I am speaking the truth in Christ—I am not lying; my conscience confirms it by the Holy Spirit— I have great sorrow and unceasing anguish in my heart. For I could wish that I myself were accursed and cut off from Christ for the sake of my own people, my kindred according to the flesh" (9:1–3). What has Paul so troubled is his growing realization that, as he did before he received a calling to serve God through following Jesus, most of his fellow Jews were dismissing Jesus' message as misguided at best and detrimental for Judaism at worst. Paul is accustomed to thinking of his Jewish people as those singled out by God for special favor, so he finds their rejection of Jesus to be perplexing. Tensions between the Gentile and Jewish believers are compounding Paul's unhappiness, as he preaches tolerance to all parties and grapples with these bewildering developments. In the past, Paul has stood up against opponents who have said that Gentiles must take on the practices of Judaism in order to enter the Christian fold. But the situation in Rome has struck at the roots of Paul's identity in God: after all Jesus, the Messiah, is a Jew, one of Paul's own kind. Already Paul is catching a whiff of the Christian anti-Judaism that later would become a shameful besetting sin. Almost as if he needs to remind himself, Paul repeats in this letter that the human need for God's saving action is universal, as is access to God's grace (see Rom. 3:9; 1:16). Another way of putting it is that God has revealed an expanded definition of chosenness in Jesus: "But now in Christ Jesus you who once were far off have been brought near by the blood of Christ" (Eph. 2:13). The membership requirements for God's in-crowd have opened up.

Jesus did not spend much time defining categorically who was in and who was out. He certainly didn't place much value in the family identity so important in his culture. When his family members came to claim him (and probably remove him from the trouble he was making), he asked, "Who are my mother and my brothers? . . . Whoever does the will of God is my brother and sister and mother" (Mark 3:34, 35). In encounters he had and stories he told involving those defined as "other," Jesus showed that prejudices can limit our ability to see God at work. One of my favorite examples, as you can tell by the number of times I mention it in this book, is the parable in Luke 10:30–37. The unlikely hero in this story is a Samaritan, who goes to great lengths to aid a traveler, presumably Jewish, who has been robbed and beaten. At first glance, the twist in the story is that it is the Samaritan rather than the representatives of the religious establishment who acts compassionately. However, it took me years and the help of a scholar to notice also that Jesus tells this story in answer to a question about who is worthy of our help and care. Instead of answering the initial question, Jesus turns it inside out by having the helper be someone whom his audience might not deign to touch were he himself the victim. To top it off, someone centuries ago named this parable "The *Good* Samaritan," which makes our hero seem to be the exception to the Samaritan norm. I liken this title to the comment from well-meaning people who say to me as a compliment, "But I don't think of you as black."

Jesus ups the ante in his encounters with those who were "double trouble" according to the norms of his day. The woman in John 4 painstakingly points out to him when they meet at a well that as a Jewish man he has no business asking her, a Samaritan woman, for a drink of water—or for anything else, for that matter. The evangelist is equally painstaking in educating his readers about the cultural context with a parenthetical remark that "Jews do not share things in common with Samaritans" (4:9). A conversation ensues that is remarkable in its candor, reciprocity, and apparent ease. After her initial caveat, the woman is assertive and unabashed, even after Jesus discloses his knowledge of her apparently checkered past. No wonder the disciples are both "astonished" and unwilling to interrupt when they find their teacher in this exchange (4:27). This meeting launches the woman's vocation as an impassioned, credible witness to Jesus. "Many Samaritans from that city," writes the evangelist, "believed in him because of the woman's testimony" (4:39).

In another surprising conversation with a "foreign" woman, Jesus himself actually displays something disturbingly akin to prejudice (Matt. 15:22–28). In response to the woman's request for healing for her daughter, he says that his mission is restricted "to the lost sheep of the house of Israel." When she persists, he says, "It is not fair to take the children's food and throw it to the dogs." She comes right back at him with the rejoinder that "even the dogs eat the crumbs that fall from their master's table." The first time I read this story, I recoiled in horror at that remark. I thought, "She's letting herself be called a dog! Where's her self-respect?" Her child gets healed, but at what cost? Over the years my view of this story has changed radically, and I now see the process of transformation it conveys as moving in several directions simultaneously. In her fierce love for her child, this woman steps forward selflessly to challenge Jesus' narrow view of his own calling. In her verbal victory, she smashes any preconceived notions of her categorical inferiority and steps forward into her full identity as beloved daughter of God. When they heard of Jesus' words, "Woman, great is your faith! Let it be done for you as you wish," early Jewish Christians had to reexamine their prejudices about the boundaries of God's love.

A mode of response to the "other" that is reflected in Christian texts and traditions is to work out a system of cataloguing and evaluating difference with the result that some folks end up being "more equal" than others, to paraphrase George Orwell's classic line in the novel *Animal Farm*. Not surprisingly, those who devise the tests often find that their own group consistently scores at the top. When we can find in our scriptures supporting evidence for our evaluation, our hierarchies take on sacred status: those at the top are closest to God and are the divinely sanctioned leaders for the rest. "Wives, be subject to your husbands as you are to the Lord. For the husband is the head of the wife, just as Christ is head of the church, the body of which he is the Savior . . . Children, obey your parents in the Lord, for this is right . . . Slaves, obey your earthly masters with fear and trembling, in singleness of heart, as you obey Christ" (Eph. 5:22–23, 6:1, 6:5). Passages like these have been readily used to justify systemic subordination of women, abuse of children, and enslavement of whole races of people. I am thankful that they do not represent the only perspectives on these subjects in the Christian Testament and that, like the woman in the story mentioned earlier, many Christians have found their voices and have not remained complicit in their own oppression.

One of my fervent prayers is that we Christians examine, repent of, and change the ways in which we have used our relationship to God in Christ as evidence of our superiority and wielded Jesus as a weapon against other children of the one God. We have also sought to protect our material privileges at the expense of the rest of the created order, banking on the belief that Jesus will come back and snatch his chosen out of the mess we have created. We Christians are obviously not alone in this kind of behavior. However, we are prey to the common temptation to selective blindness, especially since 9/11.

An alternative perspective on difference and diversity comes from one of the spirituals about heaven that I learned as a child. "'Oh, won't you sit down?' 'No, I can't sit down.' 'Oh, won't you sit down?' 'No, I can't sit down, 'cause I just got to heaven, gotta look around.'" The newcomer to the celestial realms goes on a tour, asking, "Who's that yonder?" about different groups of folks dressed in various colors of clothing. The answers come: The people dressed in red "must be the people that Moses led"; those in white "look like the children of the Israelite." In my mind, heaven in this song was the name for the place where we could identify our kin through our common relationship as children of the Creator. So, I will continue to pray with Jesus, "Thy kingdom come; thy will be done on earth, as in heaven."

6

The Mystery of
the Invisible World

With God are the keys of the Unseen,
the treasures that none know but God.
(Quran 6:59)

Muhammad's Night Journey

Every Muslim is enchanted by the story of the Prophet's mysterious Night
Journey (*al-Isra*), which is mentioned briefly in the Quran (17:1) and
described in some detail in the hadith. Rapt in prayer and meditation one
night in Mecca at a time of great sorrow in his life, the Prophet was
astounded to find himself mounted on a magical steed called Buraq. Wherever Buraq's glance landed, the next bound brought them to that place.
Clinging to Buraq's flowing mane as the steed bounded through the air, the
Prophet traveled horizontally from Mecca to "the farthest mosque" (*al-
masjidul-aqsa*) on a rocky hilltop in Jerusalem. There he was greeted by the
souls of many prophets, including Abraham and Moses, and then, accompanied by the angel Gabriel, he began to ascend a celestial ladder of light
leading upward to the royal throne of God. Along the way, the Prophet was
bedazzled by the signs and sight of mysteries all around him, including
luminous angels prostrating themselves to God in praise and gratitude.

At the furthest boundary of the seventh level of heaven stood a "Lote-tree," which was "shrouded in mystery unspeakable" (Quran 53:16). In the mystical metaphor of the Quran, the Lote-tree (today called lotus tree, probably a jujube) is a symbol of the heavenly bliss that awaits those who surrender to Allah: wild, the tree is stunted and thorny; when cultivated, it yields both shade and fruit. That the Lote-tree was shrouded in mystery suggests that Muhammad had reached the farthest extent of heavenly knowledge that humans and angels can attain. Indeed, at this place of the radiant Lote-tree, the angel Gabriel told the Prophet that the light was singeing his wings and he could go no further. But the Prophet's sight "neither swerved nor wavered" as he beheld the tree (53:17) and in the rapture of the moment "truly did he see, of the signs of his Lord, the Greatest" (53:18). Continuing his celestial journey, the Prophet ventured into two more levels of heaven before returning to earth.

The hallowed site of the Prophet's glorious ascent into the unseen world is marked by a magnificent shrine, the Dome of the Rock, built by the ninth caliph of Islam, Abd al-Malik, in the late seventh century. On the same holy hilltop, known in Arabic as *Haram al-Sharif*, stands the al-Aqsa Mosque, built to commemorate "the farthest mosque" referred to in the Quranic version of the story (17:1). In Islam, the al-Aqsa Mosque is considered the third holiest place, after the mosques in Mecca and Medina, on the face of the earth.

Whether the Prophet's Night Journey happened in a literal sense, as some orthodox Muslims believe, or in a mystical vision during a dark night of the soul, it holds profound insights about the unseen world. The horizontal journey from Mecca to Jerusalem represents our level of reality in the visible world as we participate in the bazaar of life and experience the ups and downs, joys and sorrows of earthly existence. The vertical journey symbolizes the reality of the invisible world and our connection with it through prayer, silence, meditation, dreams, and communion with nature. Both levels of reality are sacred. The secret to leading a fulfilling life, sages tell us, is to participate equally over a lifetime in the visible and invisible worlds. To skeptics who dismiss the invisible world as the product of one's fancies, Rumi asserts that it is in fact a dimension of "traffic and trade" which we should not ignore, for it is "a place of income." The visible world, which Rumi calls a "place of more or less," is, in his imagery, a "place of expenditure."

Invisible beings in the visible world

Under normal circumstances the invisible world is exactly that—invisible. But from time to time throughout the ages, the denizens of that world have come to the aid of those who have what is called an "increased necessity." At the time of the Night Journey, Muhammad had dire need of assurances from Divinity. Both his beloved wife, Khadija, and his uncle Abu Talib, his consistent protector who kept the Meccans at bay, had died and he was bereft of their support and protection. When he sought assistance at the oasis of Ta'if, the people stoned him and drove him away. The Prophet was in desperate straits, and God mercifully sent the angel Gabriel to take him on that rapturous journey to "show him some of Our Signs" (17:1). When Abraham was in deep need of assurances about the existence of One God, Allah showed him "the kingdom of the heavens and the earth that he be one of those who have faith with certainty" (6:75). When Moses was terrified by the divine command to confront the mighty Pharaoh in Egypt, God saw that he needed support from the unseen world. Thus God turned Moses' staff into a snake and back to its original state and then caused Moses' hand to become luminous with celestial light. God sent this divine support from the invisible world so that "We may show thee two of Our Greater Signs" (20:23).

The Quran mentions a mysterious "servant of Allah" who takes Moses on a mission to teach him patience in interpreting events that he cannot understand with ordinary human knowledge (18:65). This messenger has no name, but traditionally he is called *Khidr*, "the green one," either for the color of his garments or for the divine freshness of his knowledge and help. The Quran says this messenger is the one on whom "We had bestowed Mercy from Ourselves and whom We had taught knowledge from Our own Presence" (18:65). Whatever his name and provenance, Sufis believe this same messenger and others like him have appeared numerous times over the centuries to help those who are in extreme need on the earthly plane.

Why is it that some people are blessed with a sense of the Divine Presence or celestial messengers in their lives, while others are still waiting for the experience? A favorite teaching story in India is the nineteenth-century tale of Vivekananda and his spiritual master, the Hindu saint Ramakrishna. Vivekananda had been complaining to his teacher that despite his extensive devotional practices, he did not experience the presence of God in his life. One day while they were bathing in the Ganges, Ramakrishna dunked Vivekananda's head in the water and kept it there for many seconds while his disciple flailed wildly and gasped desperately for air. Then he released him and, after apologizing for the terrible fright he had caused, he told Vivekananda that when his need for God was as great as his need for air, Divinity would appear to him. Alas, says Rumi, most of us are too distracted by the "carnal screams of our lives" to hear the whisper of the Beloved.

The story of the Prophet's Night Journey also reminds us that the subtle mysteries of the invisible world can be perceived only by the heart, which, in the words of the Holy Book, "never falsified what it saw" (53:11). We need an open heart to embrace the unseen world. "O my Sustainer!" Moses cried to God. "Expand me my breast " (20:25).

Angels

One of the abiding mysteries of beauty in the invisible world is the presence of angels. These radiant, genderless beings of light act as intermediaries between God and the visible world. The root word for angel in Arabic is *malakut*, meaning "messenger." These messengers appear at least eighty times in the Quran and repeatedly in the hadith. From the popular to the esoteric, angels occupy a central role in Islam. Belief in angels is part of faith and every time an angel is invoked, an observant Muslim says "upon him be peace," the same words that follow the mention of a prophet. According to mystical angelology, an angel accompanies every drop of rain and seven angels are needed for a leaf to grow on a tree.

The primary angels in Islam are four archangels that are also known in the Jewish and Christian traditions: Jibra'il (Gabriel), Mika'il (Michael), Izra'il (Azrael), and Israf'il (Raphael). Each of these angelic messengers has a specific function. "Not one of us has but a place appointed; and we are verily arranged in ranks for service" (37:164–165). Jibra'il, for instance, has delivered divine revelations to prophets throughout the ages, as he did to Muhammad on the Night of Power in 610 CE. It was also Jibra'il who accompanied the Prophet on his Night Journey and announced to Mary that she would be the virgin mother of Jesus. Mika'il, mentioned only once in the Quran, is charged with providing sustenance to nurture humanity and knowledge for souls. Izra'il, the "angel of death," retrieves the human soul at death and returns it to the Creator. And Israf'il will sound the trumpet on the Day of Judgment, "when all that are in the heavens and on earth will swoon" (39:68). The Quran also mentions angels in heaven, overseen by Ridwan, whose name means "good pleasure," and in hell, overseen by Malik, whose name means "master." True to the idea of a taskmaster, the latter angels are "stern and severe" and will not hesitate to do as Divine Justice commands (66:6). The hadith mention three additional angels: Nakir and Munkar, who question the dead in their graves about their faith and good works, and Ruman, who subjects the dead to trials.

In addition to the major companies of angels, there are vast numbers of guardian angels in Islamic tradition. It is said that every human being is blessed with at least two of these angels, one on the right and one on the left. The Quran calls them "watchers, noble writers, who know whatever you do" (82:10–12) and a hadith says that "They mind your works; when a work is good, they praise God, and when one is evil, they ask God to forgive you." Remarkably, we are also blessed with "attendant angels before and behind" who guard us "by command of God" and encourage us to do the work of inner transformation, "for verily never will God change the condition of a people until they change it themselves" (13:11). As if these personal angels were not enough, the Quran says there are also traveling angels who throng to places of sacred worship to encourage us to pray, especially on Fridays, the Islamic day of worship. In such places the air is said to be pulsating with angelic movement.

The foregoing are the angels who dwell on earth or commute between heaven and earth. In the heavens, says the Quran, there is another class of angels, the cherubim, who have withdrawn from every work, by grace of

God, except to contemplate and celebrate the beauty of God. They "glorify God by night and day, never failing" (21:20).

Thus, angelic vibrations in heaven and on earth help the humble and sincere worshipper to have a vision of the heavenly world and do "righteous deeds." But although angels are constantly active all around us, their presence is invisible. Angels belong to the world of the unseen, and this is just as well, for on the day they become visible to the human eye, their "descending in ranks" will herald the end of the world and begin the Day of Judgment, a "day of dire difficulty for the misbelievers" (25:25–26).

Despite their general invisibility, however, many people over the centuries have reported seeing angels in human form, and the Quran and hadith concur that this might be possible. The Holy Book reveals that angels appeared to the prophets Abraham and Lot in the form of humans, and the Prophet Muhammad claimed that a stranger who asked him pointed questions on Islam and then disappeared was actually the angel Gabriel. On another occasion Muhammad told his followers that when he was an infant he was visited by "two men clothed in white, carrying a gold basin full of snow." These angelic beings split open his chest and brought forth his heart, he said, and "This also they split open, taking from it a black clot, which they cast away. Then they washed my breast with the snow." What a powerful metaphor the Prophet has given us for doing our spiritual work! It is only by grace of God, and perhaps with the help of our personal angels, that we are able to cleave open our hearts, remove the clots of self-centered ego, and bathe ourselves in the pure, refreshing snow of divine sanctity.

As a child I was naturally fascinated by the topic of angels. Their love of God and their care and concern for humanity were deeply inspiring, but some of the stories were quite disturbing. I didn't like the angels who bothered the dead, who tormented the souls in hell, who "cast terror into the unbelievers' hearts" (8:12) on the battlefield. They seemed more like demons than angels to me, but my teachers explained that angels vary in their degree of tenderness and are assigned different functions according to "the rangers in their ranks" (37:1). Also, our sages tell us, we live in a world of duality and the stern behavior of some of the angels is a reflection of our own shadow side. Their actions, seemingly terrible and cruel, are actually a form of love beyond our understanding. As Moses learned on his allegorical journey with Khidr, we need to realize that we don't know the whole story. God, whose commands the angels are obeying, is infinitely compassionate. To be sure, God can be wrathful with wrongdoers, but, says the Quran, our Sustainer is "Oft-Forgiving, Most Merciful" (6:54) and in a hadith qudsi God assures us that "My mercy prevails over My wrath."

In all of the literature on angels in Islam, most astonishing to me is the insight suggested by the Quran that we humans have the potential to rise higher than the angels: you and I have the ability to become even more luminous than angels! Angels do not possess free will, but we humans do. Angels cannot help but be luminous, but when we choose, in the face of temptations and inconveniences, to overcome self-centeredness, open our hearts, and turn them in service to God, we will become surpassingly radiant with light and exalted by God. Our human light will flow upward, say the mystics, and a mysterious light from the celestial realms will descend, and the two will join, creating an effulgence of "light upon light" (24:35). The Quran tells us that God asked the angels to bow to the human prototype, but some of them complained, whereupon the Creator gently chided them, "Truly, I know that which you do not know" (2:30). The astounding potential in each human being is a secret close to the Creator's heart. Rumi says that the all-merciful God revealed to him a secret: there is no angel so sublime who can be granted for one moment what can be granted to you forever. "And I hung my head astounded," says the poet.

As with all of the Holy Book, it is important to approach the verses about angels with an open heart and remember that many Quranic verses are metaphorical. How else can one fathom the mystery of the angels who bear the throne of God, described as "those brought nigh" (4:172), or the angels who supervise each of the "seven levels" of heaven? To many Muslims, angels represent an aspect of the ineffable spirit of God, often felt as inspiration, but nonetheless wrapped in mystery. "I will assist you with a thousand of the angels, ranks on ranks," Allah says in the Quran (8:9). Beyond that, simply remember the truth of these holy words, "Of knowledge it is only a little that is communicated to you. . . ." (17:85).

Jinns

Peculiar to the cast of invisible beings in Islam are the jinns, which are said to have been created before human beings "from the fire of a scorching wind" (Quran 15:27). The word "jinn" comes from the root word *janna*, meaning "hidden." The English words "genie" and "genius" are derived from the same root. Jinns are believed to be possessed of free will and accountable for their deeds on the Day of Judgment. Because they are not bound to the will of God, their behavior can be unpredictable. As they say teasingly in the Holy Book, "There are among us some that are righteous, and some the contrary: we follow divergent paths" (72:11). Thus jinns can be playful and supportive to humans, but also mischievous and willing to mislead. The Muslim world abounds in stories of these invisible creatures. Anecdotes over the centuries suggest that they are capable of moving things and making audible sounds. The people of my Bengali village tell count-less stories of jinns who have caused villagers to lose their way in the dark or, more seriously, to stray spiritually from the "straight path" by encour-aging them to indulge in substance abuse. Some pious elders in the village claim that they have been able to enlist the help of jinns through spiritual practices to heal and empower those in need.

Iblis—Shaitan—Satan

The true enemy of happiness and holiness in Islam is the fallen angel known as Iblis, whose name means "the disappointed." Iblis is also known as Shaitan, meaning "one who is far from God," from the root word *shatana*, "far away." Non-Muslims will recognize Shaitan as a cognate for Satan, and they will also recognize the story of Shaitan's descent into hell. When God asked the angels to bow to humanity, Shaitan (aka Iblis) "refused and was haughty" (2:34). "I am better than he," Iblis complained: "Thou didst cre-ate me from fire, and him from clay" (7:12). God then cursed Iblis and said, "Get out!" (7:13) but Iblis pleaded for a reprieve and God allowed him to continue his unhappy existence on the earth until the Day of Judg-ment (7:15). Alas for humankind, reprieve for Iblis means countless oppor-tunities in every generation to prove that humans are undeserving of the honor in which they are held by their Creator. A sulky Satan promises to "lie in wait for them on Thy straight Way" and "assault them from before them and behind them, from their right and their left" (7:16 and 17). "Nor wilt Thou find, in most of them, gratitude for Thy mercies," he taunts their Creator (7:17).

Elsewhere in the Quran Iblis is described as a jinn, a creature of lesser power, but whatever his origin, the point is the same: Iblis-Shaitan incurred divine wrath because of his haughtiness and arrogance. For all that, should he have been driven out of heaven? A number of Islamic mystics have pointed out that Adam and his spouse also disobeyed God, but because they apologized in all sincerity, God forgave them. In the case of Iblis, the weight of his pride was so onerous, and his refusal to back down so egregious, that in spite of centuries of devotion to God before that fatal day, his sustained devotion had no weight in the balance at all. The lesson for us is that the greatest cause of a downfall, for either angel, jinn, or human, is arrogance and pride.

It is highly significant, say Islamic mystics, that when Iblis promises to waylay humanity, he invokes the power and glory of God. "By Thy Power," he says in one translation, and "By Thy Glory" in another, "I will certainly cause them all to rebel and go astray" (38:82). The implication is that all the temptations, trials, and tribulations placed on our path are sanctioned in a mysterious way by our Creator and are part of the divine design for each one of us. The placement of satanic energy on earth helps us evolve into complete human beings. Without Iblis to test us, how could there be forged in us souls of sincerity, truthfulness, patience, and compassion? Both satanic and angelic spirits present us with objects of desire to awaken our power of choice.

The belief in divine omnipresence raises a disturbing question. If the Face of Allah is everywhere, is Satan also the Face of Allah? Yes, say the mystics, much to the consternation of those who habitually curse Satan whenever his name is mentioned. This does not mean that God approves of Satan's actions and temptations. Rumi suggests that we ponder the following: A doctor needs people to fall sick in order to sustain his or her livelihood. Does this mean that doctors approve of disease and sickness? A baker needs people to be hungry in order to support the family business.

Does the baker approve of people starving? Of course not. In a telling verse in the Quran, God warns that Satan will say to humanity,

> I had no authority over you
> Except to call you, but ye
> Listened to me: then
> Reproach not me, but reproach
> Your own souls. (14:22)

In a *sura*, or chapter, often recited during Islamic prayers, the Quran tells us to seek refuge in God from the "slinking whisperer" who insinuates himself into every human heart (114:1–6). According to a hadith, the Prophet told his followers that he had it on God's own authority that there were just two humans who were not subject to the "slinking whisperer": Mary and Jesus. When his followers asked if he, the Prophet, had a slinking whisperer, he replied, "Yes! But don't worry, for I have made the devil a Muslim!" In other words, Muhammad had made sure that his whisperer was surrendered to God. The question for the rest of us is, shall we listen to the slinking whisperer, or shall we heed the voice of Divinity within us? The choice is ours.

The most important message of this sura, and others like it, is that the refuge we seek should be in God, "the Cherisher of Humankind" (114:1). Rather than curse the unhappy tempter, focus your attention on God. Become aware of the idolatry of the ego, as displayed by Iblis, and lovingly work to bring God into the center of your life. Pray to your Sustainer, and know that you have many allies in the invisible world.

> Remember ye implored
> The assistance of your Sustainer,
> And God answered you:
> "I will assist you
> With a thousand of the angels
> Rank on ranks." (8:9)

Rabia once was asked if she hated Satan. "No," she replied. The questioner was surprised. "How is that?" Rabia answered, "My love of God leaves no room for hating." When we are able to love God as much as Rabia did, we shall be fulfilling God's purpose for creating Shaitan and placing him on earth in the midst of our lives.

Jewish Reflections

Every morning an angel opens his mouth and says, The Lord reigns, the Lord did reign, the Lord will reign for ever and ever. (Talmudic legend)

In this twenty-first-century age of reason, it seems that only the woo-woo fringe will admit to having anything to do with the invisible world. Yet most of us can tell stories of mysterious events in our lives: a shove that pushes us out of the way of an on-coming car, a ghostly whistle that alerts us to danger, a sudden impulse to change a flight hours before the doomed plane crashes. Many families have their lore of unexplained events that raise the hairs on the back of the neck. In my family it was three knocks on the door of a farmhouse out in the middle of nowhere in 1942. Everyone in the house heard the knock, but there was no one at the door—or so it seemed. Days later, the family learned that their son and brother, Emmett, was killed at that very hour during the Allied invasion of North Africa. It seems likely that by a phenomenon of teleportation known in Hebrew as *kefitzat haderech* ("jumping of the way," or short cut), Emmett had come to say goodbye. I never knew my Uncle Emmett, but I like to think he is reading these words over my shoulder and smiling to be remembered after all these years.

"It seems," "I like to think"—how we moderns shy away from flat-out acknowledging the invisible world that is just on the other side of a very thin veil! The ancients were not so sophisticated and proud. To them it was no stretch at all to speak of invisible beings as if they were right there in plain sight. And perhaps they are right there for us too, if we would but open our hearts to see. My rabbi often says that he believes the Eternal didn't speak to the ancients any differently from the way the Eternal speaks to us today—it's just that as a culture, we have forgotten how to listen. So perhaps the ancients were actually more sophisticated than we are!

The pages of the Torah are full of celestial beings and other-worldly phenomena. There's that talking serpent (the "slinking whisperer") in the

Garden of Eden (Gen. 3:1–5), a trio of men that morph into angels that morph into God and then back again at Abraham's camp in Mamre (Gen. 18:1ff), Jacob's celestial ladder (Gen. 28:12ff) and midnight wrestler (Gen. 31:25ff), the voice of God in a burning bush (Exod. 3:1ff), Moses' rod that turns into a snake (Exod. 7:8ff), Balaam's talking donkey (Num. 22:23ff)—all of these and more are so taken for granted that the Torah doesn't even bother to offer details for us skeptical folk. That is left for the rabbis, and Midrash is full of their fanciful explanations.

Of these stories in the Torah, I am most moved by the paranormal adventures of Jacob. In the first one, Jacob has just done serious dirt to his brother, Esau, and is on the run. Night falls while he's in the wilderness, and he improvises a place to sleep. In that lonely place he dreams about a luminous ladder or stairway into the heavens, and on it he sees angelic beings going up and down. (By at least one Islamic account of Muhammad's Night Journey, this is the very ladder on which the Prophet ascended into heaven.) Translations and illustrations of this famous scene have the ladder set on the ground, reaching into heaven, but in fact the grammar of the word *artzah* (earth) in the Hebrew original suggests that the ladder was suspended from heaven toward the earth. The direction of all this celestial energy is downward, and the lesson is powerful: as much as we humans think we are trying to reach "up" to God, the Eternal is reaching "down" to us. As Jamal says elsewhere in this book, if we take one step toward God, God comes running toward us. Jacob awakens from his dream, shaken and transformed. "Surely the Eternal is present in this place," he says, "and I did not know it!" (Gen. 28:16). Again, there is a beautiful lesson for us: just as Jacob realizes belatedly that God is present with him in the wilderness, so we can learn to open our fearful hearts to the reality of God's presence even in our darkest hours. That ladder between heaven and earth is not reserved for Jacob and the Prophet Muhammad. It is there for anyone who is willing to abandon the miasma of doubt and skepticism and step onto the first rung in a spirit of surrender to the Beloved.

In Jacob's second mystical experience, he is on his way back to the home of his youth many years later. Older, wiser, and definitely richer, he has sent gift-laden envoys to Esau in an attempt to mollify his brother for the terrible wrong he did so long ago. On the eve of their encounter, he secures his wives and children and then crosses the Jordan to spend the night alone. There are no dreams on this night—he doesn't get any sleep at all. Instead, "A man wrestled with him until the break of dawn" (Gen. 32:25). The mysterious "man" turns out to be a divine being—*El*, in fact—who informs Jacob that henceforth his name will be Israel (think *Isra-el*) because he has "striven with beings divine and human, and prevailed" (Gen. 32:29). From that day to this, the descendants of Jacob have been known as the Tribe of Israel, the tribe of those who wrestle with God. In Jewish spirituality, Jacob's wrestling match has become a metaphor for the struggle between our lower and higher selves, between the wiles of the slinking whisperer and the inner wisdom of our divine nature. Whether it is our higher self or the lower that prevails is up to us, with the grace of God and a little help from our invisible friends.

Those friends are the angels, heavenly creatures that resemble the angels of Islam in almost every way. The Hebrew word for angel is *malakh*, almost identical to the Arabic *malakut*; in both cases, the word means "messenger." In a broader sense, angels are seen as functionaries who convey God's will to human beings and see that it is done. Best-known of the angels in Judaism are the seraphim, cherubim, archangels, and guardian angels. The seraphim that Isaiah saw in a vision are six-winged creatures who surround the throne of God crying "Holy! Holy! Holy!" (Isa. 6:2). In earlier scripture, they are fiery, serpent-like creatures that chastise the Israelites when they are rebelling against God in the wilderness (Num. 21:5). The cherubim, fierce angels not to be confused with Renaissance-era cherubs, also operate in both earthly and heavenly realms: on earth they guard the gates of Eden with fiery swords (Gen. 3:24) and in the heavens they surround the throne of God (Ezek. 1:1–3). The archangels, which shuttle back and forth between heaven and earth, are known in Judaism as Micha'el, the "commander-in-chief" and angel of protection; Gabri'el, the messenger; Rapha'el, the healer; and Uri'el, the angel of light. Note that I have separated "el" from the rest of the names with an apostrophe, as they are done in Arabic, to show that the angels are personal agents of *El*, the Eternal Holy One. It is interesting to note that the archangel Uri'el of Judaism does not appear in the Islamic line-up, nor does the Islamic Azra'il, the angel of death, appear in the Jewish list. There is an Angel of Death in Judaism, but this nameless creature is not nearly as benign as Azra'il seems to be; in fact, it seems to be regarded almost as a companion of the *Sitra Achra*, the "Destroyer" from the Other Side.

This brings us to the concept of an evil spirit in Judaism. While Judaism recognizes that there are adversaries to goodness, and such entities do appear in the Tanakh (starting with the serpent in the Garden of Eden), there is no particular being named Satan (a word that means "adversary" in Hebrew). To the extent that an evil spirit has been personified at all, it is called ha-satan ("the satan") and is identified with the human inclination to evil (*yetzer ra*), an inclination that vies with the inclination to good (*yetzer tov*) in every human heart. Thus the forces of evil have no preternatural power in Judaism, and with our free will we are as able to take the high road toward union with our divine essence as to take the low road of separation and despair.

Helping us to choose the high road, according to Jewish folklore, are ranks upon ranks of guardian angels. Just as Islamic legends say that angels accompany raindrops and encourage leaves to unfold, a Talmudic parable says that every blade of grass has an angel bending over it saying, "Grow! Grow!" If a mere blade of grass has its own angel, imagine the heavenly hosts that accompany us humans on our daily journeys. According to another delightful legend, every human being is preceded and followed by a pair of angels announcing the presence of God. Think what a glorious world this would be if we paid attention to those announcements and learned to bow to the Divine in everyone we met! In all our talk about the invisible world it is the Divine Presence that really matters, and it is the Divine Presence that we each have the power to manifest in a very real sense to our fellow beings right here and now.

Christian Reflections

All night, all day, angels watching over me, my Lord. . . ." (African-American spiritual)

I recognize Kate's accounts of both the widespread disdain for and the frequent enough, gooseflesh-raising encounters with the invisible world. On one hand, we are inclined to dismiss the bogeyman with amusement or titillate ourselves by witnessing him and his posse in the virtual reality of horror movies and violent video games. At the same time, we are confronted by a multitude of intangible but powerful issues and "isms," both personal and societal. So we yearn for angelic intervention, as long as it comforts us and relieves our pain. It is refreshing, though bewildering at times, to open the Christian Testament and enter a world where, like that of the Quran and the Tanakh, the existence of the unseen world is taken for granted. The insights and responses of our ancestors in faith give substance to this dimension of reality, which is so often hidden from us. We can learn from them how to make our way in that part of God's creation, finding it "a place of income" and meeting its inhabitants—helpful, troublesome, or evil—as fellow creatures with their own roles to play in the larger story. The epistles and gospels reveal many invisible beings playing a number of roles and fulfilling a variety of functions. We see angels in their typical role as envoys from God to humans, either in solo appearances as with Gabriel's visit to Mary (Luke 1:26–38) or en masse as the "heavenly host" that appeared to the sleeping shepherds on the night of Jesus' birth (Luke 2:13–14). From time to time we get a glimpse of the pecking order of the angelic ranks, which seems chiefly to establish where Jesus stands in relation to those other divine beings. For example, Ephesians describes Jesus as ascending to reign "in the heavenly places, far above all rule and authority and power and dominion, and above every name that is named" (1:20–21).

In his earthly life, Jesus also encounters the opposing forces. Often they appear with reinforcements: "My name is Legion; for we are many" (Mark 5:9; see also Luke 8:40). In the gospel of Mark, it is only invisible beings who recognize the unique character of Jesus' relation to God. The demons (along with God and the narrator) are the only ones who call him the Son of God until he dies on the cross. Their superior knowledge about him does not give them power in their confrontations with him, where he always comes out the victor. Even Satan's apparent triumph through Judas's betrayal of Jesus to his enemies is reversed in the event of the resurrection.

The accounts of humans negotiating the invisible realms in Christian scriptures, like the wonderful hadith about Muhammad's converting the slinking whisperer into a Muslim, help me put my own dealings with the unseen world into proper perspective. I learn from Mary to respond with a wholehearted "yes" when I recognize God in the face of the angelic messenger before me. I grieve in comprehension of Judas's suicide after he realizes that he mistook Satan's cleverness as psychological insight or political wisdom. I listen closely when Jesus counsels his disciples after failure to expel a particularly tenacious demon that "this kind can come out only through prayer" (Mark 9:29).

As the Nicene Creed of Christianity says, "We believe in one God, the Father, the Almighty, *maker of heaven and earth, of all that is, seen and unseen.*" The order here is important to me. First, I believe in one God; then, I stand alongside all humanity within the ranks of "all that is, seen and unseen." I do not really need to know whether my status is a little higher (Quran 2:34; 7:11; Ps. 8:5) or a little lower (Heb. 2:7) than that of the angels. What counts is my belief in and alignment with the one God, demonstrated most clearly to my Christian perception by Jesus' total identification with the One who sent him. My orientation to God as Source, Destination, and Way can give me the discernment necessary to engage in the struggle with the unseen, systemic evils that I confront. A favorite passage from Ephesians gives me a bracing caveat in this effort. " For our struggle is not against enemies of blood and flesh, but against the rulers, against the authorities, against the cosmic powers of this present darkness, against the spiritual forces of evil in the heavenly places" (Eph. 6:12).

I need to stay mindful that I do not war against other human beings, against my own flesh and blood. Instead, all humanity is on the same side in the war of resistance against unseen powers of destruction, in the effort to work for the common good, and especially in service and love of the one God. We may find allies in unexpected places to combat the legion of demonic forces—racism, poverty, destruction of the environment, violence—that are part of our everyday experience. When Jesus heard that his disciples had tried to stop someone from using Jesus' name to cast out demons, he said, "Do not stop him; for whoever is not against you is for you" (Luke 9:50).

7

The Mystery of Death

O serene soul, return to your Sustainer,
pleased and pleasing in His Sight.
(Quran 89:27–28)

The wedding with eternity

"Every soul shall have a taste of death," says the Quran (21:35), but "No soul knows what it will earn tomorrow and in what land it will die" (31:34). We all know on an intellectual level that death is the final mystery of life, but how many of us live as if we are aware that we personally are going to face that mystery? If we truly realized that awesome fact, say the spiritual teachers, how could we possibly hold grudges against others or be so invested in our prolonged dramas of pride and petulance? The truth is that most of us deny and avoid the topic of death. We lull ourselves into forgetting that God placed us on earth for a just cause and a determined time (Quran 15:85). We get stuck in distractions and trivialities and lose track of the limited span of our lives. When the summons comes to cross over to the other side, we are not ready.

The Quran repeatedly reminds us that time is a precious resource: "Be mindful of God with all due mindfulness and do not allow death to overtake you before you have surrendered yourselves to God" (3:102). In a sharp metaphor directed to those who are spiritually hard of hearing and refuse to listen, Rumi exclaims that Death is hoarse from shouting and his drumskin is split from so many astounding blows. Sadly, we get entangled in trivialities and only as death approaches do we apprehend its mystery. The Holy Book pleads with us not to lose sight of our ultimate purpose on earth: "Hasn't the time come for the faithful that their hearts in all humility should engage in the remembrance of God?" (57:16). Hazrat Omar, a seventh-century caliph of Islam, took these insights so to heart that he retained an employee to remind him daily of the impermanence of life. Then one day he summoned the employee to thank him for his reminders and to inform him that his services were no longer required because, for the first time, a white hair had appeared in his beard and he now had his own daily reminder of mortality.

If we allow it, awareness of death can be a major teacher in our lives. The Prophet Muhammad regularly visited graveyards and meditated on his own death as an integral part of his spiritual practices. Even in fragile health in the days before he died, he spent several hours in a graveyard, meditating and praying for the souls of the departed. Following the example of the Prophet, spiritual aspirants make "sacred visits" to gravesites of loved ones, spending time there in prayer and silence. Whenever possible, they also participate in the Islamic ritual of washing the dead body and wrapping it in white cloth. They help carry the bier, dig the ground, lower the body, and join in prayers for the departed soul. Visiting and serving the dead can be a remarkably life-affirming experience that increases the beautiful qualities of humility and compassion and teaches us to be aware and fearless about our own death. Sufi teachers advise us to be fully present when we participate in these sacred activities and to be aware of our own feelings while we are serving the dead. Without mindfulness, we may be either morbid or callous in our service. Have you not noticed, they joke, that not all gravediggers or funeral professionals are saints!

Visiting cemeteries may not be your chosen method, but we all should find a way to remember that our days are numbered and our opportunities for spiritual growth in this lifetime are finite. Mindfulness of death gives us the courage to remove our masks and discover our authentic self. Understanding impermanence gives passion, urgency, and clarity to our purpose here and gently initiates the mind into the deathless state. We realize the insight offered by the Quran: "Wealth and children are adornment of the present world: but the abiding things, the deeds of righteousness, are better with God in reward and better in hope" (18:46).

One way of practicing for death with a capital D is to allow ourselves to experience our feelings around the numerous little "deaths" that occur in the course of our lives: the deaths of aspirations, jobs, relationships, and pets, and the painful losses of friends and loved ones. In those situations, may we with grace, courage, and compassion embrace the feelings that these losses evoke and not push them away or seek to dull the pain with various distractions. If we hold our feelings consciously, we will begin to understand that what we really fear is not loss and death, but the tragic waste of not having lived, of not having been true to ourselves. We fear the regret we will feel for having put off to "tomorrow" whatever it was that we could sense was the true longing of our souls. Over time, as we give ourselves permission to look at death and to experience our feelings about its terror and mystery, our fear abates and instead we begin to sense the grandeur and beauty of death. We begin to realize that in death we will be letting go of a garb that was borrowed and our essence will be soaring into higher states.

Each person's death, Sufi teachers say, is a wedding with eternity. It is the ultimate surrender. Our souls ache to be with God. The dim sight and bent posture of old age, Sufis say wistfully, are caused by the soul's tears and load of grief at having been parted for so long from God. In the mystical language of the Quran, our souls enjoy a brief reunion with God every day: Allah takes our souls while we sleep and then returns them to us "for a term appointed" (39:42). "And Who makes the night as a robe for you and sleep as repose, and makes every day a resurrection" (Quran 25:47). Sufis enlarge on this theme, suggesting that when we sleep, our souls fly to those mysterious realms in order to prostrate to God and receive divine tenderness and mercy before returning to earth. And when our souls return to God in eternity at the appointed term, there is great rejoicing:

> Oh serene soul!
> Return to your Sustainer
> pleased and pleasing in His sight.
> Join my righteous servants
> And enter my paradise. (Quran 89:27–30)

The unspeakable delight felt in the ultimate surrender is reflected in a beautiful utterance of Rumi. In my favorite translation of this famous poem, found in James Cowan's book *Rumi's Divan of Shems of Tabriz*, the poet says, "A love-sick nightingale among owls, you caught the scent of roses and flew to the Rosegarden."

The mystery and beauty of death, understood by a higher awareness, are embodied for Muslims in the story of the Prophet and his beloved daughter, Fatima. Shortly before his death, the Prophet tenderly whispered to Fatima, and she burst into tears, for he had told her that very soon he would die. But then he whispered to her again, and this time she cried out in joy: he had told her that she would join him very soon in those celestial dimensions. In her eulogy at her father's funeral, Fatima said, "It is not surprising to me that whoever catches the fragrance of Muhammad's tomb will never know another perfume. Destiny injured me with a bereavement so sorrowful and so dark that had it fallen on the days, they would have turned into eternal nights." Six months from the day of the funeral, Fatima made the transition to join her father in those heavenly Rosegardens.

The Day of Resurrection

After a Muslim dies, the body is buried immediately and tradition has it that the soul is tenderly received by God and then placed in a state of quiescence called *Barzakh* (Quran 23:100) to await the Day of Resurrection. In the era before that fateful day, which corresponds to the end of the world and is also described in the Quran as the Day of Judgment and the Day of the Gathering, there will be a period of extraordinary instability in the world leading to widespread chaos and injustice. According to the Quran and hadith, Jesus, whom God raised up "unto Himself" (4:158), will return to earth and will be followed by the Mahdi, a descendant of the Prophet and identified in some Shiite sources as the twelfth imam, who had gone into occultation. The Mahdi, like Jesus, will, according to the hadith, "fill the earth with justice and equity." Not long after this, the earth will be visited by a series of cataclysmic events, "When the heaven is split open, stars are scattered, seas swarm over and tombs are overthrown" (82:1–4).

No one knows the time frame for these eschatological events, for "indeed it is God with whom is knowledge of the hour" (31:34).

Following the end of the world comes the Day of Resurrection and Judgment, a day of triumph for the righteous and terror for the unrepentant sinner. The dead will rise from their graves and be called to account for all their deeds and misdeeds in the presence of the angels and the Divine Judge. On that day, described as "the laying bare of truth" (69:1), what is in people's hearts will be brought to Light and every part of the body will testify, even against itself. As Rumi describes it, the tongue will say, "I gossiped," the feet will say, "I went to places I shouldn't have," and the genitals will say "Me too!" On that day "neither wealth nor children will be of use but only the one who brings to God a sound heart" (26:88–89). The Quran goes to lengths to assure us that in the final reckoning "God does not wrong anyone as much as an atom's weight" (4:40) or "as much as the groove on the pit of a date" (4:124), and "whoso brings a good deed shall have ten the like of it" (6:160). Men and women shall be treated equally: "Whoever does an evil deed shall be recompensed with only the like of it, but whosoever does a righteous deed, be it male or female, believing—these shall enter Paradise" (40:40). Of all the wicked deeds to be mentioned on the Day of Judgment, the epitome of evil is female infanticide. Signaling the heinousness of that practice in a society where "extra" females were buried alive at birth, the Day of Reckoning is described as a day "when the female infant, buried alive, is questioned—for what crime she was killed" (81:8–9). In view of the reality that many women still are "buried alive" metaphorically, it seems significant that of all the evils that could be singled out for punishment, the crime against female infants is the one that was deemed appropriate for revelation in the Quran.

Heaven and hell

At the end of Judgment Day, some will enter heaven and others, hell. Heaven is described in exquisite and sensual detail: a place of "palaces" (25:10) and "gardens under which rivers flow" (2:25), where abound "wide-eyed houris" (44:54), "immortal youths" (56:17), and "all that your souls desire" (41:31).

Hell, by contrast, is a place of "evil homecoming" (48:6), an abode of "garments of fire" (22:19) where all around are "burning winds and boiling water and the shadow of a smoking blaze" (56:42–43).

The Quran devotes a large number of verses to eschatological events, a fact that scholars attribute to the intended audience, the tribes of seventh-century Arabia. The hearts particularly of men in those societies were hardened and corrupted by the savagery, arrogance, and ignorance typical of their times. Trying to dissuade them from violence and their hedonistic lifestyle, which it blames on their belief that "there is nothing but our present life" (45:24) and any talk about accountability and resurrection is "but the fairy tales of the ancients" (23:81), the Quran makes of Judgment Day a dominant theme and of hell a frightening place. On the other hand, the sensual pleasures of heaven, with luxuriant gardens watered by flowing streams, would have resonated with the people of that arid land. The specific description of wide-eyed and fair-skinned houris spoke to the desires and fantasies of Arab men of that time.

Spiritual understanding

Most Muslims realize that the Quranic passages describing what happens after death are purely metaphorical. The Holy Book is simply trying to convey the awe of those events in language that we can understand. Probing the Quranic metaphors and insights by the Prophet Muhammad, Islamic sages over the centuries have developed a more spiritual interpretation of those dramatic events. Judgment Day, they say, is a time of astonishing awareness and celebration. On that day "piercing will be your sight" (50:22) and "whoever does an atom's weight of good shall see it, and whoever does an atom's weight of evil shall see it also" (99:8). We shall recognize where we behaved righteously and where we erred. On the basis of our level of attainment on earth, we shall be placed in one of the seven levels of heaven so that we can continue to evolve into perfection and spiral into higher and higher states of unity with God. Thus, say Islamic teachers, our spiritual journey continues after our physical death; reincarnation occurs not on earth but in the mysterious realms of heaven. This belief is based partly on the Quranic verse, "Their light will run before them and on their right hands. They will say, 'Our Creator, perfect our light for us; surely Thou hast power over all things'" (66:8). Islamic mystics know that "Surely my Creator is All Merciful, All Love" (11:90), and with loving humor they pray to God, "Oh my Creator, on Judgment Day, plead on my behalf with Yourself!" and "please do what is worthy of Thee and not what is worthy of me."

In the mystical interpretation, heaven is indeed a place of eternal delights, but the deep fulfillment that we all yearn for comes from being in close proximity to the pleasure of God. In the words of the Quran,

> God hath promised to Believers,
> Men and women, Gardens
> Under which rivers flow,
> To dwell therein,
> And beautiful mansions
> In Gardens of everlasting bliss.
> But the greatest bliss
> Is the Good Pleasure of God:
> That is the supreme felicity. (9:72)

Spiritual teachers tell us that hell is, surprisingly, a place of divine mercy. It is a womb of nurturance, radical recovery, and wholeness for those whose hearts have hardened because of life circumstances. In a verse pregnant with meaning, the Quran describes hell as the sinner's mother (101:10). Just as every human spends a specified time in its mother's womb before being delivered as a whole being, those assigned to hell are actually spending a gestation period in a womb of creative compassion before continuing on the journey of union with God.

The Prophet Muhammad offers us a pair of striking insights about hell and heaven. Observing a mother who was deeply absorbed in the care of her child, Muhammad said to his companions, "Look at this woman and her concern for her child. Would she hurl her own child into a blazing fire with her own hands? I tell you, God loves us much more than this mother loves her child." On another occasion the Prophet remarked, "If heaven is so wonderful, how is it that Adam and his spouse committed errors there? If hell is so terrible because of the fierce and blazing fire, then how is it that when King Nimrod hurled Abraham into the fire, he was cool in it?"

Stories abound in Islam about the folly of being overly fearful of hell or greedily desirous of the delights of Paradise. In a Sufi teaching story, Jesus comes across two groups of people whose faces are wrinkled with worry and bodies are bent over by the weight of anxieties. "What is your affliction?" he asks one group, and they reply that their condition is a result of their terrible fear of the fires of hell. "And yours?" he asks the other group, and they answer that their condition derives from an ardent and urgent desire for the sensual pleasures and comforts of heaven. This folly of being attached to fear and desire is highlighted by a story about Rabia, who was seen rushing through the streets with a torch of fire in one hand and a bucket of water in the other. When asked what she was up to, she famously replied that with the torch she was going to set fire to Paradise and with the bucket of water quench the fires of hell "so that people may worship Allah for His Glory alone." May we draw heart-felt lessons from a well-known prayer of this saintly woman:

> O Allah! If I worship You for fear of Hell, burn me in Hell.
> And if I worship You in hope of Paradise, exclude me from
>   Paradise.
> But if I worship You for Your own sake,
> Grudge me not your Everlasting Beauty.

Ultimately, none of us truly knows what happens to us after death. The Quran says "For with God are the keys to the Unseen: the treasures that none knows but He" (6:59). What we do know, from the Quran and from Islamic mystics, is that God is boundlessly compassionate and receives each returning soul with love. A just king once approached a pious dervish on his deathbed. The king said, "Oh dervish, beloved of God, soon the Light of Splendor will descend upon you. When you step into the glory of the Divine Presence, please do me a favor. Please remember me to God." The dervish replied, "Your majesty, when I step into the Light, I won't even remember who I am. How then can I remember you?"

Jewish Reflections

The time is drawing near for you to die. (Deut. 31:14)

These words, which the Eternal speaks to Moses in the closing pages of the Torah, we could well hang on our bathroom mirrors to remind ourselves every morning that the inevitable day is coming for each of us. In a touching midrash, Moses asks God, "Master of the Universe, shall the feet that went up to the firmament, the face that confronted the Presence, the hands that received the Torah from Your hand—shall these now turn to dust?" And the Holy One replies, "Such was My thought from the very beginning." Continuing the theme of inevitability is the famous verse often quoted at funerals: "A time to be born, a time to die" (Eccles. 3:2)—such is the divine plan for us "from the very beginning." Therefore, says the psalmist, "Teach us to count our days rightly, that we may obtain a wise heart" (Ps. 90:12), for, as the psalm continues in a beautiful interpretation by Nan Merrill (*Psalms for Praying*), "our days on Earth are a mystery, a searching for You, a yearning for the great Mystery to make itself known."

Thus Jewish scriptures are typically matter-of-fact about death, and although they don't dwell on it obsessively, our teachers tell us to be mindful of it every day. "Repent one day before your death," said the first-century Rabbi Eliezer (Avot 2:10), meaning that since we don't know when we will die, we should repent every day of our lives so that at the time of death we will have spent a lifetime in preparation. For the same reason—not knowing precisely when we will die—it is a Jewish practice to say the Sh'ma continually so that the holy words, which we hope to be saying when we die, will be on our lips should the moment catch us unaware. Aside from this practice, however, it is probably fair to say that Jews, like almost everyone else, are focused more on daily life than on death and the afterlife— with one exception.

That exception is the period of the Days of Awe, more often called the High Holy Days, which occur in the fall of the year. Beginning with the new moon of the Jewish month of Elul, we enter a forty-day period of fasting and soul-searching similar to Lent in Christianity and Ramadan in Islam. At the start of the following month, Tishrei, we convene to celebrate the feast of Rosh HaShanah, the Jewish New Year and also the Day of Judgment, the day on which we stand before God individually and in community to recommit ourselves to *teshuvah*, a return to what really matters.

Ten days later we arrive at the most life-altering day of the Jewish year: Yom Kippur, the Day of Atonement. (In progressive congregations we often call it the Day of At-one-ment, the day of being at one with the Divine at the core of our being.) This is a day of complete fasting—nothing to eat or drink for more than twenty-four hours—in acknowledgment that this could be the year when our name is written in the Book of Death. Synagogues around the world overflow with penitent Jews confessing their sins and begging forgiveness in the haunting prayer *Avinu Malkainu*. "Our Father, our King" is the literal translation of these two words, but they might better be translated "Our Cherisher, our Sovereign" to reflect our anthropomorphic understanding of Divinity as both lover and judge. Like the Sufis begging Allah to "Plead on my behalf with Yourself," we invoke divine compassion while acknowledging the Eternal's right to call us on our sins. "Avinu Malkainu," we plead, "be gracious and answer us, for we have too few good deeds. Treat us with justice tempered by love, and bring us salvation." Sobered by our contemplation of death and eternity during the Days of Awe, we embark on a new year of trying to live more consciously, more righteously, and more joyously in the presence of the One who keeps us in life and brings us to each moment for blessing.

What happens when the Book of Death opens to the page with your name on it is a matter of surmise and speculation. In Judaism there is no consensus about the afterlife other than that there probably is one, given the belief that the human soul is immortal. Whether the soul enters paradise, languishes for a while in Gehenna (similar to the purgatory of Christianity and the purifying-but-not-eternal fires of hell in Islam), or transmigrates into a new human ego state (a popular belief in Jewish mysticism) is an open question. There is talk in the Talmud of a Great Day of Judgment (*Yom Ha-Din Ha-Gadol*) similar to the Day of Resurrection-cum-Judgment in Islam: all who ever lived will be resurrected, called to account for their deeds and misdeeds (Avot 4:22), and assigned to everlasting life or termination. "Life," whether on earth or in *Gan Eden* (the Garden of Paradise), means heightened knowledge and experience of the Divine. "Termination" seems to be just that: not fire and brimstone, but the end of existence and therefore the loss of any opportunity to enjoy connection with the Eternal.

The theme of resurrection is fundamental to the prayer that observant Jews say every morning upon awakening. "*Modah ani,*" we say (men say *Modeh*)—"Grateful am I to be in your presence, my Creator and Sustainer, for in your compassion you have restored my soul to me. Great is your faithfulness!" (Or, in another interpretation, "Great is your faith in me.") In the short term we mean that our soul, which some believe was journeying in celestial realms as we slept, has been returned to us for a new day of living. In the longer term, we are expressing our hope of the great resurrection, based on the beautiful words of Lamentations:

> This do I call to mind,
> Therefore I have hope:
> The kindness of the Eternal has not ended,
> [Your] mercies are not spent.
> They are renewed every morning—
> Ample is Your grace! (3:21–23)

As in both Christianity and Islam, Jewish tradition has it that the Day of Resurrection will be preceded by a dramatic era, but with a remarkable difference: whereas our sibling faiths foresee a period dominated by the forces of evil and cataclysmic events, Judaism looks beyond the cataclysm to a Messianic Age of peace and redemption. In the metaphoric language of the prophet Isaiah, "The wolf shall dwell with the lamb, the leopard lie down with the kid" (Isa. 11:6). At the time of Christ, the Jews of Palestine were hoping for a temporal Messiah to usher in that era of peace and harmony—a hope that was, of course, one of the issues that led to the schism between mainstream Jews and those who became followers of Jesus two thousand years ago. Whereas the former were focused on the desperate need of salvation from their earthly oppressors, the latter were drawn to Jesus' teachings about the need for spiritual redemption. Those teachings are more in tune with contemporary thought among progressive Jews, which is why I like to think of Jesus as one of the first Reform Jews. Though beliefs have morphed over the centuries, Orthodox Judaism still awaits a *Moshiakh* (Messiah) and progressive Judaism still hopes for a Messianic Age.

Needless to say, the world is nowhere near such an idyllic and peaceful era, so we probably shouldn't be looking for the Day of Resurrection to happen anytime soon. Nevertheless, it is wise to be prepared. "The sum of the matter, when all is said and done: Revere God and observe [God's] commandments! For this applies to all mankind: that God will call every creature to account for everything unknown, be it good or bad" (Eccles. 12:13–14).

Christian Reflections

Fight the good fight of the faith; take hold of the eternal life. (1 Tim. 6:12)

God alone is timeless, without beginning or end. In the beautiful words of the Quran, "He is Allah, the One and Only, Allah, the Eternal, Absolute" (112:1–2). The rest of us must deal with time and the confines it imposes, the most dramatic and mysterious of which is death. Death appears in many guises and at several levels of existence: for individual beings; for relationships; for societies and other groups; and eventually, according to the scriptures of the Abrahamic traditions, for the cosmos itself.

In Christianity I have run across two approaches to death and the Day of Judgment. Although both of these views find some support in scripture and have persisted through the ages, they seem to be efforts to cut the mystery down to manageable size. Understandably, both are also challenged radically by the witness of Jesus and his earliest followers in the Christian Testament, as well as by the Quran and Torah. Neither of them takes into account the fundamental interconnectedness of life and death, especially in terms of resurrection, justice, and the astounding compassion of God.

The first approach is that of denial. Jamal and Kate have already written about how natural this path seems to be for human beings, especially for those of us who are comfortable. We can get very cozy with the creature comforts of this world. Our relative success here can delude us into thinking that at the very least we may be able to pull some strings in the age to come. Sometimes we even think that our prosperity is a sign of God's blessing and favor, even a down payment of sorts. Some people would say that this mindset has taken hold of much of Western Christendom. From the fourth century on, the upper echelons of the institutional church became one with the social and political establishment, as Christianity became first the privileged state religion of the Roman Empire and then the religious matrix of Western civilization. God certainly seemed to be on the side of the Christians, and didn't Paul say, "If God is for us, who is against us" (Rom. 8:31)? This same chapter ends in a passage that is not surprisingly a favorite one at Christian funerals: "For I am convinced that neither death, nor life, nor angels, nor rulers, nor things present, nor things to come, nor powers, nor height, nor depth, nor anything else in all creation, will be able to separate us from the love of God in Christ Jesus our Lord" (Rom. 8:38–39).

Yes, Paul did write this passage, but it was in the context of dealing with "the sufferings of this present time" (Rom. 8:18), a period when the tiny Christian movement was a blip on the screen, not well enough known even to be persecuted systematically. Paul exhorts his congregations to take a stance of resistance toward the distractions of life so that they can be ready for the second coming of Christ, in Greek the *parousia*, a term used for a royal or imperial visitation. To a congregation in Thessalonika anxious about the seeming delay in Christ's appearance, he writes that "the day of the Lord will come like a thief in the night" (I Thess. 5:2). So they are to be vigilant at all times: "So then let us not fall asleep as others do, but let us keep awake and be sober" (5:6).

Jesus was quite skillful at troubling the placid waters of the comfortable with pointed parables and head-on confrontations. He told of a rich man who has so much stuff that he actually tears down all his storehouses to build larger ones. "But God said to him, 'You fool! This very night your life is being demanded of you. And the things you have prepared, whose will they be?' So it is with those who store up treasures for themselves but are not rich toward God" (Luke 12:20–21). After a mutually unsatisfactory conversation with a rich man who is reluctant to give up his wealth to follow Jesus, the teacher evokes astonishment in his disciples by saying, "It is easier for a camel to go through the eye of a needle than for someone who is rich to enter the kingdom of God" (Mark 10:25).

Both Paul and Jesus communicated to their followers that they were living in a special time and that God was beginning a new age for the entire universe. This new age—Paul called it the "new creation" (2 Cor. 5:17; Gal. 6:15)—required new behavior and transformed relationships. Paul wrote: "There is no longer Jew or Greek, there is no longer slave or free, there is no longer male and female; for all of you are one in Christ Jesus" (Gal. 3:28). No social rank or classification confers any privilege here. Repeatedly Jesus said, "The last will be first, and the first will be last" (Matt. 20:16; see also Matt. 19:30, Mark 10:31, and Luke 13:30).

As a teacher, I look at the second approach to death and judgment as a variation on the question, "What's going to be on the final exam?" The goal is to ace death and judgment by figuring out just what will be on the test and making certain to cover that material. There is no point in paying attention to anything extraneous. The strategy is to come up with a formula to identify the do's and the don'ts and then to engage in the former and avoid the latter. This method certainly has logic and efficiency in its favor. Furthermore, there are helpful passages in all our scriptures that boil the message down to the basics: the Ten Principles of the Torah, for instance, and similar passages in the Christian Testament. Paul gives an example of what not to do: "Fornicators, idolaters, adulterers, male prostitutes, sodomites, thieves, the greedy, drunkards, revilers, robbers—none of these will inherit the kingdom of God" (1 Cor. 6:9–10). He also has a straightforward solution: quoting Jewish scriptures, he says, "Anyone who calls upon the name of the Lord shall be saved." The sense of certainty that this approach confers gives those who follow it the confidence to recruit others vigorously on the basis of the fear of eternal punishment if they don't get on board.

But like the first approach, this one grasps at a way to control and second-guess a situation that is firmly in God's hands. First of all, we have no first-hand knowledge from those who have sat for the final exam. Furthermore, the lists of vices in scripture cannot be deciphered without understanding the situation of the community addressed. Then, when we look to Jesus, we are likely to be jarred by his answers, as was the rich man I spoke of earlier, who consulted Jesus to learn the formula for attaining eternal life. No doubt he was at first relieved to find that he had kept all the commandments Jesus mentioned. But Jesus took the matter beyond any checklist. "Jesus, looking at him, loved him and said, 'You lack one thing; go, sell what you own, and give the money to the poor, and you will have treasure in heaven; then come, follow me.'" To follow Jesus meant leaving strategies and formulas behind and surrendering to the will of God. On another occasion Jesus said, "Not everyone who says to me, 'Lord, Lord,' will enter the kingdom of heaven, but only the one who does the will of my father in heaven" (Matt. 7:21).

If no formulas suffice and the instruction lists depend upon their context for interpretation, how do we prepare for the reckoning to come? Christian scriptures teach me first of all by the pattern of death and resurrection. Jesus' resurrection is one of the most debated phenomena in history. Yet, as I once heard Nora Gallagher say, although we may not know exactly what happened to Jesus in that event, we surely can see resurrection in the transformed lives of the apostles. The new life that came in the aftermath of his horrific death produced a transformation in his followers that has had monumental impact on the world ever since. In the night before he died, Jesus gave instructions to his disciples that indicated that, in order for them to be transformed, he had to leave. He said, "I tell you, the one who believes in me will also do the works that I do and, in fact, will do greater works than these, because I am going to the Father" (John 14:12).

On a pilgrimage in 2006, I had a lesson about this mysterious interrelationship of death, sacrifice, and new life. Our group was in a little boat on a rainy day, returning from Skellig Michael, a stony island off the west coast of Ireland, where medieval monks had built a monastery high on a cliff. As I sat thinking about my ancestors who had crossed the North Atlantic Ocean centuries ago never again to return to their African homeland, the air seemed full of a presence. I had always had great respect for those enslaved Africans who had jumped overboard rather than continue on the ocean journey of oppression. But that day I heard a chorus of voices telling me, "Daughter, we are the ones who did not jump overboard. And you are the reason we didn't." At that moment I felt an overwhelming joy and gratitude for these unnamed kin who made a sacrifice for me that until then I had never examined and fully received. I felt resurrected.

This experience also renewed my commitment to justice. The God who brought them through is a God of justice. As their offspring, I realized that my own work for justice is directly related to their lives lived for me through the one God who is mine and theirs. My life is part of their ongoing day of reckoning. Finally, I recognized the hand of *Ar-Rahman, Ar-Rahim*—the all-compassionate One in this event, the One who reaches across the line of life and death to link us in love.

PART III

The Path of Surrender
and Provisions
for the Journey

8

The Journey of Surrender

Indeed, those who submit themselves to Allah,
while doing good, will have their reward with Allah.
(Quran 2:112)

The road is long and the sea is deep

"Witness how all affairs incline towards God," says the Quran (22:41). No matter what our religious affiliation—or lack of it—may be, our life story is about the mysterious and fascinating journey of surrendering to Divinity. Whether you are a sultan, saint, or pickpocket, say the Sufi masters, God has everyone by the ears dragging us to the divine heart in secret ways. Life is a journey from God, to God, and in God. Sooner or later we will connect to a deep inner longing to turn to God. "There is a kiss we want all our lives, a touch of spirit on the body," says Rumi. This longing is built into us, as the story of our primordial covenant with God shows. Before Adam and Eve descended to earth, says the Quran, God gathered the souls of unborn humanity—that includes you and me—and said, "Am I not your Creator?" Ecstatic at hearing God's voice, we all exclaimed, "Yes! We testify to it!" (7:172).

Despite our inherent desire for union with the Divine, too often we resist the urge to turn our hearts to God, for this might entail some serious and inconvenient changes in our lives. We make excuses, and this too is the story of our lives. This dilemma is beautifully described in a classic work of Islamic spirituality, *The Conference of the Birds*. In this long allegorical poem from the thirteenth century, beautifully translated by Afkham Darbandi and Dick Davis among others, the Persian mystic Farid ud-din Attar describes a kind of international convention of birds. As they arrive and mingle, they talk about their disenchantment with life and begin to share their longing to meet their creator, a sovereign being called the Simurgh. Sensing that this will bring lasting joy to their restless hearts, they turn to the Hoopoe bird, a messenger of the invisible world, who knows the path that leads to the Simurgh. The birds chirp with excitement at the prospect of traveling to meet the Simurgh, but the Hoopoe bird dampens their enthusiasm by talking about the perils of the journey. The road is long and the sea is deep, says the Hoopoe, warning that the path goes over seven valleys and in each valley the birds will undergo a hundred trials.

Discouraged, the birds begin to make excuses. The nightingale is so deeply in love with the rose, who unfolds her hundred petals just for him, that he can't even think of leaving her. The rose is enough for him, he says, but the Hoopoe chides him for being superficial and wasting his love on a rose that will flower once and then be no more. The parrot says that he has spent his whole life in a cage and now wants only to be free for all eternity. He has no need to see the Simurgh if the journey could cost him his life, but the Hoopoe answers scornfully, "You are a cringing slave—this is not noble, generous, or brave." Next comes the glittering peacock, turning this way and that like a proud, self-conscious bride. The peacock has tasted life in an earthly paradise, so why, he asks, should he exert himself to reach the Simurgh? Ah, the Hoopoe replies, the palace of the Simurgh far exceeds any earthly paradise. "Which matters more, the body or the soul? Be whole: desire and journey to the Whole." The duck, the partridge, the hawk, the heron, and the owl all make their excuses and receive a strong rebuke. Then comes the tiny finch, of feeble body and tender heart, and she too begs off: "I am less sturdy than a hair and lack the courage that my betters share." But the Hoopoe shows no sympathy. If we all are destined for the funeral pyre, why should she be allowed to plead infirmity? "Get ready for the road, you can't fool me—Sew up your beak, I loathe hypocrisy!"

One by one the birds keep coming with their excuses—"In an incoherent rush they came, And all were inappropriate and lame." The Hoopoe remonstrates with each of them, and then he tells a long love story that sets their hearts on fire to see the Simurgh:

> They heard the tale; the birds were all on fire
> To quit the hindrance of the Self; desire
> To gain the Simurgh had convulsed each heart;
> Love made them clamor for the journey's start.

And so the birds are off, led by the Hoopoe, to find the kingdom of the Simurgh. Many perish in the rigors of the voyage and only thirty birds arrive at the palace.

> A world of birds set out, and there remained
> But thirty when the promised goal was gained,
> Thirty exhausted, wretched, broken things,
> With hopeless hearts and tattered, trailing wings . . .

The birds watch, bewildered and astonished, as veils of ignorance are lifted and the Light of Lights is manifest. And then, in a magical moment expressed by a Persian play on words (*si* means thirty and *murgh* means birds), they grasp the true meaning of their longing for the Simurgh: there in the Simurgh's radiant face they see themselves! As one they ask, though silently, how it is that they cannot distinguish themselves from the Simurgh.

> And silently their shining Lord replies:
> "I am a mirror set before your eyes,
> And all who come before my splendor see
> Themselves, their own unique reality."

"All your journey was in Me," the Simurgh continues, "and all your deeds were Mine." The last thing the birds hear before they are dissolved into the Simurgh is the promise that by their annihilation they will find once more the selves they were before.

Like Attar's birds, we humans are propelled by an innate longing that neither food, sex, money, power, prestige, nor even human love can fully satisfy.

It is a primeval longing for reunion with our Creator. Separated from God by our human birth, we are, says Rumi, like reeds sighing to return to the bed of reeds from which they were cut. Deep in our souls we remember our primordial covenant with God and we yearn to experience that closeness once again. "Our longing," says Rumi, "is the core of mystery. Longing itself brings the cure. The only rule is, Suffer the pain."

The Quran tells us that the God for whom we long is both *Batin* and *Zahir*, both within and beyond our individual selves. To move close to the God who dwells within, we must work to remove the veils of ego that prevent us from seeing God face to face. To connect with the God beyond ourselves, we must learn to see God in all of creation, especially in our fellow human beings, and to offer ourselves in service. Our work to evolve into the fullness of our being in union with our Creator is the path of surrender in Islam.

PRACTICE

When you feel a gnawing dissatisfaction with life, don't seek to deny or avoid it. The ache is rooted in something deeper. Hold the feeling in your consciousness. Give yourself permission to be present with its energy. Embrace it with compassion and bring it into your heart. Pray to the all-merciful God for help as you go deeper with this feeling. In time, this practice will strengthen your primordial connection with God and increase your awareness that your very essence is divine.

Marry your soul

The Quran says, "God has not put two hearts in one body" (33:4). To illustrate this point, Rumi tells a delightful story about a lover who longs to be with his beloved and knocks on her door.

"Who is it?" she asks.

"It is I," replies the lover.

After a brief pause, the beloved replies sadly, "Alas, there's only room for one of us in here," and she declines to open the door.

Hurt and confused by her rejection, the lover goes away. For many years he travels far and wide, and in the process he gains a wealth of experiences and insights. Finally he returns to his beloved and again knocks on the door. This time, when she asks who is knocking, he replies, "It is you!" Joyfully she calls out, "There is enough space for both of us!" With that she flings open the door and they melt into each other's embrace.

In our search for intimacy with the Divine Beloved, we are like that lover. We knock on God's door and say "It's me," and then wonder why we're not ushered into the inner sanctum. What stands between us and God is what the Quran calls our *nafs*, loosely translated our ego, our personality, our sense of "I." To draw close to God, we need to align elements of our nafs with the pure essence of our soul. "Marry your soul," counsels Rumi; "that wedding is the way." Though we may shudder at the idea of annihilating our personality, the truth is that the personality is nothing more than a bundle of conditioned reactions to life's circumstances. It is not the essence of who we are. What is a little seed that it should not be annihilated for the sake of a tree, asks Rumi. If we mistake the ego for our essence, we turn it into an idol, what Sufi masters call the mother of all idols. We do not have to smash the ego, as Abraham smashed the idols in his father's shop (Quran 21:51–67), for the ego is a necessary instrument of the soul. We simply need to tame the ego and help it find its proper role, not as a commanding master, but as a helpful assistant. The ego needs to be transmuted or transformed so that it can open up and give way to a higher Will, so that the seed can grow into a tree.

In another metaphor, Rumi likens the ego to a candle flame flickering in the dark. We need that bit of light to find our way, but once we are ushered into the Land of the Radiant Sun, the candle's meager light is subsumed in the sun's radiance. In that sense, the flame is annihilated. But it is still very much alive, for if you touch it with anything flammable, it quickly flares again.

Transmuting the ego is a simple concept, but not an easy task. The ego does not willingly give up its role on center stage. In Rumi's imagery, the nafs is a sea of calm deception until it roars; it is an ankle-deep river in which it is easy to drown. But despite the ego's intransigence, on some level it wants us to transcend it and grow into our higher self.

The three stages of the nafs

The Quran identifies three stages of the nafs (12:53; 75:2; 89:27). In the early stage (*nafs al ammarah*), the ego can incline as easily to wrongdoing as to virtue. In the middle stage (*nafs al-lawwama*), the ego has the wisdom and ability to make good choices. In the final stage (*nafs al-mutma'inna*), the ego is peacefully surrendered to the divine will. It is our sacred task to become acquainted with our ego and transform it to that final stage of surrender. In Islamic spirituality, each of us is conceived with an inner inclination to be united with our Creator, and we have the gift of the Quran to guide us. If we ignore this task, we shall fail utterly in the purpose for which we are born. It is, says Rumi, as if a king has sent you to a distant land to accomplish a specific task, and you do many wonderful things but avoid that particular task. Upon your return, can you really tell the king you've done what he asked? Warming to his metaphors, Rumi chides us for wasting the precious gift of life. It's as if we've been given a golden pot and never used it for anything except boiling turnips, not realizing what an excellent vessel it would be for cooking the dross out of our ego. Or as if we were given a gem-studded Damascene sword and used it for nothing except cutting meat, never lifting it to slash through the ego's veils of ignorance and unawareness.

So how do we begin to tame the ego? Step by step, "little by little," as I am constantly reminding my students. We begin at stage one by shining the light of awareness on ourselves, witnessing as continuously as possible the things we think and say and do. This sacred light of awareness will reveal to us not only our shadow side, the tendency of our ego to dominate and sometimes incline toward wrongdoing, but also the ways in which we manifest the divine virtues that are part of our vast potential. Thus, awareness brings us closer to our higher self, who, says the Quran, is always a witness. "Not a word does he utter but there is a watcher with him ever present" (50:18). When we recognize the manifestation of a divine virtue, we acknowledge its Source and we nourish it. When we recognize traits that are less positive, less worthy of our divine essence, we invoke God's help and exert ourselves to transform those unworthy tendencies. In stage two we are more consistently aware of the power of choices and are able, through God's help and our own efforts, to think and act in closer connection with the divine will. Gradually, as we master this life art, we grow into stage three. Our ego has been tamed and aligned with our divine essence, and we experience a sense of deep inner peace.

The ego may complain that the task is difficult—the road indeed is long and the sea is deep—but we are not entirely on our own. If we take but a single step towards God, says the Prophet, God will come running towards us. Not only running, I would say, but bearing gifts of sustenance and guidance. In the words of the Quran, "God draws to Himself those who are willing and guides to Himself everyone who turns to Him" (42:13). So be bold: take that first step, and persist, joyful in the knowledge that you, like Attar's birds, will survive the difficulties and find yourself at last face to face with the radiant Beloved in your own heart.

Patterns, excuses, attachments, and fears

Once you have engaged that ever-present inner witness, your spiritual consciousness, you will become increasingly mindful of the ways in which your ego will seek to defend itself and sabotage your efforts to align it with your higher self. A helpful method for dealing with a recalcitrant ego is to keep a "little black book" in which you can record both successes and failures in your work of transformation. With every notation, remember to express gratitude for the awareness of soul qualities to be nurtured and ego traits to be kept in check. This technique will soon reveal your personal patterns and habits that protect your ego and prevent you from manifesting your higher self. My own little black book revealed that I had a chronic habit of procrastination and avoidance, which I blamed on external causes: it was "others" or "circumstances" that had to change if I was going to reform my ways. It took a verse from the Quran to make me look at my own behavior: "Truly God does not change people's conditions unless they change their inner selves" (13:11).

Illustrating the power of this fundamental principle is a Sufi teaching story sometime attributed to the beloved eighth-century saint Rabia. One night Rabia went looking for a lost key under the streetlight, which in those days was a small fire burning on top of a pillar. Her neighbors joined in the search, without success. "Whereabouts did you lose your key?" they asked, hoping to focus on that specific area. Rabia replied that she had actually lost her key inside her house. Surprised and bemused, they respectfully asked her why she did not look for the lost key in the house. "Because the light is so much better out here," she said. The neighbors couldn't help laughing and shaking their heads in disbelief, and Rabia seized the opportunity to make her point. (The "lost key" was obviously a setup.) "Friends," she said, "it is clear that you are intelligent people. Then why is it that when you lose your peace of mind or happiness, perhaps because of a failed relationship or a problem at work, you look for what was lost out there and not in here?" Rabia pointed to her chest. "Did you lose your joy out there or in here? Do you avoid looking inside you because the light is dimmer, and therefore, inconvenient?"

One of the most powerful tools the ego can use to defend itself is fear. My little black book revealed a number of fears that held me back from the path of surrender, and I had to learn to look at those fears gently, in measured stages. Amazingly, the more light I was able to shine on them, the more my fears began to melt away. It is in the darkness of avoidance and denial that fear vibrations grow and assume monstrous shapes that can overwhelm and undermine. The simple truth is that the things that frighten us are, in the deepest sense, things that merely need our love and attention. When we look at our fears with compassion, creative solutions emerge and our higher selves are emboldened to take flight like Attar's birds on their way to see the Simurgh.

Open for me my heart

Once we start the work of transforming our ego, the Quran says that a deep yearning pours out from the depths of our being, crying out, "Open for me my heart!" (20:25). The heart longs to open and expand, to embrace and be embraced by its Creator. The longing is mutual. In a hadith qudsi, a direct revelation to the Prophet, God reveals:

> I cannot be contained in the space of the earth,
> I cannot be contained in the space of the heavens,
> But I can be contained in the space
> Of the pure loving heart of my servant.

What an exquisite concept: Divine Heart dwells in human heart! But how do we open the lines of communication between heart and Heart? There are three major ways. The first is by cultivating spiritual practices such as prayer and meditation. "Close down speech's door and open the window of your heart," says Rumi. "The Moon will kiss you only through the window." The Quran says it more directly: "Bow in adoration and draw closer" (96:19). We will explore prayer and meditation in some detail in a subsequent chapter. In the remaining pages of this chapter, let us focus on two powerful techniques for opening our hearts to the Divine: purifying the heart, and embracing the joys and sorrows of life.

Purifying the heart

The Quran says that God knows well "the secrets of your heart" and so strive to "render your innermost heart pure of all dross" (3:154). A favorite Sufi practice is to "polish" the heart so that it reflects the Face of Allah. Expanding on this theme, Rumi says we should pay attention to what is in our hearts, for negative energies are as visible to Allah as a black hair in a bowl of white milk. Unload the unworthy baggage in your heart, he says, and fill your heart only with that which is a fitting gift for a righteous sovereign.

A heart worthy of a righteous sovereign is a heart beating with divine qualities—most importantly, says the Quran, the interrelated qualities of patience, humility, truthfulness, and sincerity. These qualities do not always come naturally to our nafs-driven hearts, and the only way to acquire them is through lifelong practice.

By nature we humans are not patient beings. In fact, quite the opposite: "Truly man was created very impatient, fretful when evil touches him . . . but not so those devoted to prayer" (70:19–22). Even prophets need an occasional admonition to be patient. When the Prophet Muhammad was beset by political difficulties in Mecca, God reassured him, "Did not Allah find you an orphan and give you shelter and care? . . . [therefore] the Bounty of thy Sustainer rehearse and proclaim!" (93:6–11). In a sterner moment, God chided the Prophet for his impatience with his enemies in Mecca. "If you find their aversion hard to bear, seek if you can a chasm in the earth or a ladder to the sky by which you may bring them a sign. Had God pleased, He would have given them guidance, one and all. So don't be among those who are swayed by ignorance and impatience" (6:35).

Closely related to patience is the virtue of humility. Indeed, humility is essential to patience. Humility is to "know our place" in the presence of our Creator. The true servants of God are "those who walk on the earth in humility" (25:63) and are "humble before the Unseen" (50:33). Inspired by the latter verse, the sage Saadi of Shiraz wrote about a raindrop dripping from a cloud. When the raindrop saw the sea, it blushed and said, "Who am I where there is the Sea?" Having seen itself with the eyes of humility, the raindrop was nurtured by a shell and became a priceless pearl. It knocked on the door of annihilation and became at last alive.

True humility is rooted in our acknowledgment that God is the Ultimate Truth. "It was to manifest the Truth that We created the heavens and earth and all that lies between them," Allah says to humankind (46:3). "A goodly Word [that is, a word of truth] is firmly rooted like a good tree, its branches reaching toward the sky, yielding its fruit at all times by the permission of its Sustainer" (14:24–25). In his whole-hearted embrace of divine truth, the Prophet Muhammad risked persecution and death to spread the word to his idolatrous community. "Even if you put the Sun in my right hand and the Moon in my left hand, I shall never waver from the Truth that there is only one God." Using the Quran's metaphor of a tree, Muhammad taught that the tree of truth must have both deep roots and branches that open to the sky of mystical knowledge. We must be willing to let go of our limited beliefs and open ourselves to higher knowledge, higher awareness, as the God of truth is revealed to us through our scriptures and through our own spiritual experiences.

Islamic teachers caution us not to become self-righteous in our pursuit of truth. As a child, Saadi of Shiraz sometimes took part when his father, a revered teacher, spent the night in prayer with his devoted students. One night all the disciples fell asleep during the vigil, but not the young Saadi. Feeling quite proud of himself, he said to his father, "Look at them! You might think they were all dead!" To which his father replied, "Beloved son, I wish you also were asleep like them, rather than slandering them." This tender but firm remonstrance always reminded Saadi in his later years to be cautious of the "truth trap"—the tendency to be self-righteous about the exclusive "truth" of our own perceptions and practices. The path of surrender is a path of humility, not of arrogance.

As important as our pursuit of truth is our ability to embrace it with sincerity. The Quran teaches us to pray, "O my Sustainer! Cause me to enter upon whatever I may do in a true and sincere way and cause me to complete it in a true and sincere way" (17:80–81). To discover whether we are truly sincere, we have only to ask ourselves why we have ventured along the difficult path of surrender. Are we doing it out of sheer longing for union with God, whom we acknowledge to be the one Truth and the Source of our existence? Or are we perhaps doing it for less-worthy motives—for self-glory, say, or to impress others with our holiness? Consider the pure "motives" all around us in nature: the sun rises and sets daily whether we thank it or not; rain showers grace the orchards of the rich and poor alike; the soil is faithful to its trust—plant a mango seed, and a mango tree grows. Walk the path of surrender because that is what you were born for, not because it will earn you glory either here or in the world to come. Daily life offers numerous opportunities to practice sincerity. Ask yourself often, Do I say what I mean and mean what I say? Am I sincere in my promises, and do I keep them? Though a sincere person does not practice sincerity for a reward, the rewards are celestial: "For the sincere is an appointed nourishment: fruits and honor and dignity in gardens of felicity" (37:40–43).

Clearly, the work of purifying the heart involves a lifetime of vigilance on numerous fronts. Do not be disheartened or overwhelmed by the scale of the task or the difficulties along the way. The divine qualities that we have just explored in the briefest manner are so entwined that any work on one means progress on the others. As you remove conditions that give rise to one unhelpful habit, you also loosen and uproot other related habits. Deepen one virtue, and you enhance many others. Rumi offers a reassuring insight: whatever dominates within you is what you are. If your gold outweighs your copper, you will be known as gold. Whatever you most are is the form in which you will resurrect.

When difficulties arise, remind yourself that what we perceive as obstacles are the Universe's compassionate way of helping us build our "purification muscles." Just as we are created "very impatient" so that we might learn to exercise our patience muscles, we are constantly presented with opportunities to commute our many weaknesses into strengths. Let's say that you make an intention to be more generous, and almost immediately are assailed by situations that challenge your sense of generosity. Are you being tested or punished? Not at all. The universe is merely smiling on your good intention and giving you opportunities to show your sincerity and to build your "generosity muscle." You may not have realized it, but this is what you asked for when you made that intention. Enjoy a wry laugh with Rumi, who was amused by the irony of seeking purity but complaining about rough handling when it's time to be polished. Take to the work of purification with a sense of sacredness, courage, and readiness.

PRACTICE

• On a regular basis, consult your "little black book" and ponder on the self-observations you have written there. Look at your "virtues" list and feel grateful for the divine qualities flowing through you. These qualities are the real you. Look at the "weaknesses" list and express gratitude for your awareness of them. These are not the real you; they are a result of reactions and patterns that your ego uses to protect itself, and you can let them go.

• Develop a weekly ritual around the lists. Be creative. For example, write down one of your virtues on a piece of paper, place the paper in a bowl, and reverently offer it to the Holy One. Make an intention to honor the Divine by practicing that virtue with special mindfulness for the coming week. Similarly, write one of your weaknesses on another piece of paper and put it in a bowl. Burn this paper in the bowl as a ceremony of release and transformation. Alternatively, write the word in water-soluble ink, place the paper in a bowl of water, and release your attachment to that weakness as you watch the ink swirl away in the water. Then pray for divine help as you make a sincere intention to bring your light of awareness to shine on that particular weakness during the coming week.

Embracing the joys and sorrows of life

"It is God who created for you sight, hearing and feelings," says the Quran (23:78, 32:9). Spiritual teachers take this to mean that feelings are a gift from God and, as such, they are sacred no matter whether they are joyous or sad. We therefore honor God by giving ourselves permission to embrace our feelings as fully as possible. As we allow ourselves to be present with our feelings, the "locks on the hearts" (47:24) break open and we experience spaciousness within.

Pleasant feelings are easy enough to deal with: our primary task is to be mindful enough to savor them fully and express our gratitude with a sincere "*Alhamdulillah*" or "Allah be praised!" More difficult are the unpleasant feelings that come our way. The human ego tends to avoid, deny, and minimize feelings that make it feel threatened or unhappy. We don't realize that unpleasant feelings such as anger, sadness, and jealousy are just energies that are begging to be acknowledged and integrated. They possess an edge only because we perceive them as something separate from ourselves. These painful feelings are exactly what we need for our healing, transformation, and empowerment. When we embrace them with mercy and gentleness, we allow them to become integrated and healed. When, with courage and compassion, we kiss our inner demons, they turn into princes and princesses. Our hearts expand, the windows open, and we take another giant step towards union with our Beloved. Thus spiritual teachers have said, "The more that sorrow carves into your being, the more joy your heart can contain." No need to run toward pain and sorrow, say the teachers, just don't run away from them.

PRACTICE

There is an excellent Sufi technique for dealing with the pain and sorrow that life has to offer. This technique, called Sacred Holding, is the compassionate art of acknowledging, accepting, and integrating feelings that are painful or negative, feelings that we tend to avoid or deny. Whenever painful or negative feelings arise, practice this four-step process at the earliest opportunity.

- First, allow yourself to experience the feeling. Tell yourself that every feeling, no matter what we call it, is energy that is begging to be acknowledged and healed. Simply give yourself permission to feel.

- Second, ask yourself, "Where do I hold this feeling in my body?" Locate the feeling. It definitely has a resting place in your body. We are able to experience a feeling because it registers as a physical sensation somewhere in the body.

- Third, receive this "holding" in your body with compassion for yourself. Encompass the physical sensations in your body with the embrace of your soul. Give yourself an affectionate name and talk to yourself with gentleness. Tell yourself, for example, "Beloved one, I am sorry you feel this. I know this is difficult. Allow me to support you in your pain." At this time there is no need to fix or analyze these sensations. Simply hold the feeling with mercy for yourself, for as long as you want.

- In the final step, focus gently on the place in your body where you are holding the pain, and intend to inhale and exhale through that part of you. Allow Divine Breath to caress you there.

If you persist with this technique, you will experience an amazing shift in the way you process life's difficulties: that which was negative and painful will become integrated and transformed into a source of strength and wholeness. Something deepens and matures within you, and the doorway to your heart is open to the Beloved.

The Divine Exchange: "Whoever belongs to God, God belongs to that one." (hadith)

As we have seen in the pages of this chapter, the path of surrendering the ego in exchange for union with the higher self is a simple journey, but not an easy one. The ego clings to its own self-interest and the heart resists the Beloved's attempts to pry it open. God wants to sell us something, says the poet Hafiz, but we keep haggling over the price. But once we pass up the shop of hagglers and seek the Shop of Abundance where "God is the purchaser," says Rumi, we will be astounded by the power, beauty, and exhilaration of the lopsided exchange. Our gracious Sustainer rewards our "counterfeit coins" and our "shabby bag of goods" with a spiritual spring that is so delicious that "even sugar is jealous of its sweetness!"

To engage in the divine exchange, so that you belong to God and God belongs to you, listen deeply to the needs of your soul. Surrender is the lifelong practice of allowing the Divine and not the ego to be the center of reality. Make it a practice in everything you say and do to ask yourself, "Am I coming from a place of divine attributes in me—truth, say, or love, compassion, or beauty—or am I coming from a place of the little self—from fear, pettiness, or jealousy?" Be mindful of the answer and make sincere efforts to act on your soul's needs, no matter how inconvenient or difficult. God will take care of the obstacles. Have faith.

> And as for those who have attained faith in Allah
> And hold fast to Him—
> He will cause them to enter into His Compassion
> And His Abundant Blessing
> And guide them to Himself by a straight way. (4:175)

Jewish Reflections

Shiviti Adonai l'negdi tamid—I set the Eternal before me always. (Ps. 16:8)

The Jewish path is not known as a path of surrender as explicitly as Islam—in fact, Jews are famous for boisterous arguments with God and with each other. Not for nothing are we named for our forefather Jacob, who, you will recall from chapter 6, was renamed Israel ("God-wrestler") after striving all night with beings "human and divine" (Gen. 32:29). Even our father Abraham, so revered in Islam as a paragon of surrender that he is considered the first Muslim ("one surrendered to God"), may be loved more for his ability to reason with God than for his surrender. The episode that would seem to set the seal on Abraham as a fully surrendered "Muslim" is known in Judaism as the *Akeda*, the binding (usually mistranslated as the sacrifice) of Isaac (Gen. 22:1–19). This is a deeply troubling story, and Abraham's behavior in it is not universally admired in Judaism. Since the rabbis began writing explanations of Torah stories two thousand years ago, Jews have been trying to understand why Abraham, who was bold enough to bargain with God to save the nameless people of Sodom and Gomorrah (Gen. 18:22–33), wouldn't say a word to save his own precious son. At Sodom he literally said, "Far be it from you, God, to punish the innocent with the guilty." But for his own flesh and blood, he offered only silence.

Early midrash, written at a time not too distant from the days of blood sacrifice, is generally sympathetic to Abraham, while midrash of our own generation often runs along the lines of *what* was he *thinking*?! In the first place it's hard for us moderns to believe that the Eternal would demand human sacrifice, even as a test; it seems more likely that Abraham "heard" the demand during a dream or a very bad "trip." And in the second place, if God really did make such an outrageous demand to test him, why didn't he stand up to God as he did at Sodom? Writing at a three-thousand-year remove, I want him to say, "Far be it from you, God, to kill my innocent son! And what about your promise to make him the progenitor of your people?!" In a rather satisfying midrash, Elie Wiesel suggests in *Messengers of God* that in fact Abraham was calling God's bluff. By going through the motions of submitting to God's will, he was defying God to renege on the promise that he would be the father "of a multitude of nations" (Gen. 16:5) through his son Isaac (Gen 21:12). As the story turns out, of course, Isaac is saved at the last minute and God promises once again that Abraham's descendants will become "as numerous as the stars of heaven and the sands on the seashore" (Gen. 22:17). All's well that ends well—if you don't count the facts that Sarah dies shortly afterward (according to one midrash the cause of death is heartbreak when she hears erroneously that her son is dead), father and son are estranged as they go home separately from the scene of the drama, and God never again speaks to Abraham in the pages of Torah.

All this is to say that surrender is not a straight-forward proposition in Judaism as it is in Islam. Nevertheless, Jews are filled with the same longing for union with the Eternal and our scriptures adjure us to follow a path of surrender as surely as the Quran admonishes its adherents. As the "Chosen People," we are no better or worse than the rest of the human race and we are not exempt from the difficult work of surrendering our hearts and minds to our Creator. We are simply "chosen" for the path called Torah, as others are chosen to follow the path of Islam, the footsteps of Jesus, the way of Tao, or any of the myriad paths to wholeness and union with the One.

The Jewish path of surrender unfolds gradually in the Torah, until it is finally presented in perfect clarity in the six words of a statement known as the *Sh'ma* (often spelled *Shema*): *Sh'ma Yisrael Adonai Eloheinu Adonai Ekhad.* "Listen, Israel: The Eternal is our God, the Eternal is One" (Deut. 6:4). Of those six words, the one that implicitly calls us to surrender is *Ekhad*, One: the only reality is God—there is only One—and we are part of that reality. From the truth contained in this word flow all the commandments in the Torah and all the commentaries in the Talmud. So pivotal is this concept in Jewish spirituality that when the beloved Rabbi Akiva was being martyred by the Romans in 135 CE, he said the Sh'ma in such a way that he died with the word "ekhad" on his lips. From Akiva's example there developed a practice of prolonging the word "ekhad" when we recite the Sh'ma to signify our willingness to surrender to the One Reality no matter what the cost.

And there *is* a cost, which we often would prefer not to pay. The price for union with the Beloved is a lifetime of hard work to tame the self-serving ego and bring it into alignment with the divinity at the core of our being. At Sinai we declare whole-heartedly, "All that the Eternal has spoken we will faithfully do" (Exod. 24:7). Actually, this is a watered-down translation of the original Hebrew, which reads much more radically: *Kol asher-diber Adonai na'aseh v'nish'ma*—"Everything that the Eternal says, we will do and we will hear." What a concept, to be willing to do God's bidding even before we fully listen to it, before we've had time to count the cost and summon our arguments and resistance! It's a powerful statement of surrender, and we really mean it—but a few paragraphs later, we have forgotten all about it and are dancing around a golden calf. From that day to this, we have repeated our covenant with the Eternal over and over, only to forget it when the gods of wealth, power, and self-gratification lure us with their siren call. "I see that this is a stiff-necked people," God says to Moses at Mount Sinai (Exod. 32:9), and it is clear that we haven't mastered the art of surrender.

Still, our hearts know that they are made for God, and like Attar's birds longing to see the Simurgh earlier in this chapter, we long to come before the face of our Creator:

> How lovely is Your dwelling-place, O Lord of hosts.
> I long, I yearn for the courts of the Lord;
>   my body and soul shout for joy to the living God.
> Even the sparrow has found a home,
>   and the swallow a nest for herself in which to set her young,
> near Your altar, O Lord of hosts. (Ps. 84:1–4)

Jewish spirituality teaches that in a very real sense we are constantly in God's presence—we have but to train ourselves to be more mindful of that reality, to "set the Eternal before [us] always." Observant Jews begin each day by greeting the Eternal with a beautiful blessing, the *Modeh Ani*: "How grateful I am to be in your Presence, beloved Creator of all that is!" The Jewish ideal is to say at least a hundred blessings a day—for things we eat and drink, the places we go and the people we see, the delights of nature, for all the things that life has to offer. This is not because God needs our blessings, but because it reminds us to live more consciously, to be more aware of the divinity that is all around us, to be more connected with and surrendered to the divinity at the core of our own being.

In addition to the practice of blessing, at which I am woefully inconsistent, I have adopted a practice based on a word in Torah that is loaded with implied surrender—a word spoken by Abraham, Moses, and the prophets, a word that is repeated every day by Jews all over the world as they prepare to say their morning prayers. That word is *Hineini*, "Here I am." When the Eternal One called to Abraham and to Moses, they answered, "Hineini" (Gen. 22:1; Exod. 3:4). Likewise, when God asked who would speak to the Israelites who had gone astray, the prophet Isaiah responded, "Here am I—send me" (Isa. 6:8). When spoken with full consciousness and intentionality, Hineini means Here I am at this very moment, all of me: a spiritual being who is breathing divine breath and exercising divine gifts, a child of God, a sister or brother of all God's children, one with the universe, one with the One. In that moment of consciousness, however fleeting, we are subsumed in the Divine, co-creating with the Creator, and in our own individual way contributing to the all-important work of *tikkun olam*, repair of the world.

Like the path of surrender, the path of Hineini may appear long and challenging, but we don't have to master it all at once. In the words of an ancient rabbi, "You are not required to finish the work, but neither are you free to avoid it" (Avot 2:16). Our life's work is to walk our chosen path one step at a time. Of the many ways to proceed, one of my favorites is the Jewish spiritual path called Mussar, a discipline that involves transformation of both perspective and action in our daily lives. In its simplest form you choose a spiritual characteristic—compassion, say, or awareness, humility, patience, gratitude—all those qualities that we associate with the Divine but find so lacking in ourselves. Keep it simple; focus on just one quality at a time.

To illustrate, let's choose compassion, a quality so desperately needed in the world today. The first step is to reflect on the ways in which compassion could improve your relations with others, not to mention your relations with yourself and with the Eternal One. Then take stock of all the ways in which you already manifest compassion and identify areas for improvement. Think about specific ways to build compassion in your attitudes and actions, and then follow through with conscious thoughts or acts of compassion throughout the day. Renew your intention every morning, and keep track of your efforts through journaling or some kind of self-examination at the end of the day. Try to be conscious of every opportunity for a compassionate act or thought, and announce to the Beloved in your heart, Hineini. Here I am. Send me, O Holy One, to do your work of compassion in the world.

Slowly but surely, "little by little," you will find that you are surrendering your judgmental, self-centered ego to the Compassionate One and you are ready to turn your attention to another divine attribute that you want to manifest in your life. "Hineini," you say to all those opportunities to practice patience, or humility, or awareness, and then the truth begins to dawn: you may still be arguing with God, you may still be stiff-necked, but with your whole-hearted "Hineini" you are truly on a path of surrender.

Christian Reflections

Not my will but yours be done. (Luke 22:42)

Shedding the light of Islam, whose very name can be translated "self-surrender to God," on Christianity has shown me the many places where submission to the Beloved shines through Christian tradition and its scriptures—in Jesus' life and teachings; in his encounters with others, especially his disciples; and in the wisdom and practices of believers through the centuries. Jesus' life is a glowing example of "a journey from God, to God and in God." His teachings about the reign (or realm) of the Holy One point his followers to both the path and its destination. The stories of their lives in the Christian Testament and later sources provide a multitude of examples, "a cloud of witnesses" (Heb. 12:1), to mirror the ache for the Beloved that pulls us onto the path; the process of transmutation of the ego; and the qualities of patience, humility, truthfulness, and sincerity that keep us going along the way.

The pattern of Jesus' life reflects the rhythm of repeated surrender. In his pre-existent unity with God (John 1:1–2), Jesus could be a stand-in for all of unborn humanity, who in the Quran acclaim their Creator (7:172). Writing in Greek, John starts out, "In the beginning was the Word, and the Word was with God, and the Word was God." The word order and syntax are precise: the Word is not identical with God, but is an entity wholly taken up in God. Like Adam and Eve in the Quran, Jesus descends from God on a mission. Throughout his life on earth there are glimpses—especially when he is at prayer—of his continuing intimacy with and surrender to the One who sent him, the One whom he calls Father. By numerous choices in his life Jesus demonstrates that he is living in submission to the plans made for him by God. For example, when he insists upon being baptized by John the Baptist (also considered a prophet in the Quran), even though John claims to be unworthy of such an honor, Jesus is seeking to "fulfill all righteousness" (Matt. 3:14–15). In the wilderness, he seizes the opportunity to build his "purification muscles" by refusing Satan's offer of political, material, and even religious power in exchange for servitude to the Adversary (or the slinking whisperer, as Satan is sometimes called in the Quran). Drawing on the Torah (Deut. 6:13), Jesus dismisses Satan with the words, "It is written: 'Worship the Lord your God and serve only him'" (Matt. 4:10; Luke 4:8). As he walks directly into the maelstrom that his single-minded devotion to God stirs up, he shows that the way of surrender can be painful and costly. He expresses his quite human reluctance to suffer by asking God to "let this cup pass" (Matt. 26:39, 42; Mark 14:35–37; Luke 22:42), but he continues immediately with a statement of his commitment to surrender: "Not my will but yours be done" (Luke 22:42). The anguish of surrender is painfully evident when he calls out from the cross in the words of Psalm 119, "My God, my God, why have you forsaken me?" (Matt. 27:46; Mark 15:34). But God did not forsake him: God in fact brought Jesus back to his Origin (Quran 4:157–158). The events that Christians call the Resurrection and the Ascension demonstrate that the culmination of complete surrender to God is new life.

In Jesus' teaching, to follow the path of surrender is to live within the Reign (or Realm or Kingdom) of God, also known as the Reign (or Realm or Kingdom) of Heaven. Just as Allah in the Quran is both the "Sustainer of all the worlds" (1:2) and "Lord of the Day of Judgment" (1:4), the Reign of the Holy One encompasses and surpasses both space and time. It is already here and now. Jesus tells a group of opponents not to look to external manifestations: "The kingdom of God is among you" (Luke 17:21). We are also meant to pursue it actively: "But strive first for the kingdom of God and God's righteousness" (Matt. 6:33). Jesus brings together the idea of surrender to God's will and to this kingdom at the beginning of one version of the prayer he teaches his disciples: "Your kingdom come. Your will be done, on earth as it is in heaven" (Matt. 6:10).

Rather than rules or judgments, Jesus often uses the metaphorical language of parables to illumine the mysterious nature of God's Reign. As a beader, I have an obvious favorite: "Again, the kingdom of heaven is like a merchant in search of fine pearls; on finding one pearl of great value, he went and sold all that he had and bought it" (Matt. 13:45–46). No haggling over the price here! One can enter the Reign of God only with the humility and simplicity of a child, Jesus says (Matt. 18:3–4); even tax collectors and prostitutes will get in faster than hypocrites (Matt. 21:31).

Because the Christian gospels skip from Jesus' infancy to his early thirties, we do not get to watch the process of his ego transmutation. However, there are snapshots of this path in the stories of those who followed him in his earthly ministry and over the succeeding centuries. The moment called the Annunciation, when the angel Gabriel appears to the teenager who is to become Jesus' mother, captures the beauty of willing personal assent to God's invitation to what the Quran calls *Khalifa*, our assignment as humans to be God's representatives in creation. Mary says, "Here am I, the servant of the Lord; let it be with me according to your word" (Luke 1:38). Daily, in the prayer practice of the Angelus, Christians rehearse that story, to make Mary's posture their own. The conversion of the apostle Paul is a prime example of what it takes to transmute the ego and surrender it to God. Paul has to become literally blind before he can see with a new consciousness (Acts 9:1–9), and his letters to the fledgling Christian communities speak of his struggle to relinquish the privileges that had defined his place in the world so that he can fully embrace what he called the "new creation" (2 Cor. 5:17; Gal. 6:15) demonstrated by Jesus' teachings. "In Christ there is no longer Jew or Greek, there is no longer slave or free, there is no longer male and female" (Gal. 3:28).

Those who come to Jesus for healing give us another view of the power of a posture of surrender. Often in their urgency to be healed they are willing to do whatever is necessary to get to Jesus for help. They must sacrifice—surrender—whatever stands in their way. For Jairus, a leader of the Jewish community, it means giving up his dignity to kneel at Jesus' feet on behalf of his daughter, whom his neighbors are already mourning as dead (Matt. 9:18; Mark 5:22; Luke 8:41). One man suffering from paralysis has such dedicated friends that, when crowds block their access to Jesus, they lower him through the roof of the house where Jesus is (Mark 2:4; Luke 5:19). Jesus often responds to such people by commending their "faith"; in fact, according to one passage, he is limited in his power to heal people by their "unbelief" (Matt. 13:58). What Jesus calls "faith" is closely akin to the notion of surrender in the Quran. It is the posture necessary for humans to receive God's power for transformation and renewal.

My favorite example of surrender among those around Jesus is Mary Magdalene, whose need for healing is so acute that she is described as having had seven demons (Luke 8:2). Because seven is the number of completion, we can assume that she was entirely consumed by destructive energy.

For some reason, however, she is able to surrender to God's power in Jesus. From that encounter, she goes on to become Jesus' most loyal supporter and the only person to appear in all four gospels as a witness to God's raising of Jesus to new life. In fact, as the "apostle to the apostles," it is Mary Magdalene who bears the news to his followers that Jesus' tomb is empty. In an early Christian writing, the Gospel of Mary, she appears as a teacher to the other disciples. The life of Mary Magdalene is an amazing example of the divine exchange: she came to Jesus desperate for God's grace to release and relieve her; she went on empowered to proclaim, teach, and lead others toward a life of surrender and freedom to serve God.

Living a life of surrender, as Kate and Jamal have shown, calls for mindfulness and intentionality, as well as willingness to develop the qualities of patience, humility, truthfulness, and sincerity. The Christian practice of reconciliation has been an important part of my strategy for integrating these attitudes into my life; it has been my version of Jamal's "little black book" and Kate's practice of "hineini." Also known as the sacrament of confession, reconciliation has a long history in Christianity. It enables individuals and communities to identify in our lives the obstacles to God's grace that stand in the way of complete surrender and to reach again for "the most trusty Handhold" (Quran 31:22) to pull us out of the ditch so that we can move on down the road.

In childhood I practiced confession as a routine part of the communal weekly gatherings for worship in church. However, it was not until I became an adult that I really grew to appreciate the richness of the practice. During a time of crisis and soul-searching, I decided to prepare for making a life confession, and since that time periodic confession has been a part of the rhythm of my life. Confession is a three-part practice that begins with self-examination, taking stock of my life. Over the years this process has kept me current with the reality of my inner workings. It helps me stay aware of my troubling tendencies; the people, places, and things that are habitual occasions for my bad choices; the maladaptive patterns I use to adjust to hurts and injustice. The second step is "'fessing up." In letting someone else in on what could otherwise become dangerous secrets, I have found over and over again the kind of empathy that reminds me that I share two traits with the rest of humanity: most of us are just garden-variety sinners, and all of us are beloved of God. The final step is receiving the reassurance of healing and revival from the One who has been waiting for the opportunity to help me move on. I am always reminded who is doing the forgiving and the restoring when the priest says at the end, "And pray for me, a sinner."

Reconciliation has been used from time to time as a formulaic procedure, robbing it of some of its many benefits. For me, however, practicing reconciliation has helped me regularly to rediscover how God works with me. Instead of wresting my idols out of my grasp or launching a rescue mission to spring me from my furnished caves, God allows me to come to awareness of my impediments and then graciously waits for me to surrender and ask for help in removing them. God painstakingly builds in humility and patience as I confess repeatedly—sometimes for years on end, early on with alarm, then with slowly emerging self-acceptance—those troublesome patterns that are so ingrained as to seem permanent. Then there are those shining moments of spontaneous right action in harmony with the Beloved when I recognize the reality of the divine exchange. "Now to [God] who by the power at work within us is able to accomplish abundantly far more than all we can ask or imagine, . . . be glory. . . . Amen" (Eph. 3:20–21).

9

Compassion

Bismillah-ir-Rahman-ir-Rahim
(In the Name of God, Infinitely Compassionate and Merciful)

The spiritual core of Islam is God's infinite compassion as extolled in the words known as the *Basmala*: "*Bismillah-ir-Rahman-ir-Rahim.*" By frequently invoking this mantra, we remind ourselves that we are trying to live and act in the name of the Eternal One. So paramount is the principle of Basmala that it opens all but one of the 114 chapters of the Quran. (The one exception, Surah 9, may have been recited originally as a continuation of the preceding chapter, so would not have had an opening invocation.) In a famous hadith the Prophet Muhammad said, "All that is in the revealed books is contained in the Quran; all that is in the Quran is contained in the *Fatiha* [the opening chapter of the Quran]; all that is in the Fatiha is contained in the Basmala."

The operative words in the Basmala are *rahman* and *rahim*, the twin elements of compassion described in chapter 3. When we set out on the path of surrender, our goal is union with the God of compassion and mercy—a God of tenderness, forbearance, and empathy. It is only logical, then, that the most important spiritual provision for the journey is that same divine virtue. The message for the spiritual seeker is clear: living in a state of Basmala—speaking and acting in the name of divine compassion—is the key to union with the Beloved, and that is the key to a life of joy and blessing. To the extent that we lack this divine quality, it reflects our separation not only from God but from our own truest selves.

Spiritual teachers tell us that the practice of Basmala requires spiritual growth on three fronts. First, we must expand our awareness that the essence of God is compassion. Second, we need to become mindful of a deep longing to taste the essence of our being, to know what Sufis call our "real name." This longing is nothing less than a desire to experience our own divine nature. And third, we must increase our spaciousness, our personal ability to live in a state of Basmala, first towards ourselves and then in relation to the rest of the world. In seeking to connect with our own divine nature and to see the Divine in others, we are following a Quranic principle that says God is both within us (*batin*) and outside us (*zahir*).

To live a complete life—or, as Sufis say, to become fully human—we have to do the inner and outer work of bonding with the Beloved. We have to evolve into the fullness of our being and offer ourselves in service to God's creation. And at every step of the way, we need to invoke the Basmala in doing our inner and outer work. A Bedouin once entreated the Prophet to reveal to him how he could invite God's boundless compassion to be bestowed upon him. The Prophet replied, "Have compassion on yourself and on others, and infinite compassion will be given to you."

To truly understand the transformative power, beauty, and sacredness of compassion, it is useful to remember that the symbol for compassion in the Quran, as in other spiritual writings, is water. "He is the One who sends down rain after they have lost all hope and unfolds His Grace" (42:28). As noted in chapter 2, water is beguiling in its power. There is nothing as soft and refreshing as water, but for overcoming the hardest stone there is nothing as strong as water. "Not hammer strokes," says the poet Tagore, "but the dance of the water sings the pebbles into perfection." In addition to its ability to purify and transform, compassion, like water, is also life-giving. Wherever water falls, life flourishes. A parched piece of earth stirs into life when nurtured by water. Thus compassion is both authentic strength and a magical bestower of life.

Compassion for self

In doing the inner work of transformation, of giving birth to our real name, compassion for self is crucial. Our divine identity grows and develops in the womb of compassion. Some Sufi teachers claim that the inner meaning of the Basmala is really about practicing continuous mercy and gentleness for ourselves. Little do we know who we are, where we come from, or where we are going. Our beings deserve to be touched by compassion every step of the way. To discover and connect to our true name, we have to transform our ego and open our heart. Only the Allah within us can know Allah. When we do this essential work of compassion for self, the ego relaxes its anxious hold, the heart unclenches, and its armor dissolves.

As mentioned in chapter 8, the Quran identifies three stages of the ego, or nafs: an ego that inclines toward wrongdoing; an ego that learns to make good choices; and an ego that is at peace. In the course of our lifetime, we are asked to become aware of our ego through constant self-vigilance and to enable its transformation from a commanding master to an assistant of the soul. When we attempt to use will power or logic to convince the ego, it counters with creative excuses and complex reasons of its own. But when we shine the light of awareness on the ego with compassion and mercy, the armor and defenses of the ego begin to dissolve, allowing the soul to expand and express its true nature. An excellent technique for developing the self-compassion necessary for this first step in transforming the ego is "Sacred Naming," described in the practices at the end of this section.

Once the work of transforming the ego is underway, an inner cry bubbles to the surface of our consciousness. With Moses we cry, "O My Sustainer! Open for me my heart!" (Quran 20:25). And how do we open the window of the heart? Primarily by embracing whatever life sends our way: the ten thousand joys of life and also the ten thousand sorrows that cause our hearts to contract in self-defense, as we discussed in chapter 8. Feelings and tears are sacred, says the Quran (23:78; 53:43), and they need to be held in the womb of compassion. When we treat our difficult feelings with precious gentleness, their rough edges are softened and healed. Slowly, they become integrated and transformed. Without the light of compassion, we are too frightened to open our hearts. In the imagery of the Persian mystic Hafiz, the rose opens its heart and gives its beauty to the world only when it feels the "encouragement of Light against its being." By learning to shine the light of compassion on our own divine nature, we are beginning to live in a state of Basmala. Helpful techniques include Sacred Holding, described in chapter 8, and a number of practices described at the end of this chapter.

Little by little

One of the most important aspects of learning compassion for self is the Quranic principle of "little by little." The very revelation of the Quran was a little-by-little process requiring twenty-three years, so that the gradual revelations might "strengthen the heart" (25:32). From this we can infer that by building our spiritual skills gradually, little by little, we are strengthening both heart and soul. The Quran states further that all of nature illustrates the principle that things take time, that we cannot hurry nature on its appointed rounds:

> So I call to witness the rosy glow of sunset
> the night and its progression
> and the moon as it grows into fullness:
> surely you shall travel from stage to stage. (84:16–19)

The message is clear: inner transformation does not happen overnight and we must be patient and gentle with ourselves. Just as ordinary stones become rubies only with the passage of time and twigs break into buds imperceptibly, we grow into the fullness of our being gradually. Spiritual progress usually happens in many small increments, occasionally punctuated with sudden leaps forward. The leaps are the result of—and a reward for—doing the necessary work patiently, persistently, and little by little.

Compassion for others

As we cultivate compassion for self and connect to our own divine light, it becomes easier and easier to invoke the Basmala in our relations with others. Acting more consciously in the name of the boundlessly Compassionate

One, we begin to recognize that every person, whether friend or foe, is precious to the Creator. Clay though our feet may be, all human beings are infused with divine breath and in our essence we all bear the true name of son or daughter of God. When we invoke the Basmala in relating to others, we create space for the divine identity to emerge and we begin to learn each other's true name. As we see in chapters 5 and 14, diversity among people and nations is part of the divine plan to teach us to recognize and respect the sacred essence of our fellow beings, even those who do us wrong. This is not to suggest that when we are on the receiving end of harmful deeds we should unthinkingly excuse or overlook the damage. All humans have to be accountable. Rather, what the sages emphasize is this: we must not allow our hearts to clench and become blind. Invoking the Basmala, emulating divine compassion and mercy, let us call the offender by his or her true name. When taking action to protect ourselves or redress a wrong, let us remember to ask ourselves, "With what energy am I taking this action? Am I coming from my ego or my soul? Am I coming from ego attributes of rage and revenge, or from soul attributes of truth and beauty?"

The soul, whose essence is compassion, discerns between behavior and being, between form and essence. Our behaviors might sometimes be evil, but our being or essence is never evil. Regardless of our offenses, inside each one of us resides a divine nature—call it Divine Breath, Allah Nature, Christ Nature, Elohim Essence, or any other sacred name that speaks to you. As Sufis have repeated over the centuries, the husk is corruptible, but the kernel is inviolable. The sheer energy of this knowledge, as it informs our actions, has the power to shift heaven and earth. Further emulating our merciful Creator, let us never lose hope for ourselves or others. No matter how far we or they may seem from divine essence, the God of the Basmala is infinitely merciful and there is always hope of transformation and redemption.

It is not only wrongdoers who need our compassion. More often it is the people in our everyday lives: co-workers who irritate us, family members who try our patience, friends with whom we have quarreled. A powerful practice in these cases is to recite one or both of these beautiful Quranic verses: "Is it not enough that your Sustainer is a witness?" (41:53) and "Make allowances for people" (7:199). Remind yourself that your primary relationship is with God. God knows your intentions and sees your efforts to act with compassion. And then remind yourself that God witnesses the other person as well. God knows the divine essence of that irritating person. Trust that Divine Heart will speak to that human heart, and be peaceful in the knowledge that it is not up to you to judge or reform anyone but yourself. The reward for such forbearance is described in yet another hadith of Muhammad: "If a man gives up quarrelling when he is in the wrong, a house will be built for him in Paradise. But if a man gives up a conflict even when he is in the right, a house will be built for him in the loftiest realm of Paradise."

"The character of a *Wali* (friend of God)," said the Prophet Muhammad, "is based upon nothing more than graciousness and generosity." One beautiful way to cultivate compassion is to be gracious and generous in forgiving ourselves and others. Because God readily forgives our offenses, any forgiveness on our part is an echo of God's graciousness and compassion. If we wish to live in the spirit of Basmala, we must extend God's forgiveness to one another. In the process of forgiving others, let us remember the Prophet Muhammad's insight about being compassionate with ourselves. When we are wronged or offended our first step must be to embrace our own pain, sadness, or anger with exquisite compassion and mercy for ourselves. It is critical that we fully understand that this tender enfolding of our pain is the most essential step, without which forgiveness of others is incomplete. The practice of Sacred Holding (described in chapter 8) is invaluable in the process of forgiveness.

The Quran tells us that in difficult times, when conditions and circumstances in people's lives cause chronic anger, fear, or hopelessness, "Truly it is not their eyes that are blind, but their hearts" (22:46). To open another person's heart, we must first open our own. Force is counterproductive, and attempts to reason with others have limitations. Only that which comes from the heart can open another heart. It is the flame of compassion in the heart that dissolves shadows within and without and illuminates the world. What we are facing in this anxious post-9/11 world is the challenge and the opportunity of learning to express and manifest compassion for blinded hearts in a balanced and authentic way.

Our obligation to act in the name of the all-merciful and compassionate Creator applies not only to our relations with each other but to our encounters with the animal, vegetable, and mineral kingdoms of God. The Holy Book reminds us that animals and birds are "communities just like your own" (6:38). And the Prophet's love for animals is well known. The earth, too, is the face of God. Sages say we must tread carefully upon the earth and treat it with the same respect that we show to the Holy Book.

The Quran admonishes us to strive repeatedly to live the Basmala. "After the difficulty there is the easing," the Holy Book says, and then it repeats, "After the difficulty is the easing. So when you are finished, strive again and in your Lord aspire" (94:5–8). Living the Basmala is not easy, but the rewards are magnificent. One's being, graced continuously by the practice of the Basmala, takes on a beautiful fragrance. Just as a mirror cannot help but reflect an image, the sincere aspirant cannot help but be perfumed by the fragrance of divine compassion. The servants of the infinitely Compassionate One, says the Quran, are "those who walk on the earth in humility, and when the ignorant address them, they say, 'Peace!'" (25:63).

PRACTICES

- To help sustain compassionate awareness of the ego, Sufi teachers suggest a technique called Sacred Naming, which addresses our tendency to engage unconsciously in negative self-talk. Choose a term of endearment for yourself—for example, "beloved" or "dear heart"—to evoke compassion for yourself, and use it whenever you become aware that you are getting down on yourself. For example, when I discover that I am in the middle of an unhelpful inner conversation, I interrupt it with words such as, "Brother Jamal, I am so sorry you are experiencing this difficulty. Please know that I am here to support you. Let us hold this feeling together. Brother Jamal, let us together invoke God's boundless compassion and mercy to help us in this process." This simple technique has a powerful effect on our spiritual growth: the ego softens and becomes more willing to join in partnership with the soul.

- The beautiful Sufi technique of Sacred Light fosters the practice of Basmala in our relations with others. As often as you can remember, send light from your heart to everything and everyone with whom you come in contact. Simply intend to send out light and, if possible, love from your heart. Intention equals action in the subtle realms. If you meet someone you do not like, remind yourself that you are sending light and love from your heart to the other person's soul or essence, which is pure and sacred. You are not condoning his or her personality or behavior. For that, let your Sustainer be a witness. With this technique, you are naming the person by his or her true divine name and doing it with the divine energy at the core of your being. Graced by God's compassion, you will evolve more and more into your own divine essence and enable others to do the same.

- To open a doorway between human heart and divine heart, Sufis practice a technique called Gazing upon the Heart. Try to make it a lifelong habit to bring your attention to rest on your heart during quiet moments and even as you are engaged in speech and action. Continuously, as you go about your daily life, be mindful of your heart. In the practice of meditation, rest your attention on your heart. If your mindfulness wavers or is distracted, compassionately bring your attention back to your heart again and again. As this habit takes hold, you will become deeply centered and amazingly present to each moment and the window of your heart will open magically. A beam of light from the divine heart, infused with compassion and mercy, will illuminate your heart and guide your life.

- To take Gazing upon the Heart a step further and deeper, adopt the practice of Adoring the Heart. In your waking state or in meditation rest your attention on your heart space and, with feeling and tenderness, tell your heart repeatedly, "I love you . . . I love you so much . . . I really love you." If the words do not resonate, change to "I am willing to love you," or change the word "love" to "cherish" or "honor." No matter how awkward it may feel, say the words to your heart repeatedly. Know that God, who not only exists outside of you but also resides in your heart, longs to hear these words from you. Your ego might resist, so persist! Eventually, the ego lets go, for in the face of genuine, abiding love and compassion, the ego is helpless. With continuous practice, a supremely compassionate divine vibration goes from the tongue into the mouth, into the chest, deep into the heart, and deeper still into the mysteries within, healing you, empowering you, and transforming you.

Jewish Reflections

A kindly man benefits himself. (Prov. 11:17)

And a kindly woman benefits herself, I hasten to add in the spirit of inclusiveness. The point is that in Jewish spirituality, any thought, feeling, or act of compassion, whether directed towards ourselves or towards someone else, redounds to our own benefit and is a blessing to the world.

The preeminence of compassion in all the Abrahamic traditions has its origins in the Torah, the Holy Book of Judaism. The daily mantra of observant Jews, endowing every moment of existence with grace and meaning, is the six-word declaration of faith known as the Sh'ma: *Sh'ma Yisrael, Adonai Eloheinu, Adonai Ekhad.* "Listen, Israel: The Eternal is our God, the Eternal is One" (Deut. 6:4). This statement of the Oneness of God is tantamount to the Islamic *"La Ilaha Il Allah,"* meaning "no reality but God." Taken to the nth degree of its implications, the Sh'ma means that all of creation—including each human being—is part of God and, as such, is part of Oneness. It's all one. *We* are all one. And we all partake of the nature of God.

That nature is, above all else, one of compassion. Among the many Hebrew names for God, one of my favorites is *Ha–Rakhaman*, the Compassionate One. Readers will notice the strong similarity with the Arabic *rahman* and *rahim* discussed in chapter 3, and indeed the divine name is based on the Hebrew word for compassion, *rakhamim*, which in turn is rooted in the semitic word for womb, *rhm*. The message bears repeating: compassion is a nourishing, life-giving womb without which it is impossible to grow and develop into the likeness of God as Torah commands us to do. Ours is "a God compassionate and gracious, slow to anger, abounding in kindness and faithfulness" (Exod. 34:6). As in the Quran, there are other passages that show a less gracious God, but the overriding message in Torah is that God will show kindness "to the thousandth generation of those who love Me" (Exod. 20:6). Reinforcing this image of the Eternal are numerous touching and fanciful midrashim. In one legend, God first thought to create the world through the quality of judgment, but upon realizing that the world could not survive divine judgment, God added the quality of compassion. In another, the Holy One sits on the throne of judgment to judge the world every day, but upon seeing that the world is so wicked as to deserve extermination, the Holy One rises from the throne of judgment and moves to the throne of compassion. (As an aside, this pattern must have begun after God destroyed the wicked world in Noah's flood! Indeed, it was after the flood that the Eternal promised "Never again will I doom the earth because of man" (Gen. 8:21).)

The compassion of God is extolled throughout the Hebrew Bible and Midrash, but nowhere is it described in more practical terms than in the writings of the Jewish mystics. In a fascinating little book called *Tomer Deborah* (*The Palm Tree of Deborah*), Rabbi Moses Cordovero, a sixteenth-century Kabbalist, describes each of the "thirteen Qualities of Divine Mercy" in which we should strive to resemble our Creator. Following each description, which he bases on examples from Torah, he exhorts the reader, "So should every man act" and offers both spiritual and practical examples. Like many men of his time, Cordovero had little regard for the female intellect and his male-focused writing can be maddening to contemporary women, but with a little paraphrasing his message is invaluable to men and women alike: just as we conduct ourselves below, so do we merit that the Divine Qualities above should be opened for us. The Influence that is sent down from above is exactly of that quality wherewith we conduct ourselves; and therefore we cause the Divine Qualities to shine in this world.

The overall message of both Torah and teachers is that Judaism is a religion not so much of faith as of action, and our relationship with God is played out primarily in relations with ourselves and with our fellow human beings. In the *parashah* (portion) of Leviticus called *K'doshim* ("[Be] Holy"), the Eternal instructs Moses to tell the Israelites that they are to be holy, "for I, the Eternal your God, am holy" (Lev. 19:2). There follow numerous instructions in what scholars now call the Holiness Code, some of it inscrutable to our modern sensibilities but much of it focusing on justice and compassion for each other, both familiars and strangers. God promises that when we follow the code, "I will establish My abode in your midst, and I will not spurn you. I will be ever present in your midst: I will be your God, and you shall be My people. I the Eternal am your God who brought you out from the land of the Egyptians to be their slaves no more, who broke the bars of your yoke and made you walk erect" (Lev. 26:11–13). What a beautiful statement about the power of compassion! It is just as Muhammad said to the Bedouin and Cordovero says in his mystical writings: our compassion attracts the Holy One of Compassion to dwell with us on earth, loosens the yoke of slavery to our commanding egos, and enables us to walk erect with the Beloved on the path to surrender and holiness. Forget the burnt offerings, God tells us through the prophets Micah (6:8) and Hosea (6:6); what is pleasing to God is how we manifest divine compassion to the rest of the world. Not by faith, not by acts of worship, but by acts of mercy and kindness do we experience and express our oneness with *Ha–Rakhaman*, the Eternal Source of compassion and love.

Christian Reflections

God is love, and those who abide in love abide in God, and God abides in them . . . We love because [God] first loved us. (1 John 4:16, 19)

One of my favorite songs as sung by beloved reggae icon Bob Marley is called "One Love." Indeed, if God is love and God is one, then there is only one Love. Although it is a shape-shifter *par excellence*, showing up under a variety of aliases and in different forms and circumstances, this one love is rooted in that force expressed in the divine names, Ar-Rahman and Ar-Rahim, translated here as compassion. All of our traditions proclaim God as the initiator and source of this fundamental provision of our spiritual journey. God is the ongoing invitation to, as well as our host and guest at, the eternal feast of love. As I mentioned in chapter 3, an important Christian insight into this kind of love places it alongside faith and hope at the heart of a triad of powers with which God equips us to live out God's purposes for us.

The other triad of love mentioned in the Christian scriptures mirrors the one that begins this chapter; it is love of God, self, and neighbor. In my experience, most humans have relatively easy access to at least one of these manifestations of the one Love, which becomes their point of entry and sustains them as they move into the entire banquet. For Christians, Jesus—especially as described in the gospel and letters of John—is the major guide and connection point for participating in all three of these dimensions of compassion. To continue the metaphor, Jesus is the maître d', the wait-person, and the chef for the dinner. No wonder the Christian sacrament of communion is thought of as the foretaste of the celestial banquet.

One of the most significant lessons I learned in seminary was in a Christian scriptures class that addressed the apostle Paul's view of faith, hope, and love. Paul saw this triad as three catalytic forces that enable the dynamic of Christian life. Of the three forces the greatest is love, he said (1 Cor. 13:13), because it focuses on the present moment, bringing God-consciousness to bear on the here-and-now. Faith does the same for the past and hope for the future, but love is what activates them both because it makes them part of the current reality. In Paul's famous words, love "bears all things, believes all things, hopes all things, endures all things" (1 Cor. 13:7). Paul understood that when we bring love into a situation, God can transform it. My professor in that class firmly stated that love in this sense is not simply a feeling. We can and do feel it, of course, but the emotional sensation happens because we have decided to open and use the gift that God has given us. Although God uses compassion on us, God never forces it on us to use for ourselves. It is a key. God shows us how it works by loving us; we choose to put it into the lock in our hearts and turn it.

When asked to identify the foremost commandment from the Torah, Jesus said, "The first is, 'Hear, O Israel: the Lord our God, the Lord is one; you shall love the Lord your God with all your heart, and with all your soul, and with all your mind, and with all your strength'" (Mark 12:29–30). Continuing, he also said, "The second is this, 'You shall love your neighbor as yourself.' There is no other commandment greater than these" (12:31). God gives us a jumpstart in fulfilling these commandments by loving us first and imbuing us with an innate desire to seek our Creator. In my numerous conversations about love with people over the years, I have heard that often people have a built-in inclination toward at least one of the three dimensions of love and use their obvious strength as a tool to grow into the other areas. I seem to have been wired to love and trust God from the womb and in my earlier years I was amazed to encounter people who had no belief in, not to mention love for, God. Loving others also seemed natural to me, but the love of self has been a challenge, even through years of spiritual practice, direction, sobriety, and therapy. I have found some reassurance and company in the words of St. Bernard of Clairvaux, who once wrote that of all its forms, "the love even of self for only God's sake" is the one that comes after the longest struggle. Little by little and largely through a Christian form of sacred naming, at some point I came to the realization that I needed to move another human being out of the center of my heart in order to make room for the One who had given me the heart in the first place; the Owner needed the space. Much to my delight and astonishment I discovered that the Owner would not inhabit it without me. Then, to my further astonishment and chagrin, I found that although the house had much more room than I had realized before, quite a few of the doors were locked. So the project of key-making keeps me busy now. Love School never ends.

For Christians, Jesus is the building manager of the heart and the master teacher in Love School. Sent by God, he taught compassion by presence, word, and deed. In this prophet, the medium was the message. His intimacy with God radiated from him as "glory, the glory as of a father's only son, full of grace and truth" (John 1:14), though it scandalized many of those closest to him. He also told stories of outrageous compassion. One of my favorites is the one we call the parable of the "good" Samaritan (Luke 10:29–37). (Never mind that the title betrays a cynicism, doubtless unintentional, that nearly reverses one of the points Jesus is making.) A lawyer in the crowd has just asked Jesus, "Who is my neighbor?"—in other words, "Who is eligible to receive my care?"—and Jesus turns the tables on his audience, challenging their stereotypes of others and of themselves by making the exemplar of compassion a man who, in the minds of Jesus' listeners, was neither worthy nor capable of compassionate action (Luke 10:29–37). At the Last Supper, as Jesus prepares to depart from his earthly ministry, he offers the key of compassion to his disciples, leaving them with the commandment to love one another as he has loved them (John 13:34). For Christians, Jesus' death on the cross mysteriously turns that key and enables us to embrace the new life offered by his way of compassion.

In *The Revelations of Divine Love*, fourteenth-century mystic Julian of Norwich expresses the all-encompassing significance of love: "And I saw full surely . . . that before God made us, he loved us. Which love was never slaked, nor ever shall be. And in this love he hath done all his works. And in this love he hath made all things profitable to us. And in this love our life is everlasting. In our making we had beginning: but the love wherein he made us was in him from without-beginning. In which love we have our beginning. And all this shall we see in God without end."

10

Knowledge, Wisdom, and Awareness

O my Sustainer, increase me in knowledge.
(Quran 20:114)

To advance along the spiritual journey, says the Quran, it is necessary to grow continuously in spiritual knowledge and awareness. Indeed, the second-most-used word in the Quran, after "Allah," is "knowledge," or *ilm*. So vital and valuable is our God-given capacity for spiritual evolution that, in Rumi's imagery, when grapes turn to wine, they are longing for our ability to transform ourselves; when stars wheel around the North Pole, they are longing for our growing consciousness. The Prophet Muhammad is famous for exhorting his community to seek knowledge unceasingly. "Go as far as China" in pursuit of knowledge, he said, and know that it is incumbent on every Muslim to seek knowledge "from cradle to grave." His daily prayer, he said, was "O God, make me see things as they really are."

So inspired were Muslims by Quranic and Prophetic admonitions to seek knowledge that for the first thousand years of Islam, beginning in the seventh century, there was an outpouring of enthusiasm for increased knowledge in every field of endeavor. This was a golden age of advancement in the arts, sciences, literature, architecture, and mystical sciences through-out the Muslim world. Sadly, the Muslim pursuit of knowledge has been relatively stagnant during the last three hundred years owing to a variety of sociological, economic, and political reasons that are beyond the scope of this book. Nevertheless, in every age there have been scholars and mystics who have continued to explore the expansive and vibrant world of Islamic spirituality, and we are the beneficiaries of their wisdom and example. There is an excellent lesson in these historic periods of growth and stagnation: we humans also experience periods of astounding spiritual growth from time to time, followed by periods of quiescence or doubt, but always the soul knows what it seeks and will achieve its goal if we can silence the clamoring ego and follow the innate wisdom of the heart.

Knowledge that has been transformed into wisdom and awareness is an essential provision for the spiritual journey. God's whole purpose in creating us, says the Quran, is "in order that ye may learn wisdom" (40:67). Elsewhere the Holy Book says that Allah grants wisdom "to whom He pleases" and those who receive it are graced with "a benefit overflowing," but this message can be grasped only by people "of understanding" (2:269). Book knowledge is valuable, spiritual teachers explain, but we have to avoid the trap of getting stuck in it and thus suffering from what Rumi calls "scholarly vertigo" or an "exhausted famousness," which forms barriers to the acquisition of wisdom. If we become addicted to subtle discussions of the mind for their own sake, says Rumi, we are like a bird that has learned to tie and untie a knot around its legs. Again and again the bird creates ever more complex snares around its legs and unfastens them to show off its strange skill, forgetting that the point is to escape! Rumi reminds us to "sail the mountain air and smell the sweetness of the high meadows." The pure joy of such heart-wisdom far outshines the pleasure of mental gymnastics.

It is not necessary to be a scholar to acquire this kind of wisdom; in fact, book learning can be a detriment if it is used to support the ego instead of the heart. Simple village elders often have more wisdom than university theologians who have not received the "benefit overflowing" from their dry and strict study of the Quran. It is possible to commit Quranic knowledge to memory, but it does you no good if you are not in love with it. In a well-known teaching story, a famous theologian came to a village and berated a pious elder there for being unlettered in Arabic, the language of the Quran.

Chastened, the elder promised to come to the university to learn Arabic from the scholar. The teacher began the first lesson by writing an *alif*—the first letter of the Arabic alphabet—on the blackboard. So moved was the elder by the beauty of that simple stroke that he burst into tears and asked the teacher to end the lesson there and then so that he could spend time really getting to "know" the alif. When he returned the following week, the theologian sarcastically asked him if he remembered the first letter. Face beaming and eyes aglow, the elder rushed to the blackboard and gripped the piece of chalk. As he slowly made the stroke, the board crumbled into pieces! Such is the power of knowledge when it is infused with the wisdom of the heart.

Birdsong in the egg

Inherent in each human being is a perennial knowledge that the Quran calls "an inner truth" (10:5) and some teachers call "second intelligence." Rumi describes this gift from God as a freshness in the center of the chest that neither stagnates nor turns yellow. Unlike first intelligence, or book learning, which moves from the outside to the inside, second intelligence moves from inner knowing to outer expression. It is "a spring overflowing its springbox." With this knowledge, we begin to recognize the divine essence in all that is, to hear what Rumi calls "birdsong in the egg." The Quran tells us that God "imparted to Adam the names of all things" (2:31), that is, gave humanity the grace of inner knowing, and then asked the angels to bow to humanity in acknowledgment of this precious gift.

Spiritual commentators point out that during the Night of Power, when the angel Gabriel appeared to Muhammad and commanded him to recite, the command was to proclaim "In the Name of thy Lord and Sustainer" (96:1). Alas, we humans usually recite in the name of our ego and are veiled from access to a sacred tablet that is already preserved and complete in our inner essence. When we do the work of transforming the ego and opening the heart, by Grace of God, some mysterious veils lift and that second intelligence becomes available to us. Then, says Rumi, we realize that the delightful sciences known to us are just two or three bouquets from the celestial garden.

When we operate from this higher awareness, our life journey with its usual ups and downs becomes an adventure marked by joys and sorrows that ennoble and enrich us. Without such awareness, we feel angry and frustrated during downturns and are suspicious of good times. We fail to realize, the Quran suggests, that every event in our lives is part of a larger, mysterious, and ultimately compassionate story. When knowledge is limited, we are quick to make judgments. The Quran elaborates on this point in a wonderful story that we touched on in chapter 6. Moses wanted to accompany Khidr, a mysterious being described as a servant of God "on whom We had bestowed mercy from Ourselves and whom We had taught knowledge from Our own Presence" (18:65), as Khidr went about his mission in the visible world. Khidr was reluctant to have Moses come along, but yielded when Moses agreed not to question his actions. Along the way, this esoteric being damaged a boat belonging to poor people, killed a youth, and repaired a wall in a town inhabited by rude people who did not deserve such kindness. In each instance Moses was so disturbed that he couldn't stop protesting despite his agreement to keep silent, and Khidr kept saying, "See, I told you that you wouldn't be able to bear it." Finally, at the end of the journey, he told Moses the reasons for his inexplicable actions. In the first case, a despotic king was seizing every ship by force, but the damaged boat was spared because it could not sail. In the second instance the youth's life was taken away because he would have brought bitter grief upon his godly parents by his "overweening wickedness and denial of all truth" (18:80). In the third situation, there was treasure hidden underneath the wall belonging to two orphans, and Allah wanted them to be able to retrieve their buried inheritance upon reaching maturity. Each of these actions, said Khidr, was "an act of mercy from your Sustainer and I did not act by my own commands" (18:82).

Endowed with higher awareness, the heart is comforted by epiphanies such as the one Rumi received about joy and sorrow. Joy is a most precious treasure and needs to be hidden in a secure place just as we would hide a treasure of gold. It would be foolish to hide treasure in plain sight. And so, says Rumi, "Joy is hidden beneath sorrow." But that doesn't mean we should go running toward sorrow, our sages tell us—we just shouldn't run away from it. The spaciousness of second knowledge enables us to see that there is mercy hidden in wrath and wrath concealed in the heart of mercy. The aware person possesses equanimity in times of deep distress and also in times of wild exhilaration. Imbued with this greater awareness, the heart is able to distinguish between pleasure and bliss and rejoices in the truth of the Quranic verse: "The (blessing) from the Presence of God is better than any amusement or bargain!" (62:11).

As we discussed in the previous chapter, higher awareness mandates that in judging others we make a distinction between behavior and being. A person's behavior may be unacceptable, but the person's being is sacrosanct—it is imbued with the divine breath of God. Graced by this knowledge, we know at a core level that nothing exists but God. All spiritual practices in essence revolve around techniques that help us to be conscious of God all around us, to become aware of what Rumi calls the Invisible Hand that moves around our birdcage. Such inner knowledge reassures us that what is mortal and transient is actually rooted in eternity, that evil is simply an energy that is separated from the Light and eventually will be enveloped in it, and that all is perfectly well. Deep within each one of us is an eternal hidden smile that sometimes shows itself in love and laughter rising from the core of our being. This laughter, says the poet Hafiz, is the sound of a soul waking up.

The three stages of knowing

How can we attain to higher knowledge? A Sufi insight offers an essential clue: in this created world we see things not as they are but as *we* are. To be graced with second intelligence, we have to do the inner work to change the way we are and surrender our hearts to God. According to a beautiful hadith qudsi, "The heart of the believer is between two fingers of the Merciful, who turns it wherever he desires." As we surrender to the Compassionate One, let us pray in the Prophet's words, "O God, O Turner of Hearts, turn our hearts towards thee."

In the process of doing our inner work, we need to learn the practice of silence and the art of listening. Our souls begin to hear the constant Quranic refrain, "Will you not listen? Will you not pay attention?," and as we truly listen, our awareness expands organically. The difference between a thinker and a spiritual practitioner who genuinely listens, says Rumi, is that a thinker collects and links up proofs whereas a mystic puts his or her head on a person's chest and sinks into the answer. Most important of all, what expands our awareness is our willingness to participate in the experiences of life with the fullness of our being, with both mind and heart, by fully embracing both thoughts and feelings. As we have seen in other chapters, those who taste, know.

The Quran enumerates three stages of knowing. The first is *ilm-ul-yaqin*, a knowing through reasoning, reflected in the Quranic verse, "Nay, were you to know with certainty of mind" (102:5). The second stage is *ayn-ul-yaqin*, a knowing by sight or personal witnessing: "Again you shall see it with certainty of sight" (102:7). The third stage is *haqq-ul-yaqin*, an experience of inner certainty: "Surely it is the certain truth" (69:51). The third stage taps into the divine sense of knowing from within and is characterized, spiritual teachers emphasize, by silence, humility, and a knowing that "unto God is our limit" (53:42). In other words, the expansiveness of our knowing is directly related to the degree and stages of our inner growth as we advance in union with God.

These three stages of knowing are beautifully and succinctly summarized in the treasures of Native American wisdom: "When I hear something, I remember it; when I see something, I understand it; and when I experience something, I know it.

The limits of human knowledge

"Truly, the noblest of you in the sight of God is the one who is most mindful" (49:13). What makes us noble and, by grace of God, expands our awareness, is humble mindfulness that our human perceptions are limited by the conditioning of our lives and the customs of our society. In an Islamic story about Abraham, our revered forefather had a daily practice of delaying his breakfast until a hungry sojourner came to join him. But even that great prophet limited his hospitality to people of similar belief. One day the stranger with whom he shared his meal turned out to be a Zoroastrian, and Abraham was quite upset. No "fire-worshipper" should eat at his table, and he sent the man away. As the story goes, God was displeased and scolded

Abraham, saying, "I have given this man life and food for a hundred years. Could you not give him hospitality for one day, even if he does homage to fire?" Abraham immediately went after the old man and brought him back to his tent. The lesson is that even Abraham had to do the inner work to increase his spaciousness and thereby earn the title "Friend of the Merciful." In an illustration of the conditioning that tribal customs have on one's psyche, the Prophet lamented to God that he had no surviving male heir—a liability in a society where a man's honor and status depended on his ability to produce male offspring. Although Muhammad is considered by Muslims to be the world's most revolutionary champion of women's rights, he was susceptible to the taunts of his detractors. Immediately after he expressed his sadness to Allah, he received a revelation: "To thee have We granted the Fount (of Abundance)" (108:1). Having received a fountain—a "benefit overflowing"—of grace and spiritual guidance, what need had the Prophet of any worldly accoutrements of success? Abundance in this life or the next does not depend on satisfying social customs and expectations. Rather, we drink from that Fount of Abundance by being conscious of our Source and by bringing a heart turned in devotion to God. This is the ultimate knowledge, the ultimate wisdom that will guide us on our lifelong journey to the Beloved.

Jewish Reflections

Happy is the one who finds wisdom, who attains understanding. (Prov. 3:13)

As the first "People of the Book," Jews have been seeking and celebrating knowledge and wisdom for at least three millennia. In Jewish writing, the two concepts are nearly always linked. Of course we need to pursue knowledge in the practical sense of facts and figures, but we are empty shells proudly showing off our fund of information if we have not achieved a "second intelligence" incubated in the womb of compassion and understanding. We are expected to spend time every Shabbat reading and trying to plumb the depths of the weekly Torah portion, not only to glean new knowledge about the ancient text but, more important, to apply its hidden wisdom to our own lives.

The theme of wisdom runs throughout the Hebrew Bible and really constitutes the core of at least two books, Proverbs and Ecclesiastes. Open the book of Proverbs to any page and you will find a paean to *Khokhmah*, the divine trait of wisdom. "Her ways are pleasant ways, and all her paths, peaceful. She is a tree of life to those who grasp her, and whoever holds on to her is happy" (Prov. 3:17–18). So closely do these words parallel the Way of Torah that they have become part of the Torah service in synagogue, sung to extol the Torah as the embodiment of wisdom and guidance. As one who frequently cringes upon encountering what Jamal would call "difficult" or "awkward" verses in the Torah itself—scenes of gratuitous mayhem and destruction—I can't quite bring myself to say all her ways are pleasant and peaceful, but in the broader sense of the "Way of Torah," the way of compassion and mindfulness, I do delight in the deep wisdom that we are invited to pursue. I also delight in pointing out that *Khokhmah*, the Hebrew word for wisdom, is feminine—as is *Torah*, the Hebrew word for teaching. This brings us back to my opening words about the womb of compassion and understanding: both Khokhmah and Torah are life-giving and our souls become most fully alive when we bathe them in the amniotic fluid of spiritual teachings and an ever-deepening awareness of the enfolding presence of God.

And how do we achieve that womblike experience? In the only way possible: by doing the hard inner work that has become a mantra in this book. Continuing a theme mentioned in the previous chapter, "as below, so above," we develop wisdom from the ground up:

> The beginning of wisdom is—acquire wisdom;
> With all your acquisitions, acquire discernment.
> Hug her to you and she will exalt you;
> She will bring you honor if you embrace her. (Prov. 4:7)

In other words, the Eternal is more likely to increase our wisdom if we "seed" the project with our own sincere efforts. In a delightful midrash from the medieval period, a merchant whose customer wants him to fill up the hold of his cargo ship first goes to the pier and sniffs around. If his nose tells him that the hold has been used for wine, he fills it with wine again; if it has been used for honey or oil or fish brine, that's what he puts in. Likewise the Holy One, upon sensing the fragrance of wisdom, fills us with more.

In addition to knowledge and wisdom, one of the most important provisions for our spiritual journey is mindfulness, a topic on which Jamal touched briefly at the end of his section. Numerous books have been written on the subject and it is not possible to give it the play it deserves in these few pages, but I would go so far as to say that mindfulness is the *raison d'etre* of Jewish living. All our studies, practices, prayers, blessings, and dietary laws have but one focus: to make us mindful of God both transcendent and immanent. Does God need our constant prayers and blessings? Of course not. *We* are the ones who need them, for those moments of spiritual mindfulness lead to what Michael Fishbane, in *Sacred Attunement*, calls "moral mindfulness": they remind us who we are, where we are, and what we are doing so that we may do it compassionately and responsibly in the name of our Creator. Does God care whether we eat pork or mix dairy with meat? I will go out on a limb and say certainly not. The God who worries about that kind of thing is an anthropomorphic deity of our own devising. The real God has bigger fish to fry, such as looking out for people who have nothing at all to eat. What the dietary laws of Judaism and Islam do is make us mindful of what we choose to put in our mouths. In the twenty-first century this is a major issue as we grapple with tainted foods and the horrific prospect of worldwide food shortages caused in part by the mindless choices we make every day. "Kosher" takes on a whole new meaning when we realize that it's not some god in the sky telling us what to eat—it's the divinity of our own essence telling us to be aware, to count the social cost, to make moral choices in what we consume on this mortal planet. Indeed, this kind of mindfulness has led to an "eco-kosher" movement that focuses not on the traditional dietary laws but on the consumption of food that is organic, grown with respect for both laborers and ecology, and marketed by fair trade. This is a prime example of the practical way in which the ancient words of Torah can be interpreted and implemented in the twenty-first century.

The Hebrew Bible, like the Quran, frequently reminds us to cultivate spiritual awareness and to surrender our hearts to divine guidance so that we may live righteously and responsibly. "Trust in the Eternal with all your heart, and do not rely on your own understanding" (Prov. 3:5). What these words really mean, I believe, is to trust the divine wisdom that whispers to your heart. Human understanding can be tainted by the frantic machinations of the ego to defend its own interests, but the more we surrender ourselves to the Divine at our core, the more we live in a state of sacred wisdom and mindfulness.

Christian Reflections

I thank you, Father, Lord of heaven and earth, because you have hidden these things from the wise and intelligent and have revealed them to infants; yes, Father, for such was your gracious will. (Matt. 11:25–26)

This strange prayer shows the tension Jamal and Kate have mentioned between different kinds and levels of spiritual knowledge. Some Christians have used passages like this one to "prove" that there is little room in faith for "worldly" knowledge, an attitude that has haunted Christianity and bred an anti-intellectual strain in the faith. (Christian suspicion of education led some of my highly educated relatives to be downright antagonistic when they heard that I was going into the ministry. My father, a civil rights attorney, said, "If you want to help someone, be a lawyer!")

Jesus' prayer, however, is more about breadth of access to knowledge of God and the necessity of a certain childlike mentality in order to receive such knowledge than it is about a ban on smart or learned people in the church. The knowledge Jesus is speaking of comes to us within the context of our eager response to the command to love God with our entire being, of which our mind and consciousness are important parts. Jesus' reference to infants reminds us that receiving God-consciousness often requires "unlearning," as well as learning. It happens when we are able to maintain an openness to miracles and new expressions of God's sometimes alarming creativity. An essential experiential learning environment for my formation has been the liturgy of the church. Even though I "know" what to expect there, I often come away from the ritual refreshed and renewed by some surprising flash of grace shining through the familiar, age-old rhythms of worship. I also recognize in my fellow worshippers the eternal company of saints and angels and am grateful to bask in their collective wisdom, faith, and praise.

In his book *Nothing Personal* with Richard Avedon, the writer James Baldwin once remarked that an American may never give the vast country of

China a second thought until he or she falls in love with someone from China. In a similar way, a profound spiritual encounter often awakens a dormant desire for knowledge about the Beloved. I felt such a hunger when I returned to the Episcopal Church as an adult. After "tasting and seeing," to paraphrase Psalm 34:8 ("O taste and see how gracious the Lord is!"), I discovered I was famished for any kind of contact with the sacred. As a result, I sought out texts and teachers and fellow seekers.

Something that always renews my enthusiasm and curiosity is watching and working with young children as they come across new people, places, and things in the world. My three-year-old godson is a constant reminder of the marvels of creation, and he is blessed to have parents who always seem to have the spaciousness to let him stop and examine these amazing phenomena. His quest for knowledge is never purely academic; he wants to interact and experience. The adults around him are privileged to see the answer to one of the prayers that is a traditional part of the baptismal rite: "Give them an inquiring and discerning heart, the courage to will and to persevere, a spirit to know and to love you, and the gift of joy and wonder in all your works" (Book of Common Prayer, p. 308).

Another metaphor related to the revelation of knowledge to babes is that of being born again, or born "from above," as the Greek in John 3:3 can also be translated: "Very truly, I tell you, no one can see the kingdom of God without being born from above." Nicodemus, Jesus' conversation partner here, responds with astonishment and a bit of sarcasm: "How does this work, exactly? We climb back into our mother's womb?" Being born for the first time is not necessarily a smooth and easy process, for mother or baby. Being born again is, perhaps, even more jarring. I call to mind scriptural stories in which an epiphany of God results in being struck blind like Paul (Acts 9:4–5) or mute like Zechariah (Luke 1:18–22). Spiritual growth sometimes requires deconstruction first: "I experience every breakthrough as a breakdown," a wise person once said.

It occurs to me that this chapter on awareness is perfectly placed after the one on compassion. We must be grounded in compassion to pursue knowledge, given that our pursuit eventually will bring us face to face with seeming failures in ourselves and others or with a need to unlearn some firmly entrenched conviction or comfortable behavior. Recovery from addiction of any kind, for example, necessitates this disruptive awareness; but without compassion, such awareness is worse than useless because we tend to wield it as a weapon. Paul's teachings on love referred to in the previous chapter were inspired by a congregation rich in spiritual gifts of knowledge and discernment, but short on compassion for their brothers and sisters who, in their opinion, were spiritual laggards. He writes, "Knowledge puffs up, but love builds up. Anyone who claims to know something does not yet have the necessary knowledge; but anyone who loves God is known by him" (I Cor. 8:1–3). Paradoxically, although we need to be willing to have a childlike humility to receive sacred teaching, such openness puts us on the pathway to true maturity and wisdom. Again I turn to Paul: "When I was a child, I spoke like a child, I thought like a child, I reasoned like a child; when I became an adult, I put an end to childish ways. For now we see in a mirror, dimly, but then we will see face to face. Now I know only in part; then I will know fully, even as I have been fully known" (I Cor. 13:11–12).

11

Prayer and Related Spiritual Practices

Bow in adoration and draw closer.
(Quran 96:19)

Quranic guidance on the subject of prayer is simple and direct: "Celebrate the praises of God, and do this often; and glorify God morning and evening," says the Holy Book (33:42). Not only morning and evening, as it happens, but also at midday, late afternoon, and sunset —five times a day—it is customary for Muslims to cease what they are doing and engage body and soul in the primary spiritual practice of Islam, the ritual prayer known in Arabic as *salat*. In Muslim lands a call to prayer is broadcast from minarets to the entire community, reminding the faithful to put aside their worldly distractions and know that "in the remembrance of God do hearts find rest" (13:28). From far and wide the faithful assemble at the local mosque to perform a ritual ablution, symbolizing the yearning of the human soul to be cleansed and purified before standing intentionally in the presence of God, and then together they bow to the Compassionate One in the direction of the Kaaba in Mecca. As the Earth revolves through one time zone after another, an unceasing wave of Muslims bowing to God turns the planet into a magnificent prayer rug.

The ritual body prayer is derived, many scholars opine, from the Prophet's mystical Night Journey (described in chapter 6). As the Prophet ascended the seven levels of heaven, he was dazzled by the sight of myriad angels bowing and prostrating to God, while from their lips poured words of praise and thanksgiving. The Prophet saw this as a sign that prayer must consist essentially of praising God and expressing gratitude and that we, like the angels, must use the gift of our bodies to express our adoration. Thus Islamic prayer consists of standing, bowing, prostrating, and sitting on one's knees in sweet surrender to God, while the lips are heartfully reciting verses of the Quran that express praise and thanksgiving. At the end of the ritual prayer, devotees turn their heads to right and left, offering greetings of peace to the host of angels who always gather in sacred spaces. Then, cupping the palms of their hands and pointing heavenward, they ask God to bless their families, friends, and themselves. Mystics have pointed out that by prostrating to the ground in submission and supplicating heavenward, we are probing spaces where the veils between humanity and God are especially thin and the forces of darkness are not lurking to intercept our prayers. Though Satan said that he would waylay humanity from front, back, right, and left (Quran 7:16–17), he made no mention of spaces downward and upward!

Pray early and pray often, says the Quran, for "Regular Prayers . . . are enjoined on Believers at stated times" (4:103). The "stated times" in fact are not stated in the Holy Book, but since the earliest days of Islam the "Regular Prayers" have been said five times a day. Legend has it that this is the number agreed upon by God and Muhammad on the night of his mystical journey into heaven. As the Prophet was descending the seven levels after his audience with God, the story goes, he told Moses that God wanted the community to pray fifty times a day. "They'll never pray that much!" Moses exclaimed, and he urged Muhammad to return to God and ask for a lesser number. Back went the Prophet to discuss the matter with God. "Twenty times a day" was the result. "Still too much," said Moses, and he kept sending Muhammad back to bargain with God. Finally, when the number was down to five, the Prophet told Moses he was too shy to bargain any further, and ever since the number has been affixed at five times a day.

The holy day of the week in Islam is Friday, which in Arabic is called *Jumaah*, meaning "gathering." On that day Muslims make a concerted effort to gather in mosques and elsewhere for the midday prayer and fellowship. It is said that particularly during Jumaah prayers, places of worship are thronged with angels blessing the worshippers. According to a hadith qudsi, God said to Muhammad, "I remember every devotee who remembers Me, but I remember even better when devotees remember Me in a group."

In our interfaith community, many non-Muslims who are faithful followers of their own religion incorporate the body prayer into their daily spiritual practices. They report that the body posture of prostrating to God increases intimacy between praiser and Praised, whether they call the object of their worship Adonai, Jesus, or any other sacred name. On a heart-level they connect to the words of the Quran addressed to humanity, "Bow in adoration and draw closer." It is this nearness and intimacy that made the Prophet say, "The freshness of my eyes is given to me in prayer." Mystics rhapsodize that the inward savor of a single prostration is sweeter than a hundred empires and a humble but passionate cry arises from within: "I want no kingdom except the kingdom of that prostration."

Mindfulness and intentionality

"Remember Me and I shall remember you," Allah tells us in the Quran (2:152), meaning among other things that we should perform our prostrations with a sacred sense of presence. The Prophet told his followers to worship "as if you can see God, and if you cannot see God, know that God sees you." And, he warned, "God does not regard a prayer in which the heart does not accompany the body." So focused was the Prophet during prayer that his intimates often heard throbbing sobs, like the sounds of a boiling pot, coming from his breast. Such singular focus is beautifully illustrated by the story of the seventeenth-century emperor Akbar of India, who was once praying in the forest. As he was prostrating, a young woman appeared from nowhere and carelessly stepped in front of him. The emperor was furious: "How dare you cross my prayer path!" he demanded to know as his guards seized the girl. Trembling with fear and with eyes lowered, she replied that she had not seen the emperor and confessed that she had been lost in thoughts of her beloved. Then, turning to the emperor, she asked him how was it possible for him to see her if he was lost in remembrance of his Beloved. Shamed, the emperor ordered her to be released and gave her a handsome reward for teaching him about mindfulness in prayer.

Spiritual teachers advise that when we are supplicating for divine favors and blessings, we need to come from a place of increased necessity, from the depths of our soul. Without increased need, says Rumi, God doesn't give anything to anyone. Have you not noticed, he continues, that only when the baby is born does God graciously fill the mother's breasts with milk? In one of his prayerful utterances, Rumi exclaims, "I shall cry to Thee and cry to Thee until the milk of Thy Loving Kindness boils over."

Praise and gratitude

The angelic praise and gratitude that Muhammad witnessed on his mystical Night Journey is the model for our human prayers. The Prophet told his followers that the angel Gabriel taught him three prayers of praise: *Subhan Allah* ("Glory be to Allah"), *Al-hamdu lillah* ("Praise be to Allah"), and *Allah hu Akbar* ("Allah is Incomparably Great"). It was part of his spiritual practice to recite each of these praises ten times after prayers and thirty-three times before falling asleep.

Though God truly welcomes every type of communication with humanity, prayers of praise and gratitude are at the top of the recommended list—not because God needs our praise, but because *we* do. To God already belong the ninety-nine (and counting) beautiful attributes; when we prostrate ourselves before the Beloved, we too partake of those divine attributes. Thus God does not become holy from our prayer, *we* do. In Islamic spirituality it is said that when we praise God we are creating feathers and wings for the bird of Spirit within us. This insight originates from a Quranic story in which Jesus infused some birds of clay with his breath and the birds magically stirred into life "by God's leave" (3:49). Muslim mystics say that the life-giving element in this story was the praise of God with which Jesus always perfumed his breath. Therefore, they say, we should heed what the Quran says: "To God belong the most Beautiful Names" (59:24).

An integral part of praising God is the expression of gratitude, a practice that just happens to be a primary technique to attain happiness and fulfillment in life. "Whatever is in the heavens and on earth extols the limitless glory of God," says the Quran (62:1), and by joining the cosmic chorus we move our personalities into alignment with all of Creation. The Holy Book urges us to grow in this essential practice. "Which of your Sustainer's blessings will you deny?" it asks repeatedly, and it reminds us that if we were to count God's blessings, we could never compute them. "So remember with gratitude the blessings that God has bestowed upon you" (3:103).

> Don't you see that God has made in service to you
> all that is in the Heavens and on earth
> and has made His Bounties flow to you
> in abundant measure, seen and unseen? (31:20)

Gratitude is a magical touchstone that enables us to truly enjoy our times of blessings and transforms our times of affliction into grace. "Any who is grateful does so to the profit of his own soul," says the Holy Book (31:12), and God promises that if we are grateful, "I will add more (favors) unto you" (14:7). The psychological power of gratitude has been demonstrated by the astonishing results of several international studies of mental and emotional wellbeing in my native country, Bangladesh. In this impoverished and densely populated nation, which is often devastated by natural disasters, people overall are remarkably happy and content. While scholars grapple to define the exact reasons, village elders know that it is because the vast majority of rural villagers have mastered the art of gratitude. In times of plenty, their heart-felt gratitude allows them to experience the fullness of joy. In times of affliction they continue to give thanks for unknown blessings already on their way because a habit of gratitude enables them to trust their Sustainer,

> Who has made the earth your couch,
> And the heavens your canopy;
> And sent down rain from the heavens;
> And brought forth therewith
> Fruits for your sustenance. (2:22)

In this attitude of trust the Bangladeshi villagers are emulating the Prophet himself. Muhammad's wife Ayesha reported that when he was pleased with something, he would say, "Praise be to God, whose Grace brings all goodness to perfection." If he was displeased, he would say, "Praise be to God under all conditions."

Dhikr

Dhikr is the Arabic word for remembrance, a practice that the Quran urges us to continue outside of ritual prayers. "When you finish your prayers," says the Quran, "remember Allah while standing, sitting or lying on your sides" (4:103). Muhammad once advised a simple Bedouin who came seeking a singular spiritual practice, "Keep your tongue forever moistened with the name of God." To illustrate the beauty and power of this practice, the Prophet used the example of rust: for every kind of rust there is a polish, and the polish for rust of the heart is the constant invocation of "Allah." Other words are equally effective: one of the ninety-nine divine attributes of Allah (appended at the end of this book) or a sacred verse such as *La ilaha ilallah* ("There is no God but God"). The idea is to choose a sacred mantra and repeat it silently as often as possible in the course of the day. The continuous repetition of the sacred word or phrase creates vibrations that can go deep into your being and create abiding transformations. Sufi teachers liken the practice to dipping fabric into a vat of dye. Upon first immersion the cloth becomes imbued with a beautiful color, but over time the color begins to fade. If you keep dyeing the cloth again and again, however, there comes a point at which the color is permanent. Thus, in the words of the Holy Book, "We take on God's dye and who has a better dye than God's?" (2:138).

The practice of dhikr can be done silently "and in the secrecy of your heart" (7:55) or in rousing chants with fellow worshippers. Devotees often gather in a circle to recite, chant, or sing sacred verses in sessions that can go on for hours at a time. Many practitioners experience an expansive opening of the heart during these sessions and report that they have tasted what Rumi calls "a sweetness that existed before honey and bee." Rumi often felt an indescribable Presence in the midst of his circle just before dawn, and exclaimed that "the human body and the universe grew from this, not this from the universe and the human body." In a wonderfully human story, Rumi tells about a dhikr session in which a conservative practitioner, who was uncomfortable with music as a spiritual expression, was getting increasingly annoyed by the nonstop songs of praise. Finally he burst out, "What is all this singing and singing!" and Rumi replied, "It's the sound of the creaking of the doors of Paradise." Not to be mollified, the unhappy man exclaimed, "Well I hate the sound of creaking." To which Rumi retorted, "That's because when *you* hear the sound of creaking, the doors of Paradise are closing!"

The prayerful practice of silence

Even as a young child, Muhammad practiced prolonged periods of silence, and as a young man he often ventured into the caves of Mecca to spend days and nights in deep contemplation. One fateful evening while he was on a personal retreat (*chilla*) of forty days and nights of silence in a Meccan cave, the angel Gabriel appeared to Muhammad and commanded him to recite. What emerged from Muhammad's lips were the first revelations of what came to be known as the Quran. It is highly significant for Muslims that both the Quran and the Prophethood of Muhammad were birthed in the womb of silence. The Quranic description of that Night of Power can also be taken as a description of the unspeakable majesty, beauty, and power of silence itself:

> The Night of Power
> is better than
> a thousand months.
> Therein come down
> The angels and the Spirit
> by God's permission,
> on every errand:
> Peace! . . . This
> until the rise of Morn! (97:3–5)

True silence, which is the absence not of sound but of the little self, is filled with divine vibrations and an exquisite sense of peace. All the earthly noise, turmoil, and disturbances of daily life are, in Sufi parlance, outside the veil; inside the veil is the Night of Power, infused with divine properties. From time to time we need to go inside the veil so we can become refreshed, renewed, and restored in spirit. Inside the veil, the balm of silence begins to heal, nourish, and revitalize our beings. We feel more connected to our Source. Disconnected from that Source, we are like fish out of water, thrashing and quivering on the banks. We suffocate when we get overly mired and entangled in this world. Desperately we need to step out of this frenetic and frantic back-and-forth movement that fragments the soul. Our souls need to breathe by diving often into those life-giving waters. We need to practice some kind of silence every day. "Close down speech's door," Rumi says, because in silence we awaken to deep insights and truths. In that state and space, he says, the secrets of the universe are revealed to us.

The wise ones tell us that all the theologies of the world are as nothing compared with one whisper of the Beloved. Thus it behooves us to make the practice of silence a regular part of life. Be practical: choose a realistic time period when you can be silent, be it for five minutes or half an hour, and build your schedule around that. Don't fall into the trap of thinking you will meditate whenever your schedule allows; it will never happen! In addition to your daily silence, try to choose one day a month when you can be fully silent. Turn off the phone, television, radio, and computer; ignore newspapers and other trappings of the secular world; control the natural tendency to dwell on various thought forms—mentally composing to-do lists, writing letters, solving personal problems, and the like; and just let your soul abide in pure, peaceful silence.

Once the practice of silence has become a habit, it becomes easier to engage in personal or communal retreats for prolonged periods of time. Advanced Sufi aspirants undertake a ten- to forty-day personal retreat or chilla of silence under the supervision and guidance of a teacher. The practitioner spends the days in silent prayer, meditation, and contemplation. A sparse meal is provided daily and the teacher checks in from time to time to provide insights about issues that come up, interpret dreams, and offer guidance. For many, this chilla is a life-transforming experience. In the words of the Prophet, "Fountains of knowledge in the heart will gush out of the tongue of that person who dedicates himself wholly to God for forty days."

Fasting as a form of prayer

Every year during Ramadan, the ninth month of the lunar calendar and the month during which the Night of Power occurred, Muslims abstain from food, drink, and sex from dawn to dusk in fulfillment of the Quranic instruction "so that you might remain conscious of God" (2:183). So important is this practice that it is one of the five pillars of Islam. If a Muslim is unable to fast for reasons of health or difficult circumstances, he or she is obligated, whenever possible, to feed a needy person as a form of "ransom." The fast is not only physical, and our attention is not to be focused on what we are giving up. Rather, the purpose of the fast is to remind us to dedicate ourselves to the taming of the petty impulses and negative patterns of the ego so that we may evolve in compassion, awareness, and righteous deeds. Thus, by disciplining our bodies we nourish our souls. In the imagery of our friend Rumi, the body is like a flute. If the soundbox is stuffed, there can be no music of "Allah! Allah!"

Call upon Me; I will answer you

At some point in all our spiritual practices, most of us wonder whether God is paying any attention. God offers a clear and unambiguous answer in the Quran: "I listen to the prayer of every supplicant when he calls on Me; let them also, with a will, listen to My call, and believe in Me" (2:186). Elsewhere God says, "Call upon me; I will answer you" (40:60). Sometimes that "answer" is silence, which we are inclined to interpret as divine indifference. But the wise advise us not to grieve for what doesn't come. Sometimes we pray and fast for things that are not truly in our best interest, says the Quran, "for people are inclined to be hasty" (17:11). So instead of indifference we might interpret God's silence as a compassionate reminder that we don't see the whole picture. At such times we need to heed our Sustainer's words—"Let them . . . believe in Me"—and simply take refuge in that comforting verse, "Of knowledge We have given you but a little" (17:85).

In a beautiful story that illustrates the subtlety of God's response to prayer, Rumi tells about a pious man who spent years in diligent prayer, meditation, and fasting, always crying out from the core of his heart, "Allah! Allah!" One day a cynic approached him and asked, "Well! Have you ever gotten a response from Allah?" The question pierced his heart and he was speechless. Feeling defeated and forlorn, he gave up praying. One evening he had a vision in which Khidr, the esoteric being described in chapter 6, came to him and asked why he had stopped praising Allah. "Because I never got back any reply," he said. Then Khidr gave him a message from God: "The deep longing you express is the return message. The grief you cry out from is what draws you towards union. Your pure sadness that wants help is the secret cup." Continuing, Khidr asked the man, "Have you ever listened to the moan of a dog for its master?" And then he delivered an insight: "That whining is the connection. There are love dogs no one knows the names of. Give your life to be one of them."

Personal spiritual practices

One of my most persistent spiritual practices these days is my interfaith study and ministry. The more I come to understand and appreciate the truth and beauty of other faiths, the better I understand and appreciate my own tradition—not by contrast, but by completion of the picture. According to the renowned religion professor Huston Smith, when we view an object from one angle we gain just one perspective, but when we view it from different angles we see it with greater depth and clarity. Christ's teachings on non-violence illuminate for me Quranic verses about turning our enemies into bosom friends. The Jewish insight about wrestling with God reinforces my understanding about the ego barriers that stand between me and God.

My interfaith ministry is sustained and enhanced by several practices that I would like to be able to say I do every day. This does not seem to be humanly possible, but I do the best I can, with compassion for myself when I fall short, which is what I recommend for anyone who has a sincere desire to walk the path of surrender. I find my motivation in two Quranic verses: "Be conscious of God" and "Truly in the remembrance of God do hearts find rest."

The first practice is the Islamic body prayer, which involves prostrations to God. Each time I prostrate, my parents' words invariably come to mind:

"One prostration of prayer to God frees you from a thousand prostrations to your ego." I also draw inspiration from God's words to Moses in a poem by Rumi: "I look inside the humility; that broken open lowliness is the Reality, not the language! Forget phraseology. I want burning! burning!"

The second practice is a daily period of silence. Following the Prophet Muhammad's example of practicing silence regularly and often, I try to meditate for short periods at least twice a day. I recall often the utterance of Rumi, who advises us to be silent and allow our Sustainer who gave us language to speak, "for as He fashioned a door and a lock, He also made a key." My favorite meditation technique is to focus quietly on my heart and, from time to time, repeat a Quranic verse or, more often, the words directed to the Divine in my heart, "I love you." Quite frequently I combine this technique with Christian centering prayer. I repeat the sacred words until I usher into a spacious emptiness, open to receiving the grace of Spirit. When thoughts and images intrude, I start repeating the words until I re-enter this magical space.

My third practice is to keep my tongue "forever moistened with the name of Allah," as the Prophet instructed the Bedouin. The wise have counseled us that we, like the angels, should make the glorification of God our sustenance. My favorite tongue-moistening words are *"Allah," "La ilaha il Allah,"* and *"Estakhfurillah,"* a word that means, "O my Sustainer, I beg repentance." It touches me to know that the Prophet uttered "Estakhfurillah" so often that he was called "the Prince of Repentance." I also moisten my tongue with repeated words of gratitude to God. My favorite expression is the one my parents taught me when I was a child, "O God, favor upon favor have you bestowed upon this handful of dust. Thank you."

My fourth practice is to prioritize my daily tasks using a technique called "Closest to the Light." This technique is based on the following hadith: "Make all your concerns one single concern and God will look after all your other concerns." Simply ask yourself which of the things on your to-do list are closest to the Light and attend to them. Use whatever time and energy are left for the other items on the list, and you will find that the Light takes care of them. As an example, let's say that that you need to raise money for your business, prepare for a lawsuit, attend a religious ceremony, and care for your ailing mother. Ask yourself which activity holds the greatest sacredness and meaning for you. Maybe you decide that taking care of your mother is closest to the Light. Willingly and lovingly focus your activities on tending to her, and as for the others—the fundraising, the lawsuit, and the religious ceremony—give to them whatever is left of your energy and time without avoidance or aversion. The Light will honor you for honoring it and will take care of your other concerns. Islamic sages say that there is a great secret in this for anyone who can grasp it.

Lastly, the wisdom of the Native American tradition has made me more aware of the many images of nature that adorn the Quran and enhanced my appreciation of the Quranic verse, "On the earth are signs of inner certainty" (45:3). I find myself spending more time in nature as a spiritual practice and learning from its signs. Islamic mystics have become my guides as I meditate on trees and sunsets. They say the world is like a tree and we are its half-ripe fruit. Unripe fruit clings tightly to the branch because, immature, it is not ready for the Palace. During sunset and sunrise, the Sun of the world stammers in rapture, "My God!" I truly appreciate the insight from primordial traditions that when people lose their sense of awe and wonder, that's when they turn to institutional religion. Though all the Abrahamic faiths in fact have become codified and institutionalized over the centuries, neither Islam nor any other religion can ever be a substitute for the innate desire to bow in adoration and draw closer to the Sustainer and Cherisher of all humankind.

Jewish Reflections

Let your prayer be a window to heaven. (Baal Shem Tov)

Hebrew scriptures and legends are so rich with exhortations to pray, and the Book of Psalms is so full of magnificent examples, that it seems impossible to encapsulate the themes in a few short pages. So I will preface these reflections with a prayer that is familiar to Jews and Christians alike: "May the words of my mouth and the meditations of my heart be always pleasing to You, Holy One, my Source and my Redeemer" (Ps. 19:15). This heartfelt request is the first step in Jewish prayer: a declaration of *kavanah* (intention) and acknowledgment that it takes two to tango. At a deep level the prayer originates in the recognition that, as Khidr reminded the pious man in Rumi's story, our longing to pray is God's part of the conversation. And so we say, as we stand before the Eternal, "Holy One, open my lips that my mouth may declare Your Glory."

In many respects the Jewish approach to prayer parallels that of Islam—or vice versa, depending on your point of view. We too have prescribed times for daily prayer, but just three times per day (morning, afternoon, and evening) instead of five. Evidently Moses was bolder than Muhammad in his negotiations with God, though I have not discovered any midrashim on the subject! The types of prayer also parallel those in Islam: communal, private but formulaic, and free-form personal prayer.

Jews do not perform ritual ablutions before communal prayer, but most men (and women in progressive congregations) will don a prayer shawl and head covering (called *tallit* and *kippah*, respectively). The custom of the kippah originated in ancient times when men were required to cover their heads in the presence of royalty. Since the Eternal is the Supreme Royalty, *Melech ha-Olam* (Ruler of the Universe), we cover our heads during prayer to remind ourselves that we are in the ultimate Royal Presence. The tallit is required for men during Torah service, but progressive men and women also use it as a personal tent or shelter encompassing self and the Eternal One during moments of sacred intimacy. (As an aside, one of our most beautiful customs is that the prayer shawl also serves as a shroud at the end of a faithful Jewish life.) Having donned our prayer apparel, we engage in ritual prayer that strongly resembles Islamic prayer, even including a rudimentary type of body prayer: we stand for the formal prayers, and at every blessing we bend our knees and bow our heads. Only at the High Holy Days does the knee bend become a full prostration, and there are variations even on that: some prostrate on knees with forehead to ground à lá Islam, and others prostrate flat out—a serious challenge to execute in a crowded synagogue! For the more senior among us, this is a dramatic body prayer in the most fundamental sense: the increasing difficulty with which we lower and raise our creaking bodies from year to year is a stark reminder of the swift passage of time and the urgent need to put aside our temporal concerns and focus on the Eternal.

The content of Jewish communal prayer, like that of Islam, consists primarily of blessings and scriptural recitations, particularly from the Book of Psalms. What one might call the centerpiece of our ritual prayer, both in community and in the private-but-formulaic mode, is *ha-Tefillah* ("the Prayer"), more commonly called the *Amidah* ("standing") because we stand while we say it. The Amidah is a series of prayers beginning with paeans to the God of our forefathers (and foremothers, in progressive circles), continuing with supplications for knowledge, forgiveness, healing, and all the other gifts we humans think will enrich our lives, and concluding with praise and thanksgiving. To me, the most meaningful thing about the Amidah is the way it is said: standing as one, we pray as individuals within the group, each at our own pace in a barely audible voice, and then one by one we sit down when we are done. Some race through the prayers, some sing them quietly, some pray in English and some struggle through the Hebrew—but all of us are united in that unbelievably sacred moment as the murmur of voices floats heavenward. Everything else stops until the last person sits down, signaling that the mystical minutes of the Amidah are finished—until the next time.

Ideally we would all be able to pray communally every day, but the reality of life in a multicultural, secular society precludes that life-giving practice for most of us except on Shabbat, the Jewish day of worship and rest. Even so, nothing truly prevents us from engaging in the next-best thing: what I call private-but-formulaic prayer. In the privacy of our own homes, many Jews say some version of ritual prayers every day. As I mentioned in chapter 7, it is customary to rise with the *Modah ani* ("How grateful I am") on our lips, often in song. So quickly ingrained is this beautiful custom that after only a few months of living as a Jew I found myself waking every morning with the melody singing itself in my head. A friend reports that her cat sleeps through her nocturnal trips to the loo, but the moment she begins to sing Modah ani in the morning, the cat hops off her bed and is ready to be fed! My own ritual prayer continues, after a latte and a shower, with the *Barkhu* (a call to blessing) and the Sh'ma, a few chants of my own devising, and then my favorite portions of the Amidah. Again, this has become such a part of my morning routine that I am already humming the Barkhu unconsciously as I step out of the shower. No credit to me—it is simply an illustration of the power and beauty of this kind of habit.

Equally powerful are the blessings that we say throughout the day. The farther I go along the Jewish path, the more convinced I become that the essence of living Jewishly is to live in a state of blessing. As noted in chapter 8, we Jews have blessings for just about everything life has to offer: the things we consume, the sights and sounds we savor, the people we cherish (and the ones we do not)—the possibilities are endless. These brief blessings are a kind of drumbeat in our daily lives, helping us to stay centered and sanctifying the mundane. They all begin with the same formula: "Blessed are You, Eternal One, our God and Sustainer of all that is," and if we are really up on our Hebrew, we can probably finish the prayer by rote, but that is not the point. The formula gets us started, and then our hearts take over, with whatever words of gratitude or petition rise authentically from the depths of our being. That is the beauty of "private-but-formulaic" prayer.

There is one last formulaic prayer that many Jews say as they are turning out the light at the end of the day: *"Ribono shel olam,"* an astonishing prayer of forgiveness and apology composed by Reb Nachman of Bratslav (1772–1810). Addressed to the "Majestic Presence of the Universe," the prayer offers forgiveness to all who have wronged us in any way and begs for release from our own hurtful patterns and behaviors. Such a prayer, spoken mindfully every day, has the power to heal the world.

And then there is plain old private prayer, personal conversation with the Holy One in the quiet of your own heart. This kind of prayer is beyond sectarian style or description. It can be informed by theological or spiritual mindsets, but it is a strictly heart-to-Heart affair. The only thing I would say is, be yourself and find your own voice. Sing to God, or share a funny story, or throw yourself in God's arms and have a good cry. Praise, gratitude, entreaty, complaint—all are fair game. There are no rules. Rabbis have debated for centuries about the correct times and styles of prayer—the books of legends are full of their exhortations to pray in certain ways and with certain levels of concentration. Some say it is sacrilegious to pray with anything but one hundred percent attention to God, but I respectfully disagree. A magnet on my refrigerator reminds me, in the words of the Sufi poet Hafiz, that vegetables prefer to be cut "by someone who is singing

God's name." So sing God's name while you are cooking, mowing the lawn, or driving to your next appointment—but spare some attention to the task at hand for safety's sake! Going about your daily tasks with God's name on your lips is pure prayer just as surely as singing psalms and hymns in church or synagogue, and it will transform whatever you are doing into a blessing on the world.

As for the question of whether prayer has any practical effect, I have a little story. A few years ago several of us went to Israel with our rabbi to do the usual sightseeing and then spend a week in retreat in the Galilee. One day while on retreat we went to Kfar Nahum (known to Christians as Capernaum, the center of Jesus' ministry) to visit the remains of the synagogue there. As it happens, the site is now under the control of a religious order of Catholic priests and we were cautioned that public prayer is not allowed in the synagogue ruins. In fact we hadn't been planning to hold a "demonstration" there, but it was a shocking and painful thing to be forbidden to pray as a group in our own historic place. We wandered for a while, took photos, tried to make our individual peace with the place and the situation. And then we began to hear the faint sound of a familiar melody. Ears and hearts perked up. It was our rabbi, quietly humming the tune to which we sing Moses' prayer for healing (Num. 12:13): *"El na r'fa na lah*—Please God, let healing be now." One by one we joined our humming voices as we drew closer and closer to each other, and the good fathers never suspected that "their" preserve had been hit with guerrilla prayer-fare! It was a profoundly healing moment and we left that place not in anger but in peace. From there we went to the site where Jesus is said to have delivered his Sermon on the Mount, and in the space of *shalom* (spiritual wellness) created by that wordless prayer in Kfar Nahum our rabbi opened a Bible and read to us the words that Jesus spoke to his followers two thousand years ago: "Happy are the poor in spirit, the gentle, the merciful, the peacemakers, those who hunger and thirst for justice . . ." (Matt. 5:3–10). In that timeless moment, it was all restored to us: the synagogue, where the stones still whisper Talmudic stories and debates; our own Rabbi Jesus, who has been co-opted by a church that has wounded his people so grievously; and Jesus' teachings, which are Jewish to the core. Such is the power of a simple prayer, hummed wordlessly with "increased necessity."

Christian Reflections

Rejoice always, pray without ceasing, give thanks in all circumstances; for this is the will of God in Christ Jesus for you. (1 Thess. 5:16–18)

At the outset of these reflections on prayer and spiritual practice, I must confess that I have been very resistant to writing about these topics. At first I thought it was because prayer seems too deeply personal to share. It's one thing to talk about being in love, another to talk about making love. Except for a few passages in which Jesus is said to address God as *Abba*, "Papa," the gospels provide little information about Jesus' intimate prayer life or spiritual practices. Jesus himself offers no details. Yet I have the sense that his wisdom and grace are continually fed from the wellspring of ongoing communion with the One who sent him.

Then I recognized that my resistance probably was caused by a sense of insufficiency about my spiritual practice. I do not pray ceaselessly, as Paul instructs in the passage above. I feel as if I should, but I don't. For much of my life, I have seen prayer as an obligation that I was shirking, or as a therapeutic procedure I should be following for my health. However, as my friends Jamal and Kate have said—and as I have found as I have moved more deeply into a prayer practice—spiritual practices are not about proficiency or obligation. True, they require effort; they are part of the work we talked about in the last chapter. Prayer is the labor of love that makes concrete our intention to attain the fullness of wisdom and compassion we seek.

Spiritual disciplines also may be prescribed by our traditions and, in that way, become an obligation. However, in my experience, they become their own reward when they give me a whiff of the perfume of heaven and keep me moving "further up and further in," as C. S. Lewis writes in *The Last Battle*, toward the Beloved. When I understand the "personal" prayer about which I am so self-conscious as simply my participation in the continual chorus of praise and supplication flowing from all corners of the universe toward the Creator, I can begin to ease my ego out of the way and be swept up in the flow. Finding my own voice and daring to sing my part in the cosmic orchestration of prayer continues to be an adventure, some of which I will share in the hope that doing so will encourage others in their efforts.

Jamal's wonderful image of planet Earth as a prayer rug for the cease-less wave of Muslims bowing and rising in salat has a Christian parallel—some might say antecedent—in the practice of the Daily or Divine Office. It should be noted that both sets of practices—salat and Divine Office—originate from the pattern of daily prayer in Judaism. (After all, Moses was Muhammad's coach on the subject.) Religious communities such as monasteries and convents preserve the most complete expression of this kind of prayer in Christianity, though some forms of the Office still continue in other Christian venues. In the Episcopal parish of my childhood, the service of Morning Prayer—consisting mainly of sung psalms, readings from scripture, hymns, and a sermon—was the principal mode of worship most Sundays of the year. As a child chorister, I learned the choreography of worship—kneeling, standing, bowing—to the rhythms of that ritual.

As important as the Daily Office has been, the central act of communal worship in many Christian traditions is the Eucharist, the holy meal in which Christians remember (re-member, put back together again) Jesus' last meal with his disciples. This sacred ritual is also known by many other names, including the Mass, the Lord's Supper, the Divine Liturgy, and Holy Communion. Even as a child, I loved going forward to receive the bread and wine of that holy meal. Taking Communion made me "know" in a way that no doctrine could convey the free and gracious offering of God's self to integrate into my deepest being. When I returned to the Episcopal Church as an adult, my parish was one where the Eucharist was the principal service celebrated not only on Sundays, but every day of the week. There I "fell in love" again with God in the liturgy. The word "liturgy" comes from Greek for "the people's work," which concords with Jamal's and Kate's remarks about the need to strive for the transformation of our consciousness. (Liturgy can also mean "public work," indicating that our prayers are offered on behalf of the world.) Not only did I feel again the offer from God to move into my heart, I also was aware of the weekly retelling of the story of divine faithfulness in sending prophet after prophet to recall humans to our true sense of self, culminating in the birth, life, death, and resurrection of Jesus. This dramatic repetition has shaped my soul over the years; it always leaves me renewed and empowered to live for God. Like

Kate, I take the music from worship with me as an inner soundtrack that lingers and resurfaces throughout my days.

Even when I am not physically in church, however, I am being informed by my life in the worshipping community. Like the music, the sacredness of the time and place of worship seems to expand into the rest of my days and perfume the spaces where I live and work. Observing the seasons of the church year keeps me grounded in holy time. Walking into church, I know by the colors of the hangings and the vestments whether we are in the four weeks of Advent, the season of preparation for both the first Christmas and the Day of Judgment to come; the twelve days of Christmas; the forty days of Lent; or the fifty days of Easter. By reading the coming Sunday's scripture passages in advance, I can be prepared to receive the sermon on a deeper level. As a Christian of African descent, I consider the simple act of dressing for church a part of the weekly celebratory activity that has reminded us of who we really are. We have owed it to each other and particularly to our children to radiate the glory of our identity as beautiful and precious children of God. To this day I can recall some of the fabulous Easter outfits of my girlhood. But how do I get from a lovely straw hat and linen dress on an Easter Sunday long ago to a sustaining devotional routine in my current life? What did Jesus do?

Jesus follows his own advice about prayer. In Matthew, just before he teaches his disciples the Lord's Prayer, he says, "Do not be like the hypocrites; for they love to stand and pray in the synagogues and at the street corners, so that they may be seen by others . . . But . . . go into your room and shut the door and pray to your Father who is in secret; and your Father who sees in secret will reward you" (Matt. 6:5–6). Accordingly, we get only glimpses of Jesus in prayer in the first three gospels, while in John the longest prayer we have from Jesus is on behalf of his disciples and those who will come after them (John 17:1–26). The passage that gives me the clearest window into his communication with God is in Hebrews:

> In the days of his flesh, Jesus offered up prayers and supplications, with loud cries and tears, to the one who was able to save him from death, and he was heard because of his reverent submission. Although he was a Son, he learned obedience through what he suffered, and having been made

perfect, he became the source of eternal salvation for all who obey him, having been designated by God a high priest according to the order of Melchizedek. (Heb. 5:7–10)

From this description of Jesus at prayer I learn that I may bring my true feelings to prayer and can even struggle with God. I also must note that, although Jesus "was heard," he still went to his death on a cross—and before death, at least according to Mark and Matthew, he suffered a moment of desolation: "My God, my God, why have you forsaken me?" As he resorted to the lament from his own scriptures, Psalm 22:1, Jesus did not necessarily find immediate peace and reassurance. Each word from Jesus to God was part of an ever-deeper relationship, the heart of which was hidden from all but the parties involved. I also glean from these passages and the Christian Testament as a whole that Jesus' interactions with God revolved around his particular identity in, and calling from, God. So too each of us develops his or her own patterns of interaction and engagement with the Beloved that are of a piece with who we are and who we are becoming. While we can get support and ideas from one another, our most intimate interactions with God will be as distinct as we are from one another. There is truth in the saying that "your life is hidden with Christ in God" (Col. 3:3).

My hidden life of spiritual practice so far has revolved around my calling as a musician, preacher, teacher, and pastor in the church. Some of my earliest intense and tender encounters with God took place in the nursery I shared with my two younger sisters, as my mother sang us to sleep with spirituals. My first and longest-term spiritual director instructed that the one part of my personal rule of life I should never abandon was singing. My voice is a barometer of my soul, registering its most minute conditions. Moreover, my job as a paid soloist in a church choir was the vehicle that brought me back to the Episcopal Church as an adult; four years later I left my parish—one whose traditions included confession (as I wrote about in chapter 8), quiet days, retreats, and spiritual direction—to enter seminary.

As a priest, I have depended upon the worshipping life of the larger community as the basis for much of my personal spiritual discipline. To fulfill my calling to preach and teach, I have had to deal seriously and regularly with scripture; to be an effective pastor and spiritual guide, I have had to be consistent in addressing my own inner dynamics. A speaker at a conference for seminarians once talked about the priest (or minister) as parable, referring to the fact that our lives will be the sermons that people really hear and heed. During my seminary years, my abiding love for texts, contexts, languages, and cultures converged in an excitement about scriptural studies and a calling to be a scholar for the church. Preparing to teach is part of the bedrock of my spiritual discipline. I have jokingly said over the years that God knew that I am a person for whom regular attendance at church and study of scripture are not optional, so God has made certain I have been paid to show up there—my definition of divine economy. As I have let go of my conception of the "perfect" spirituality and instead followed the path of my heart's most profound inclinations and my communities' needs, my devotional life has budded and begun to flower. In turn my spiritual practice nurtures and empowers me to continue to follow the path, and so it goes.

The person in whom I have been most able to see the amazing exchange of energy between disciplined spiritual practice and joyous, committed engagement in life is Archbishop Desmond Mpilo Tutu. God has so graciously arranged it for my benefit and delight that I have been able to encounter the archbishop a number of times during my life so far. On the day of the announcement that he had received the Nobel Peace Prize, Archbishop Tutu was resident at the General Theological Seminary in New York, where I was then a tutor. The seminary was predictably abuzz that day, and at chapel that evening the excitement still lingered in the air. I don't think I was alone in assuming that the archbishop would be at home recuperating from his busy day. However, as we filed out of chapel, I noticed that back in the corner he was quietly kneeling at prayer. The seminary official who had been designated to run interference for him was standing at the end of the aisle, and as I paused to speak to him he asked if I wanted to talk to Archbishop Tutu. I sputtered, incoherent with embarrassment at the thought of intruding. He said, "Oh, I'm sure he would love to talk to you." After a mild protest I left, pausing to sit for a moment on the bench outside. A few minutes later, out burst the archbishop. "I'm so sorry to have kept you waiting," he said as I rose to my feet in amazement, "but I just had to stop to give credit where it was due."

In a way, this story is enough. But I know that Archbishop Tutu, wherever he is in the world, celebrates the Eucharist every day in the company of the people around him. I know that he is quietly, seriously, intently consistent in his own practice of prayer and in his gratitude for others' prayers for him. His own abundant graciousness, irrepressible good humor, and holy and tender outrage at injustice all flow directly from this solid grounding in communion with the God with whom he is so obviously on intimate terms. He shows me not only what it looks like to "rejoice always, pray without ceasing, [and] give thanks in all circumstances," but also what that behavior yields in compassionate, loving action.

PRACTICES

In recent years, praying with beads has become part of my spiritual practice. Beads made from stones, seeds, and other natural materials connect me deeply to the Creator. I am grounded in the here and now through my sense of touch even as I reach for the divine. Guides to making and using prayer beads are readily available; a fine example is *Bead One, Pray Too* by Kimberly Winston.

12

Balance

We have appointed you a moderate nation.
(Quran 2:143)

The spiritual life is like a beautiful Sufi prayer dance. With right hand raised to receive light from heaven and left hand extended to convey the light to earth, the dervish whirls and whirls around the sacred space of the heart. It is unutterably beautiful to watch—and very difficult to do without a good sense of balance. Requiring supple movements and adjustments from moment to moment, the dance of the dervish is a good metaphor for the flexibility and balance needed to negotiate the sometimes-tricky steps of the "straight path" (Quran 1:6). In another metaphor, Sufi sages say that just as a bird flies by the beautiful rhythm of its wings opening and closing, the human heart is in a constant dance of expansion and contraction. What keeps the heart alive, both physically and spiritually, is the balance between the expansions and contractions. Thus whether we want to spread our metaphorical wings and fly to the Beloved or wrap our arms around the Compassionate One in our hearts, a sense of balance is an invaluable provision for the journey of surrender.

The importance of balance is a recurring theme in the Quran. "Verily, all things have We created in proportion and measure," it says in God's revelation (54:49), and it tells us repeatedly to observe the signs and lessons of balance in the natural world. Take the planetary movements as but one example:

> And the Moon,—
> We have measured mansions for her to pass through
> until curved like a withered date stalk she returns . . .
> The sun is not permitted to overtake the moon
> Nor can the night go beyond the day,
> But each moves in its lawful way. (36:39–40)

Lest we miss the point, the Quran spells out the teaching explicitly:

> The sun and moon follow their designated paths
> and the herbs and the trees both bow in adoration
> and He has raised high the heavens
> and He has devised a balance
> so that you might not measure wrongly. (55:5–8)

The exhortation not to measure wrongly applies not only to the practical matters of everyday life—buying and selling honestly in the bazaar, for instance—but also to our personal dealings with God and our fellow beings. In a culture where it was the norm to avenge a wrong with disproportionate and devastating force, the Quran sought to impose a sense of balance. If we cannot fully control our vengeful impulses, says the Quran, then "mandated is the law of equality" (2:194). What that law means is clarified in a later verse: "The recompense for an injury is an injury equal thereto (in degree): but if a person forgives and makes reconciliation, his reward is due from Allah: for Allah loveth not those who do wrong" (42:40). Of the one who is patient and forgives an injury, the Quran says "that would truly be an exercise of courageous will and resolution in the conduct of affairs" (42:43).

Being patient and forgiving does not mean that we allow ourselves to be abused. Our noble aspirations to follow the high road must be tempered with a sense of due measure and proportion, as delightfully illustrated in the following story about a snake that had been terrorizing a village. The frightened villagers enlisted the help of a sage who was known for his ability to communicate with animals, and the sage spoke at length to the snake. Deeply repentant, the snake asked for forgiveness and made a commitment to practice non-violence. After a year or so, the holy man re-visited the village and found the snake in a ragged and pitiable condition. "O Seer, what did you teach me!" complained the snake. "Children practice throwing stones at me, and grown-ups delight in kicking me." "O snake," replied the seer, "I simply asked you to stop biting. When did I ever ask you to stop hissing?"

Commit no excesses

Of particular importance to us who are focused on spiritual guidance, the Quran cautions us, "O People of the Book! Commit no excesses in your religion" (4:171). A major spiritual failing is a tendency to over-do, to not know when to stop. To his companions who fasted all day and prayed all night, the Prophet counseled moderation and warned against excesses. He famously said, "Your body has a right over you, your soul has a right over you, and your family and wife have a right over you. So give everyone the right it has over you."

The Quran also asks those who tend to be zealous when elaborating to others on the beauty of Islam to be gentle and gracious in their speech. "Invite to the way of your Sustainer with wisdom and beautiful urging and discuss with them in the best and most gracious manner" (16:125). As for overly aggressive and self-righteous proselytizers, spiritual teachers rebuke them for ignoring the divine design of diversity as it is stated explicitly in the Quran (e.g., 2:136, 3:63, 5:48, 49:13), telling them that they are like the sincere and self-righteous monkey who made it his life's mission to go to neighborhood ponds and pluck the fish out of water to save them from a watery grave!

Throughout our book the word "God" appears repeatedly, which is appropriate in this context. In daily life, however, the invoking and usage of "God" can be overdone if we become self-righteous about it and we nag, preach, and harangue others about devoting themselves to God. The Sufis have a popular tongue-in-cheek prayer: "O Merciful God, protect me and save me from all these God-lovers!"

In our individual religious practices, it may seem harmless to focus excessively on one virtue or another, but in fact such over-emphasis can create a counterproductive imbalance. Over-emphasis on clarity, for example, can cause us to magnify moments of confusion or bewilderment out of all proportion, leading to inner chaos rather than the clear vision we want to have. Similarly, an excessive ego attachment to "truth" can result in hurtful remarks that serve neither charity nor truth itself. The wisest spiritual practice is moderation in all things—even in moderation!

Thus it behooves us to meditate on the repeated teaching in the Quran that "In true proportions did God create the heavens and earth" (29:44). If it were always summertime, say Sufi teachers, the sun would burn the soil and roots and there would be no flourishing of fruits and vegetables. Rumi remarks that December can be grim, yet kind; summer is all laughter, yet it burns. In the seasons of our lives there are times of withdrawal and times of return, times of quietude and times of activity. Muslims withdraw from the hustle and bustle of the world five times a day to be in communion with God. And every year during Ramadan, one entire month is dedicated to a prayerful withdrawal from physical satisfactions to cleanse and purify the body.

In another illustration of the importance of balance, both laughter and tears are sacred. If we laugh all the time, even in times of pain and suffering, we are missing out on the holiness of the tears that water our inner growth. On the other hand, if we shed tears all the time, it is, in the words of the poet Tagore, like crying all night long for the daylight and missing out on the beauty of the stars.

The need for sacred balance also applies to the care with which we treat the physical body that houses the breath of God. The human body is the "Face of Allah" and the temple of Divine Spirit. To eat and drink things that nourish the body, to practice physical exercises that vitalize and strengthen the body, and to develop a lifestyle that does not overstress the body—these are profoundly sacred practices. As I age, I remember the long-forgotten advice of my teachers that paying attention to the body in times of illness is a sacred practice. Pay attention to what needs nourishment and care in your body. Your cells are working heroically for you. This is a sacred time for awareness, a period of listening and learning, an opportunity for growth, grace, and a mysterious opening in the heart. In one of his utterances Rumi tells us to keep looking at the bandaged place because that is "where the light enters you," and "don't believe for a moment that you are the one who is healing yourself."

First tether your camel

Before entering the mosque to pray, a Bedouin asked Muhammad, "Should I tether my camel or trust in God alone?" The Prophet replied, "First tether your camel, then trust in God."

Mystics say there is an important teaching here. The Spirit and the body need different kinds of attention and carry different loads. We often make the body do what the spirit does best and place burdens on the spirit that the body could carry easily. In Rumi's words, "Too often we put the saddlebags on Jesus and let the donkey loose in the pasture." To illustrate this, let's say that a student aspires to an excellent grade in his exams, but rather than study he spends his time in prayer and fasting. Spirit cannot be expected to do the work that his body and mind need to do.

There is another lesson in the story about tethering the camel. We are not the solitary agents of our lives, and lest we forget that, the Quran advises: "Don't despair over things that pass you by nor exult over blessings that come to you, for God does not love a vainglorious boaster" (57:23). In other words, keep a sense of balance about what you can do to help yourself and what should be left—and credited—to God. This principle is illustrated by a Sufi teaching story about a sultan who was deeply struck by the wisdom of the above-mentioned Quranic verse. As sovereign of a large empire, he was often exceedingly blessed by successes and would become overly exhilarated, overconfident, and arrogant. Almost always this led to devastating failures and in those times he suffered from gloom and depression. Upon reading the Quranic verse about the transitoriness of failure and success, the sultan asked his council of elders to come up with a short sentence that captured the essential meaning so that he could have it inscribed on his ring and reflect on it in times of blessings and of difficulties. The elders came up with four words, "This too shall pass."

Let Allah be angry

As we have seen, balance requires an understanding of measure and proportion along with a sense of moderation. Add to those qualities a willingness to be flexible about what goes on in your life, knowing that the All-Merciful God has your interests at heart. A favorite saying in my family is, "Blessed are the flexible—for they shall never be bent out of shape!" Most important in the quest for balance is compassion for self as you work to become more and more conscious of God's action in your life. Eventually you will come to see that compassion, awareness, and balance are all of a piece in the spiritual life. All three qualities flow naturally in the following story, which found a tender home in my mother's heart.

There was a holy woman who practiced authenticity in her life by praying, fasting, and joyfully serving everyone she met. As her inner light grew, the heavens were so pleased that they created one star, and then another, to shine in the skies in her honor. One day as she was fasting and praying in the holy month of Ramadan, her little niece came and begged her to come for a walk in the forest. Off they went, and soon the little girl felt thirsty but refused to drink unless her aunt also drank with her.

"But I am fasting," said the aunt.

"Then please, break your fast," pleaded the little girl.

"Allah will be displeased with me."

"Let Allah be angry. I just want you to drink with me."

With trepidation, but moved by compassion for the little girl's thirst, the holy woman broke her fast. And lo! A third star appeared in the skies in her honor!

Jewish Reflections

Like a gold ring in the snout of a pig is a beautiful woman [or a handsome man!] bereft of sense. (Prov. 11:22)

Paging through the Book of Proverbs, the Biblical source most likely to provide a pithy quotation on the subject of balance, I came across this amusing simile, which is a perfect illustration of the need to combine the beauty of religious observance with a degree of common sense. It was, in fact, the common-sense practicality of the Jewish path—the ability to sanctify the mundane through mindfulness and blessing—that first drew me to Judaism many years ago. A life focused on the oneness of God and the interconnectedness of all God's creatures, with the ensuing awareness of the divine in every aspect of life, seemed so genuine, so natural, so . . . balanced.

This is not to suggest that Judaism is a perfectly balanced religion or that its adherents are paragons of moderation. One has but to read the pages of the Torah and other Hebrew scriptures to see wild mood swings on the part of deity and humans alike. As the original People of the Book, the early Israelites were also the first Abrahamic extremists, and alas there are Jews today who can be just as extreme as some of their Muslim and Christian counterparts. I'm not talking about political extremism that masquerades as religion. Rather, I'm thinking about the extreme interpretations of scripture and related rules and regulations that teachers in all three traditions have imposed in all good conscience because they forgot to pack a healthy sense of balance in their spiritual kitbags.

To many readers, a typical example of religious extremism is the ancient law of an eye for an eye and a tooth for a tooth (Exod. 21:24). We moderns read that passage and shudder at how vicious people could be in ancient times, but in truth this passage is not about revenge to be extracted; rather, like the similar passage in the Quran (42:40), it is about moderation and self-restraint in response to a wrong. The *worst* you may do if someone knocks out your tooth is to knock out one of his. It is also permissible—and recommended, as Rabbi Jesus taught (Matt. 5:38)—to forgive the wrong and, under the right conditions, even turn your enemy into what the Quran calls your bosom friend. The words you read just a few pages ago bear repeating: "That would truly be an exercise of courageous will and resolution in the conduct of affairs" (Quran 42:43).

So "an eye for an eye" turns out to be a statement of moderation, but Torah contains other perfectly innocuous passages that have been interpreted to lengths that I would call extreme. Take for example the proscription against cooking a kid or a calf in its mother's milk (Exod. 23:19 and 34:26; Deut. 14:21). This is an eminently merciful law meant to show compassion for the animal whose offspring has been killed, and it is clearly an important law since it is stated three times. Its implementation would seem to be simple and straightforward—in an agrarian society you'd know which calf came from which cow and if you wanted beef stroganoff you'd use sour cream made from some other cow's milk. In a more complex society, however, it's not possible to know with one hundred percent certainty which milk came from which cow, so by a practice known as building a fence around the Torah to protect against any possible infraction of the law (Avot 1:1), the early rabbis decreed that Jews may never mix flesh and dairy in the same meal: no cheeseburgers, no butter on your baked potato if you're having steak—not even chicken a la king, even though it is not physically possible for a hen to produce milk in which her chicks could be cooked. My own non-rabbinic opinion in the case of chicken is that the law of compassion should decree that a hen not be dipped in its own egg, but this would mean the end of an old favorite in many a Jewish kitchen, breaded chicken cutlet! To this day, Orthodox and many Conservative Jews observe the law religiously—and I do mean "religiously," for it has become a matter of religious observance with only the most tenuous connection to Torah and no connection at all to common sense.

This interpretation of a simple law seems extreme enough, but that's not the end of it. Jews who are really intent on keeping kosher will decline invitations to dinner at non-kosher households, with at least two unfortunate results. First, they foster their own isolation from the broader society, and second, their perceived standoffishness breeds resentment and distrust among some non-Jews who read it as a message that they are not considered good enough for "those people." Thus a lack of balance has transformed a simple law of compassion for a cow and its calf into a major impediment to the kind of easy fellowship and understanding that happens so naturally when people share a good meal.

The same penchant for absolutism led some early rabbis to make outrageous remarks about the study of Torah as the be-all and end-all of existence. "If three have eaten at one table and have not spoken words of Torah, it is as if they had eaten sacrifices offered to the dead" (Avot 3:3). No small talk at the dinner table for these guys! (On the other hand, in the next chapter you will see the positive side of Torah talk at the table.) A rabbi named Yaakov said that if one were walking along a road while studying Torah, and stopped to admire a tree or a lovely field, "such a person would be considered by the Torah to have sinned against one's own soul" (Avot 3:7). This takes me back to the practice of "custody of the eyes" during my convent days forty years ago! Part of our self-discipline then was to keep our gaze straight ahead and not relish the beauty of our surroundings—a discipline that I could not adopt because it seemed an insult not to notice and praise the Creator's handiwork.

Fortunately, consciousness has evolved in the centuries that have passed since the early fathers were interpreting Torah, as has the sense of balance and realism that first attracted me to Judaism. The sage Maimonides, writing in the twelfth century, advised his followers to habituate themselves to righteous conduct and to appraise themselves continuously so that they would follow a "middle way" to perfection. (Never mind that this same Maimonides catalogued not ten but 613 commandments contained in the Torah!) The "middle way" involves not only spiritual practices but also the physical pleasures of everyday life. In a collection of Chasidic precepts called *Torat Avot* (Teachings of the Fathers), Abraham of Slonim says it is possible to come closer to God during material pursuits such as eating and drinking than during religious activities because "when the heart opens up due to the sense of pleasure, and there is a feeling of satisfaction and happiness, then is the fit time to come close to holiness."

Just as it is possible to go too far in interpreting the dictates of our faith traditions, it is easy to go overboard in our pursuit of spiritual growth. Seeking the instant gratification of surrender, we throw ourselves on our Sustainer's generosity and sing as if there were no tomorrow: "Though I walk through a valley of deepest darkness, I fear no harm for You are with me" (Ps. 23:4). But "tomorrow" arrives, darker than we imagined it could be, and we sing another tune: "My God, my God, why have You abandoned me?" (Ps. 22:2). The sultan in Jamal's story could well have recited the psalmist's words:

> When I was untroubled,
> I thought, 'I shall never be shaken,'
> for You, O Lord, when You were pleased,
> made me firm as a mighty mountain.
> When You hid Your face,
> I was terrified. (Ps. 30:7–8)

What is needed as an antidote to these spiritual mood swings is a sense of balance born of the quiet, steady knowledge that there is no reality but God. *Sh'ma Yisrael, Adonai Elohenu, Adonai Ekhad.* Everything we are, everything we do, is part of God. It is not possible for God to abandon us: our Sustainer is part of the air we breathe, our Cherisher is closer to us than our jugular vein (Quran 50:16). Compassionate awareness of this reality will help us keep our balance as we turn, turn, and turn again in the sacred dance of life.

Christian Reflections

I know your works; you are neither cold nor hot. I wish that you were either cold or hot. So, because you are lukewarm, and neither cold nor hot, I am about to spit you out of my mouth. (Rev. 3:15–16)

So much for balance! The final book in the Christian Testament can be—and often is—seen as the prime scriptural evidence of extremism in our tradition. At least one of my seminary professors described its theology as one of "revenge," through which members of a beleaguered, tiny religious sect that saw itself as marginalized and scapegoated could cling to a vision of God's ultimate triumph over their imperial foes. I am saddened when I see Christians in the wealthiest, most privileged society on the face of the earth wield this text as an ideological weapon in the twenty-first century. We live in a culture where the label "liberal" is the kiss of death for politicians while "extreme" in the title of a television show gives it a chance at success. I have heard the charge that my own mainline denomination, historically known as *via media* (the middle way), is "soft on sin"—an accusation one bishop countered by saying, "No, we're not soft on sin; we simply don't believe in shooting our wounded in the back." At the same time, those of us who might wear the badge of liberalism proudly (although we often prefer the word "progressive") can hardly do so when we start complaining about "those conservatives" or "those fundamentalists."

What is so refreshing and instructive about Jamal's and Kate's remarks is their implicit message that we must start at home, with our own behavior and attitudes, when dealing with the tricky topic of balance. To avoid the pitfall of hypocrisy, we need to diagnose our own lack of balance. Jesus wisely said, "How can you say to your neighbor, 'Let me take the speck out of your eye,' while the log is in your own eye? You hypocrite, first take the log out of your own eye, and then you will see clearly to take the speck out of your neighbor's eye" (Matt 7:4–5; see also, Luke 6:37–38).

Extremism does seem to go hand in hand with zealousness for God. In our ardor to be good and righteous, we often get overly ambitious and forget that, like the sun and moon in their appointed schedules, we have limits. Again, we tend to be able to see other people's denial much more easily than our own. One reason many Christians identify so strongly with the disciple Peter is that he is always overestimating his capabilities or doing something dramatic and ridiculous out of his great love for Jesus. My favorite episode is when, out of apparent embarrassment, after realizing that the stranger on the shore dispensing fishing lessons is the risen Jesus, he "put on some clothes, for he was naked, and jumped into the lake" (John 21:7). Peter's wild moves always bring a rueful grin to my face, a reminder that humor—along with remembrance of God—is another antidote to extremism. In fact, I believe that some of Jesus' instructions that we take so seriously were initially told with a twinkle in his eye. For example, the directive to turn the other cheek after someone hits you (Matt. 5:39) has the slapstick wisdom of a Charlie Chaplin routine. By the way, that advice also seems to be about restoring balance to a situation that threatens to escalate into greater violence. By getting the opportunity to strike again, the aggressor is first caught off-balance and then is able to choose emotional and spiritual equilibrium over the reflex of anger.

Jesus faces an example of extremism in a story to which I have referred before, that of the rich young man who is striving for eternal life. What higher stakes are there? In Mark's version of the story, after the man blurts out—no doubt with great relief—that he has kept all the commandments since he was a boy, the evangelist observes: "Jesus, looking at him, loved him." Jesus' response of compassion in this moment is telling. I doubt that I have ever been able to meet anyone as self-righteous as this man apparently was with love rather than a desire to strike out, at least in words. I realize from Jesus that those who differ from me in political or theological perspective usually love the same God I love and for the sake of that love I can at least consider the possibility of loving them, even as I challenge their assumptions.

There are many examples of imbalance and extremism in our current culture. Take the issue of rampant materialism: we seem to have lost all sense of proportion in terms of how much stuff we need to have a decent life. In the process of acquiring more and more things, we overlook the toll our obsession with possessions is taking on our relationships with other human beings and the rest of creation. One of the best-kept secrets in Christian scriptures is this passage from Acts 2:44–45: "All who believed were together and had all things in common; they would sell their possessions and goods and distribute the proceeds to all, as any had need." While not a simplistic formula to be yanked out of context and applied willy-nilly, this passage does suggest that there are some alternatives in Christian tradition to the extreme materialism of our time.

Another face of imbalance is addiction to alcohol, drugs, gambling, and sex, to name but a few of the dysfunctional behaviors that plague our planet. As a person who has been in recovery from alcoholism for over twenty years, I have seen the ravages that this deadly imbalance causes if it is allowed to go unchecked. There is alarming evidence that if we do not choose to address the addictions and planetary distortions for which we are responsible, creation itself will enforce the natural checks and balances established by the Creator. One of the approaches in Christian scripture to such lopsidedness is in Jesus' oft-repeated refrain, "The first shall be last, and the last first." The good news is that we can choose to be agents of the restoration of balance, especially if we can attend to the logs in our own eyes with tender humor and abundant compassion.

13

Community

Ah! What a beautiful fellowship!
(Quran 4:69)

We humans are social creatures and most of us gravitate naturally toward some kind of community that shares and supports our interests and goals. There are book clubs, athletic clubs, collectors' clubs, investors' clubs—and spiritual clubs. In a broad sense all our co-religionists are members of the same "club," though of course we don't use such a mundane word to describe our spiritual affiliation. Instead we call it our "faith community," and we all need the support of such a group. "Truly," says the Quran, "human beings are in loss except those who have faith and do righteous deeds and encourage each other in the teaching of truth and of patient perseverance" (103:1–3). Elsewhere the Quran urges us to "Make room for one another in your collective life; do make room; God makes room for you" (58:11). The spiritual benefit of belonging to a faith community is spelled out sweetly in the Quran:

> All who obey God . . .
> Are in the company
> Of those on whom
> Is the Grace of God . . .
> Ah! What a beautiful Fellowship! (4:69)

The primary purpose of a faith community is, in the words of the Quran, to "help one another in righteousness and piety" (5:2). Even prophets need a spiritual network for support and counsel. Despite the many days he spent in solitary meditation, the Prophet Muhammad lived in community and took an active role, both advising his followers and seeking advice from his trusted inner circle. The Holy Book advises us to do the same: those who "hearken to their Lord," pray regularly, and "conduct their affairs by mutual consultation" are among the ones who will have their reward with God" (42:38). Like the Prophet, we need to surround ourselves with companions with whom we can share mutual love, trust, and thirst for the truth. These are the people who keep us real, encourage us to be our most authentic selves, and show us the face of God through their loving presence and support.

In a perfect world, this kind of community would be available to us wherever we go to church, synagogue, or mosque. But not everyone belongs to an established religion, and those who do know that the congregation at large, while supporting the spiritual life in general, cannot really supply the intimate kind of support that we need for our individual journey. For this we need a community within the community, an inner circle like the Prophet's companions. These are the ones who, when the going gets hard, will hang in there with us, holding fast, "all together, to the rope of God" (3:103). This circle of companions is vitally important to our spiritual growth and the overall quality of our lives.

The poet Rumi calls this intimate community a "circle of love," and in one of his most famous utterances he urges us to "come out of the circle of time and enter the circle of love." In image after image he describes how essential it is to have such a circle. A wall standing alone is useless, he says, but if you put two or three walls together, they will support a roof and keep your grain safe and dry. Reeds and rushes, when woven together, make a useful mat. If they are not interlaced, they blow away in the wind. When wool meets a gifted carpet maker, it becomes a miracle of rich design. Earth in the hands of bricklayers and architects can become a thousand-windowed palace.

Other sages have illustrated the same principle with images drawn from nature. A single star is lovely to behold, but myriad stars light up the sky. A small stream trickles away into nothingness, but joined together with other streams in a larger tributary, it becomes part of a river and eventually flows into the ocean. A wild elephant may wreak havoc, but yoked with tamed elephants it learns how to behave peaceably. A single bee may gather nectar, but it needs a community of bees to turn that nectar into honey.

Let me offer a few ideas about how to develop your own spiritual community or circle of love. The people you choose should be able to pass through what I call the three gateways of love, trust, and truth. First, of course, you would consider the pool of family and friends who love you. Are there any who, like the Prophet's companions, are able to be vulnerable with you and will support you in your own vulnerability? Any who "with their lives bear witness to the truth" (4:69) and already support you in your spiritual life? If so, you already have a circle of love. If we possess one, two, or more such people in our lives, we are deeply blessed. For many, however, this ready-made circle does not exist and it doesn't seem possible to create one from the available pool of family, friends, and acquaintances. Do not despair! You can create an inner circle of love instantly and reap similar benefits!

Inner circle of love

It is possible to create authentic community at any time in the inner reality of your meditative state. In that inner landscape, you can summon anyone you believe is able to pass through the gateways of love, trust, and truth. This can be literally anyone who has ever lived: a prophet or a saint, a personal hero, or a loved one living or deceased. It can also be a sacred being of light, an imaginary friend, a pet, a tree—the choices are limited only by your imagination and belief system. It can be a single being or a crowd—again, the choice is up to you.

Having chosen the members of your inner circle of love, go into your inner landscape—that is, get into a meditative state—and create what Sufis call a "sacred sanctuary." This is a place of majestic beauty, absolute safety, unalloyed love and compassion, and pure magic. It can be a real place that you have seen in person or in pictures, or a place that exists in your own rich imagination. You can walk to this space down a garden path or fly there on a magic carpet—again, the possibilities are endless. Settle into this space for a few minutes and let the healing begin.

Now you are ready to summon your circle of love. In the safety of your sacred sanctuary, simply allow the members of your circle—your ideal authentic community—to bond with you and love you. Know that it is in their nature to love you, and allow yourself to be cherished, honored, nurtured, and nourished by them. Give yourself permission to receive. If possible, see, feel, and experience them touching, holding, and embracing you. Your inner circle feels ecstatic joy in showering you with love, compassion, and healing.

The power of this imaginative practice lies in the simple, overused but essential truth that all of our dramas, melodramas, posturings, and acrobatics revolve around the need for love. It's all about being loved, not being loved, and wanting to be loved. The subconscious does not differentiate between fact and fiction, and all the realms—earthly, heavenly, and imaginative—are mysteriously "real" and interconnected. If one can experience authentic love at any level, by anyone or anything, true healing and transformation occurs.

I have had the opportunity to share this practice with some who in their public lives have had to profess love for God and faith in humanity, but in their hearts, because of a series of life situations, have become deeply cynical and mistrustful of both God and humans. I recall one friend in particular who was frightened because in private he felt an aversion to God, family, and friends. In attempting to conjure an inner circle of love he could think of no one that he wanted to invite into his sacred sanctuary. When pressed, he said the only activity he liked was hiking, and he liked trees. So we started the session with one tree as his inner circle of love. Over time, the circle grew and included more trees and eventually became a grove. The trees became his family, friends, and community. The love, compassion, and nourishment that he experienced through trees opened his heart. Now he is joyously in love with Divinity, and his faith in people has been restored. He still likes to meditate under trees and he uses his own experience to teach others about signs of God in nature.

Personal circle of love

The Quran says that one of God's wishes for humanity is that there might grow out of us a community of people "inviting to all that is good, enjoining what is right," so that we might "attain felicity" (3:104). In my personal life I am blessed with three circles of love whose members "help one another to righteousness and *taqwa* [mindfulness of and closeness to God]" (5:2). My first circle is my beloved family: my brother and sister and their children, my own daughter, and my former wife, who remains a constant friend. Their unalloyed love, graciousness, and generosity fill me with joy and inspire me to "bring to God a heart that can respond" (50:33). The second circle includes my close friends who love the truth and help me to walk the earth "on spacious paths" (71:20). The third circle consists of my treasured colleagues and teachers who counsel me as a Sufi master says, "not with the tongue of words but the tongue of deeds." I also have an inner circle of love, which includes my precious and beloved parents and grandparents— all on "the other side"—as well as angels and the "Glow of Presence." From the unconditional love of my parents and grandparents, I experience indescribable nourishment and guidance. From the Glow of Presence, I feel extraordinarily uplifted and empowered by the deep sense that all is well because "God is the Lord of Grace unbounded" (8:29).

Jewish Reflections

If two sit together and words of Torah are between them, the Shekhinah rests between them. (Avot 3:3)

Shekhinah is the Hebrew name for the presence of God, and no greater blessing could a devout Jew hope for than to bask in her presence. (Yes, *Shekhinah* is feminine!) The mere possibility of experiencing that presence is reason enough to bring observant Jews together for communal study and worship, but of course there are other reasons as well. Judaism, like Islam, began in a tribal society and to some extent we Jews are still a tribe. The minute I stepped out of the *mikveh* (ritual bath) as a brand-new Jew, my witness wrapped me in a fluffy towel and said, "Welcome to the Tribe!" Those were four of the most beautiful words I'd ever heard. In that moment I was joining Ruth, that famous Jew-by-choice, who said "Your people shall be my people and your God my God" (Ruth 1:16), and I was finally a member of the community of faith that I had longed to join for half my life. This is my path and these are my people, and I can only repeat the exuberant words of the Quran, "Ah! What a beautiful Fellowship!" (4:69).

As in days of old, when there were actually twelve Israelite tribes, Jews today are not one monolithic body of believers any more than Muslims or Christians are. There are many types of Judaism (see chapter 1) offering many different kinds of community, from intimate shuls to large urban synagogues. My own community within the tribe is a meditative synagogue that is inclusive, progressive, and welcoming to Jews and non-Jews alike. Originally founded for Jews who don't go to synagogue, it has become a place of learning, deep spirituality, and mutual support for a goodly number of like-minded folk who want to follow the path of Torah as authentically as possible. It is "community" in the truest sense, and Shekhinah is palpable whenever we meet for Torah study or Shabbat services.

The role of community is never more powerful than on Yom Kippur, the Day of Atonement. As described briefly in chapter 7, this is the day when we all stand together and make a public confession of our sins and failings of the past year—not as individuals praying together, as we do when we say the Amidah, but as a community speaking in one voice. "We have sinned before you by hardening our hearts . . . We have sinned before you through acting against our own morality . . . through deceit . . . through obstinacy . . . through self-indulgence. . . ." The list is long and we have all had a hand in it. It is deeply healing to know that we are not alone in our sinfulness, to hear our loved ones, our leaders, and even our personal nemeses confess to the same failings, and to unite our voices as we pray, with what Jamal calls increased necessity, "For all our sins, God of Forgiveness, forgive us, release us, grant us atonement." The prayer itself grants a sense of at-one-ment, soothing the personal ache caused by feelings of inadequacy and unworthiness and strengthening the community by mending interpersonal rifts that may have developed in the past year.

Community living is not always easy, and other rifts will surely open in the coming year as we relax back into our bad old habits and forget to pay attention to the Shekhinah in our midst. There's an old saying, funny but true, that for every three Jews there are at least four opinions. But there's another old saying: "[Fill in the blank]: can't live with 'em, can't live without 'em." Mostly, I wouldn't want to live without 'em. One of the best-known sayings of the early rabbis is that the world stands on three things: Torah, sacred service, and loving acts of kindness (Avot 1:2). Community is where all three elements come together, and that is surely where Shekhinah is to be found.

Christian Reflections

For where two or three are gathered in my name, I am there among them.
(Matt. 18:20)

Our Western mindset can barely wrap itself around the communal cultural norms of our ancestors in the Abrahamic faith traditions, norms that much of the world still takes for granted. I remember the amused and bothered look on the face of an African graduate student when I asked her whether or not she had a family. "Ann," she said, "how could I be human if I didn't have a family? I think you want to know whether or not I have a husband and have borne children." Her answer nailed the truth on two counts: by our very existence we are members of the human family, and it is "family" in the sense of community that enables us to be fully human. Some scholars would argue that ever since St. Augustine's intense focus on his own sinfulness we Christians in the West have tended to privatize our lives in faith and "downsize" our relationship with God to the contours of our individual souls. The question that is so important to some of us, "Have you accepted Jesus Christ as your personal Lord and Savior?" bespeaks this kind of bias. We easily forget that our personal lives are inextricably interwoven into the fabric of our common life.

My Christian tradition acknowledges the communal in the idea of common prayer. In fact, most Anglicans across the globe—no matter what language they employ to sing God's praises or even whether they can themselves read—use words that come from a book with those very words, "common prayer," in its title. They also meet around a communion table to share the ritual meal of the faith. However, as is true in Judaism and Islam, the roots of Christian communal life go even deeper, all the way to our understanding of God.

The unique way in which many Christians think about God-as-community is manifest in the belief that causes our Abrahamic siblings to shake their heads (and sometimes their fists) in consternation: that is, the doctrine of the Trinity. We Christians have been using the idea of the Trinity as a way to love God with our minds for so long that we sometimes forget that it is an *idea* and not God's very self. The Trinity is our way of saying that our interconnectedness with everything that exists is grounded in the life and being of the One. I think of Jesus Christ's participation in the Trinity as being representative of the special covenant God has with humanity. To me, Jesus represents not only humans, but the whole created order, in harmony and communion with the Creator.

I must confess that sometimes I find it easier even to contemplate the Trinity as God-in-community than I do to live compassionately with my brothers and sisters in the church. If loving one another were easy, Jesus would not have had to make it his parting commandment to his disciples and a repeated refrain during the Last Supper: "I give you a new commandment, that you love one another. Just as I have loved you, you also should love one another. By this everyone will know that you are my disciples, if you have love for one another" (John 13:34–35). After all, the disciples were together because of their mutual love and regard for their teacher, not necessarily because they cared for each other. Ever since their time, Christians have labored over this test—with varying degrees of success—of loving whoever happens to show up in Jesus' name. Thank heavens for some of the level-headed guidelines he gave. The most basic rule of thumb for communal life is, whether you are the giver or recipient of an offense, to go to the other party and deal with the situation. In Matthew 5:23–24 Jesus says, "So when you are offering your gift at the altar, if you remember that your brother or sister has something against you, leave your gift there before the altar and go; first be reconciled to your brother or sister, and then come and offer your gift." In Matthew 18:15 he advises someone who has been sinned against to "go and point out the fault when the two of you are alone," then to take an arbitrator if the first encounter doesn't yield reconciliation.

Jesus knew the toxic consequences of festering contention in a circle of love. So did Paul. He warns his troublesome Corinthians that if the strife among them goes unacknowledged and unchecked, it will eat away at the life of the community and all of its members. When people show up for the holy meal without "discerning the body," he says, they "eat and drink judgment against themselves" with potentially fatal consequences (I Cor. 11:29–30). But sometimes we can see in that same setting the opposite side of the coin, a glimpse of the eternal heavenly celebration. The mystery of the communion of saints dawns on me from time to time in a very special way, often in church but elsewhere as well. It happens when all of a sudden a roomful of people whose names I have never known and whose faces I may have seen only once all look familiar. I can't recall who they remind me of, or why, but I know I am recognizing a profound truth: those who moments ago were strangers are now—and always have been and will be—kin in God. As a popular Christian hymn begins, "What a fellowship!"

PRACTICE

A good practice for deepening communal life is that of intentional, engaged listening. There are a number of formats that facilitate genuine communication—Compassionate Listening, Appreciative Inquiry, Conversation Cafes, and Re-evaluation Counseling to name just a few. Common to all these formats is the establishment of an environment of trust by mutual agreement on a style of communication that offers equal opportunity for uninterrupted expression of ideas in the safety of no commentary. Confidentiality is essential in these conversations. Speaking for oneself, in the first person, safeguards integrity and authenticity. Listening with appreciation and refraining from judgment are also important ingredients.

14

Service

The likeness of those who spend their substance, seeking to please God and to strengthen their souls, is as a garden, high and fertile.

(Quran 2:265)

"It is not this world or the next I crave," said the Sufi saint Rabia, "but for one moment to be called Your slave." Rabia, who lived in Basra, Iraq, in the eighth century, is well known for her extravagant and heartfelt flights of fancy when expressing her adoration of God, whom she called her Beloved. Though she herself never wrote a word, her poems and sayings were carried by word of mouth for four hundred years and eventually recorded by the Persian poet Farid Ud-Din Attar. In this couplet from *The Conference of the Birds* (translated by A. Darbandi and D. Davis), Attar imagines Rabia in the ecstasy of total surrender to her Beloved. And who among us cannot relate to the sentiment, if not the language, of Rabia's prayer? True lovers ache to serve each other, parents would give their very lives for their children, men and women give their lives in service to justice. Service is the natural outgrowth and expression of an ego that has begun to transcend itself, a heart that has begun to expand beyond its own selfish concerns. Once we have begun the work of transforming the ego and opening our hearts, we, like Rabia, long to be of service to God and to all of creation.

Do what is beautiful

In Islamic spirituality, authentic service is a thing of beauty. Says the Quran, "Do what is beautiful. God loves those who do what is beautiful" (2:195). The possibilities for serving God and creation are endless: "Let the beauty you love be what you do," says Rumi; "there are hundreds of ways to kneel and kiss the ground." In case we need suggestions, the Quran reminds us that righteousness is not to turn your face in prayer to east and west but to love your fellow beings (2:177) and "walk softly upon the earth" (25:65).

To be of service is both a privilege and a responsibility. Out of divine graciousness, we humans have been appointed God's "viceroys" on earth (6:165) and have been given the earth and all its creatures in trust—what the Quran calls *amanat* (33:72)—not for our ownership but for our use in accordance with the wishes of our Creator. Thus we need to remind ourselves constantly that we are God's representatives on earth and we must pray to be worthy of that privilege. Illustrating the concept of service as a sacred responsibility, Sufis tell the story of a saintly man who travels through many countries and is deeply affected by the poverty, pain, and injustices he witnesses. One day, when he sees yet another poor, starving orphan child covered with sores and shivering in the cold, the man breaks down and cries out, "God! How can you allow this misery? I beseech you, please do something!" The answer is silence, but that night God appears in a vision and says to the man, "Beloved one, I did do something. I created you."

Help God!

"God wants to turn to you," says the Quran, and in the pages of the Holy Book we read this plea: "Help God!" (47:7).

> Who is it that will loan to God a beautiful loan?
> For God will increase it manifold to his credit,
> And he will have besides a liberal reward. (57:11)

What an astonishing idea! God wants help from us mere mortals, the Creator wants help from the created! Everything we have is from God. We are debtors to the core. And yet, from debtors God is begging for a loan! In a hadith qudsi, God asks, "Child of Adam, why did you not visit me when I was unwell and in need of food and drink?" The human is utterly dumbfounded. "But you are Lord of the Worlds," he stutters. "What could you possibly need from me?" God's answer is a message to each of us: "When one of my servants is ill, you will find me with him. When you offer him food and drink, you are offering them to me."

With an exquisite sense of humor, God has created us with a triple purpose: to serve both our Sustainer and ourselves by serving our fellow beings. Service of our Sustainer is illustrated by the fourteenth-century mystic Hafiz as rendered by Daniel Ladinsky in *The Gift*:

> God revealed a sublime truth to the world, when He sang,
> "I am made whole by your life. Each soul, each soul completes me."

Just as our life and actions "complete" our Creator, our generosity to others is also generosity to ourselves because we are all one in the One. What we give to others is only what God has already given us, and our generosity creates "space" for us to receive more of what God gives us so magnanimously and repeatedly. If we truly understand this truth, how can we not be generous with our fellow beings? Once when he was being praised for his compassionate politics, Gandhi said, "I am here to serve no one else but myself: to find my own self-realization through service to others."

Clear guidelines

The Quran gives clear guidelines about the practice of service to others. First, know that "you are invited to spend freely in the way of God" (47:38), and do not refuse the invitation, for "by no means shall you attain righteousness unless you give freely of that which you love" (3:92). Do not be faint-hearted or miserly about it, "for God is with you, and will never put you in loss for your good deeds" (47:35). Second, give to those who ask (2:177)—and, Islamic teachers say, even to those who don't ask. Third, don't boast about your generosity. "It is noble even if you make your charity public, but far superior is the charity that helps the needy in secret; it will atone for some of your wrongdoings. God is well acquainted with what you do" (2:271). "Is it not enough," asks the Quran, "that your Sustainer is a witness?" (41:53).

The path of service is not always easy or convenient, and it can be tempting to avoid climbing what the Quran calls "the steep incline" (90:11). But God has given us two eyes, a tongue, and a pair of lips, the Quran says pointedly (90:8–9), so that we may climb that path. Notice that the path requires not physical strength but mental awareness—the ability to witness and to speak. And what is the steep incline? It is, in the simplest terms, the pursuit of social justice: "freeing a slave from bondage," says the Quran, "and the giving of food in a day of privation" (90:13–14). This is a critical verse. As servants of our Merciful God, we are obliged to work for structural and systemic changes within our own communities in order to free our fellow humans from the bondage of poverty and oppression. "Be just," says the Quran; "this is closest to God consciousness" (5:8). A popular hadith tells us that when an orphan cries, "the Throne of God shakes." Our responsibility as viceroys of the Divine is to use our God-given eyes to witness the pain in the world and our God-given tongues to speak out against injustice wherever we see it. Mindless of the personal cost, we need to heed the dream of the saint who pleaded with God to "do something": we need to remember that we are agents of the Divine and offer ourselves in just action. The Prophet Muhammad said, "Whosoever of you sees an evil action, let him change it with his hands; and if he is not able to do so, then with his tongue; and if he is not able to do that, then with his heart—and that is the weakest of faith."

Prayer and righteous deeds

In Islamic theology, service in the form of *zakat*, the practice of tithing for the poor, is one of the "Five Pillars of Islam." In fact, zakat stands squarely in the middle, between the pillars of faith and prayer on one side and those of Ramadan and Hajj on the other. Thus service is inextricably linked with prayer, and indeed, whenever the word "prayer" occurs in the Quran, the phrase "righteous deeds" is sure to follow. This interconnection between prayer and service is illustrated by a popular Islamic insight. Night and day, Muslims all over the world are prostrating in prayer in the direction of the Kaaba in Mecca. (The Kaaba, thought by Muslims to have been built by Adam and later by Abraham and Ishmael [Quran 2:125], symbolizes the

House of God.) What happens if you take the Kaaba away? You see human beings prostrating to one another! Thus prayer is about serving the other—and serving the other is a kind of prayer. The words "righteous deeds" appear repeatedly in the Quran, and the performance of such deeds is absolutely prerequisite for attaining closeness to God and securing entrance to heaven. Whether you are male or female, says the Quran, whether you are a Jew, a Christian, a Sabian, or a Muslim, what assures heavenly rewards is having faith in God and engaging in righteous deeds.

> If any do deeds of righteousness
> Be they male or female,
> And have faith,
> They will enter Heaven. (4:124)

In your spiritual journey, therefore, always be mindful of the urgent need to be of service to the Beloved wherever you perceive the opportunity. God never asks for more than we have to give. "From a blind man," says Rumi, "two drops of light are enough." Faith and surrender are surely important, but the Quran tells us that "good deeds, the fruit of which endures forever, are best in the sight of your Sustainer and yield the best return" (19:76). At the time of death, money and power will be left behind; family and friends will accompany you only as far as your gravesite; beyond that, only your righteous deeds will bear you onward.

Sacred mission

Each of us has a sacred mission, a special service to perform on earth. The Indian poet Tagore says, "We spend our days and nights stringing and unstringing our instruments but the song we came here to sing remains unsung." At some point in our life we shall connect to our inner yearning and give expression to our song, our life purpose. Every event, circumstance, and relationship in our life has been a preparation and a readying for this mission. At the time of death, we shall realize that our life has been a perfect plot.

How do we go about discovering our unique mission? The sages say, "Deepen your desire to serve and a chance of service will be granted to you." Rumi advises, "Do not seek water. Increase your thirst and water will gush from above and below." There is no need to be anxious about our grand and sacred mission. The ancient teachers tell us to cultivate a sincere attitude of service in our everyday life, to focus more on sharing and less on accumulation, more on collaboration and less on competition. Our unique mission will grow out of this attitude, and in time we will come to understand what our special purpose has been.

An attitude of service can make the difference between heaven and hell on earth. Take, for example, a popular story about the dining halls in the afterworld. In both heaven and hell the tables are laden with delicious foods, but the denizens are allowed to eat only with spoons that are four feet long. The people in hell go through all kinds of contortions in order to eat. They scoop food in the spoons, throw it in the air, and position themselves to catch it in their mouths as it falls. Food is splattered everywhere and the people are groaning with hunger and frustration. In heaven, on the other hand, the people scoop food in their spoons and feed one another. Because they are serving each other, they are all well fed and content. Heaven resonates with peace and joy. And that is how we, by deepening an attitude of service, can make of earth a little bit of heaven here and now.

In doing what is beautiful, the Prophet Muhammad was a model of the compassion and bounty of God for his followers, and he constantly reminded his community to follow his example. "Do good deeds according to your capacity," he said. "God does not grow tired of giving rewards unless you tire of doing good. The good deeds most loved by God are those that are done regularly, even if they are small."

PRACTICES

- Take time for yourself—be of service to your own being. Receive your own pain and suffering with mercy and gentleness. Honor and nurture your soul. This expands your ability to serve others in an authentic way.

- Make it a habit to send light and love from your heart to the "essence" of the people you meet and the entities of nature that catch your attention. Pray for those in need—both people and the world of nature.

These practices will expand your heart and increase your awareness of your connection to all of creation.

• Act on the little things in life where you can be of help: offer a smile, a kind word, a patient ear, a helping hand, a donation. These small acts of service are essential parts of your sacred mission. They enable you to become, in Rumi's words, "a lamp, lifeboat, or ladder." Or, in Rabia's words, a slave of the Beloved.

Jewish Reflections

If I am only for myself, what am I? (Avot 1:14)

In a deeply moving quotation in Yaffa Eliach's *Hasidic Tales of the Holocaust*, a death-camp survivor says, "I learned about friendship in Auschwitz. When I was cold, strangers shielded me with their bodies from the blowing winds, for they had nothing else to offer but themselves." Mercifully few of us will ever find ourselves in such desperate circumstances as the death camps of World War II, or so literally stripped to the core of who we are, but this quotation speaks to the essence of what it means to give ourselves in loving service. Our responsibility as people chosen for the path of Torah is to act as the hands and feet of the Eternal by performing the mitzvah of *tikkun olam*, repair of our broken world. We are here on this planet not only to work on a private love affair with God but to assist our Creator by performing acts of loving-kindness, working for justice, and doing whatever small thing is in our power to make this world a better place. If we have nothing left but our own breath, the way of Torah is to spend that breath in the service of the One in whom we all are one.

In Jewish thought, the command to serve, like the summons to surrender, is based on the Sh'ma, the declaration that God is the only reality. When we feed the poor, visit the sick, or free the slave, it is as if we are serving the Eternal One. And, for those of us who are motivated by a little self-interest, the Sh'ma reminds us that since we are all one, the service we give to others we are actually giving to ourselves.

Lest we fail to infer the kinds of service we are called to do, Torah provides a number of examples, both expressed and implied. In Western literature the Pentateuch is the oldest extant guide for living a righteous life in community with our fellow beings. As with the Quran, it is easy to get turned off by the negative aspects of the tribal mentality of the times in which it was written, but try to remember that these ancient scriptures are the record of humankind's first recognition of a Divine Being who is not only transcendent but also intimately involved with our everyday lives. Even in the mists of biblical history, there are hints that the way of Torah is to reach beyond purely tribal interests. When God tells Abraham that he plans to destroy Sodom for its wickedness, Abraham pleads not only for his own relatives who are living there, but for any righteous inhabitants of the doomed city (Gen. 18:20–33). Over the centuries, tribal mentality has been transformed by the values and commandments that still guide our lives in the twenty-first century—a century with its own violence and troubling mentality, a century still in need of the "thou shalt" and "thou shalt not" commands that tame our baser instincts.

The Eternal One who spoke to the early Israelites—and who speaks to us today—does not just say, "Love your neighbor because I'm telling you to." Throughout Torah, divine authority for the commandment to deal justly and kindly with each other is rooted in God's own compassion in delivering us from slavery in Egypt. Virtually every instruction of this type ends with the statement, "I am the Eternal, Who brought you out of Egypt." Whether or not the bondage and deliverance actually happened (there is no direct archeological evidence that it did) is not the point. The truth is in the metaphor. The word for Egypt in Hebrew is *Mitzrayim*—literally, a narrow place. Today when we talk about *mitzrayim* (notice the lower-case "m"), we are referring to the narrow places in our own lives—the self-destructive attitudes and habits that enslave us in the restricted world of our own egos. When, by grace of God, we get free of those stuck places—when we begin to transform our egos and open our hearts—we are able to extend a helping hand to those who are still stuck in the mitzrayim of poverty, oppression, or psychological depression.

Just as Muhammad is a beautiful model of service in Islam, the ultimate model in Judaism is Moses, who shepherded us out of the narrow place of Egypt and put up with our whining and faithlessness for forty years. Reviewing the whole adventure towards the end of his life, he tells us how angry the Eternal was when we worshipped the golden calf. "Let me at them and I will destroy them!" God exclaimed, and Moses says that when he saw what danger we were in, "I threw myself down before the Eternal— eating no bread and drinking no water forty days and forty nights . . . For I was in dread of the fierce anger against you which moved the Eternal to wipe you out" (Deut. 9:18-19). In the words of another great Jewish prophet, Rabbi Jesus, "No one has greater love than this, to lay down one's life for one's friends" (John 15:13).

All of the biblical admonitions to serve God by serving our fellow beings are summed up in an exquisitely simple statement by the prophet Micah nearly three thousand years ago. "He has told you, O people, what is good for you: to do justice and to love kindness and to walk humbly with your God" (Mic. 6:8). According to the commentary *Etz Hayim*, there are two interpretations of this passage. One is that the demands are a graded series: first keep the law, then go beyond the law in a spirit of loving-kindness, and finally, don't toot your own horn about how good you are. The other interpretation is that humility before God is the starting point, and only from there can we truly live in justice and goodness. I tend to favor the latter interpretation. Nowadays we have a warped concept of humility—we often think it means we should dismiss ourselves as nobodies. In fact, a better word in this context would be "self-integrity." Humility is to know our own worth, to know that in our essence we are the expressions of God's own being. When we have done the hard inner work to become conscious of our own divine nature, it is almost second nature to manifest our sacred identity with deeds of justice and loving-kindness.

For nearly two thousand years Jews have also drawn inspiration from a non-biblical source, the famous words of the beloved Rabbi Hillel:

> If I am not for myself, who will be for me?
> If I am only for myself, what am I?
> If not now, when? (Avot 1:14)

If I don't do my own inner work, no one can do it for me. "He who does good to his own person is a man of mercy," says the author of Proverbs (11:17). But if I focus only on my own navel without reaching out in loving service to my fellow beings, what kind of person am I? And if I don't have time or inclination to do it today, when is it going to happen? It is in my own best interest to shush my selfish ego and use my God-given abilities right now to help repair the world. In the words of the great medieval theologian Maimonides, "No joy is greater or more glorious than the joy of gladdening the hearts of the poor, the orphans, the widows, and the strangers. Indeed, anyone who causes the hearts of these unfortunates to rejoice emulates the Divine Presence."

Christian Reflections

I am among you as one who serves. (Luke 22:27)

One summer when I was in college, I worked for my father at his downtown law office. On the days I went out to buy lunch my father would give me a briefcase or some other official-looking bag in which to carry it. "It must not appear that you are fetching some white man his lunch," he said. Much earlier in my life, I had learned never to call any man "sir," in defiance of the polite ways of Southerners, black and white.

With this background, it is little wonder that I resonate with the passage in the Gospel of John where Jesus says, "No longer do I call you slaves . . . but I have called you friends" (15:15, my translation). As the great-granddaughter of enslaved persons, I was explicitly raised *not* to be either a slave or a servant. However, I *was* raised with a strong ethic of service—on behalf of my people, African Americans, and suffering humanity in general. This distinction is important to me in reflecting on Christian service.

Keeping in mind the intimate relation between prayer and righteous deeds that Jamal mentioned is a crucial element for maintaining sound intentions in doing service. Prayer keeps our work grounded in gratitude toward the Source of any resources we can use to share with others. Jesus, as one who looks for no reward and who calls others to join him in the task, stands as a model for Christians as we seek to serve the God who called both him and us. A deacon (from *diakonos*, a Greek word for "servant") in any Christian community is a living reminder to the entire body of believers that the attitude and activity of service belong to every member of that community. Where service is a common calling, there are no slaves and no masters among humans, only brother and sister servants of God.

As in Judaism, the Sh'ma provides a basis for service in Christianity, especially in tandem with the commandment that Jesus referred to as "like unto" loving God with one's whole self. That second commandment was to love neighbor as self. If there are any formulas in spirituality, the priority of first loving God and then loving self and neighbor is such a formula. Prayer helps us keep the strategy effective: although we certainly can and do go to others for assistance, our prayer begins and ends with God, who in turn infuses our hearts with the power and love to engage in right action. The Christian Testament parallel to the hadith qudsi mentioned in Jamal's section shows what that right action looks like. In speaking about the day of judgment, Jesus says that those "blessed by my Father" will be separated from the others and invited to "inherit the kingdom prepared for you from the foundation of the world" because they fed, welcomed, clothed, and tended to Jesus when he was in need (Matt. 25:34). The astonishment of the blessed equals that of those who failed to come to Jesus' aid, whose destiny is "the eternal fire prepared for the devil and his angels" (25:41). Jesus enlightens them all by saying that by serving—or failing to serve—the lowliest of his brothers or sisters they were reserving their place in the age to come. It was the righteous intention of the blessed that permitted them to act compassionately without calculating future payoff. I often feel a similar connection being made when I receive the bread and wine at the table of Communion. Those alarming words, "The body and blood of Christ," make a profound impression when I understand them to mean that God's communion with me essentially puts the well-being of humanity, Christ's flesh-and-blood brothers and sisters, in my hands.

Servanthood is central to the message of Jesus—expressed both in his own ministry and in the work he leaves his followers. In contrast to worldly rulers, he says, "I am among you as one who serves" (Luke 22:27). The route to greatness for his disciples is to imitate him, becoming "servant" of the rest (Matt. 20:26, 23:11; Mark 9:35, 10:43). In John's gospel, unlike the first three, there are no accounts of Jesus sending the disciples out on their own to preach, teach, and heal. However, in John's account of Jesus' last night with them, Jesus to their amazement first washes their feet and then tells them, "So if I, your Lord and Teacher, have washed your feet, you also ought to wash one another's feet" (13:14). In a number of Christian

traditions, the importance of servanthood is literally ordained; traditionally all bishops and priests start as deacons, symbolically grounding them
in an essential characteristic of Jesus' identity.

Deacons are not to form a closed caste or servant class in the church,
however. Just as priests are to be icons of what we call the priesthood of all
believers—that is, the notion that each of us is made in the divine image
with a sacred mission as a "viceroy" of the Beloved—deacons are to remind
us Christians that all of us are set apart for service. It is refreshing to realize that such streams of thought and practice run through all our traditions. I have an evangelical Christian friend who inspires me with the
thought that service may provide a hospitable meeting ground for Muslims, Jews, and Christians. Service maps out for us a territory where, by
answering the Creator's call heard in all our scriptures to serve the most vulnerable creatures of an endangered creation, we can engage in the delicate
work of healing the dysfunctional Abrahamic family of faith. Just as Jesus
eggs on his disciples to compete to be each other's servants, in the Torah
Moses rejoices, over his jealous assistant's objections, when Eldad and
Medad join the ranks of the prophets. "Would that all the Lord's people
were prophets, and that the Lord would put his spirit on them!" (Num.
11:28–29). So too Allah in the Quran challenges all of us. "And if God
had so willed, God could surely have made you all one single community:
but [God willed it otherwise] in order to test you by means of what God
has vouchsafed unto you. Vie, then, with one another in doing good works!
Unto God you all must return; and then God will make you truly understand all that on which you were wont to differ" (5:48).

APPENDIX I
Recommended Readings

For an enjoyable read on each of the three Abrahamic traditions, we recommend the following:

Dodge, Christine Huda. *Everything® Understanding Islam Book*. Avon, Mass.: Adams Media, 2003.

Falcon, Rabbi Ted, and David Blatner. *Judaism for Dummies®*. New York: Hungry Minds, 2001.

Woodhead, Linda. *Christianity: A Very Short Introduction*. Oxford: Oxford University, 2004.

Of the many books offering spiritual guidance, each of us has prepared a list of our favorites in our own tradition.

From Islam

Ali-Karamali, Sumbul. *The Muslim Next Door: The Qur'an, the Media, and that Veil Thing*. Ashland, Ore.: White Cloud Press, 2008.

Armstrong, Karen. *Muhammad: A Prophet for Our Time*. New York: Harper Collins, 2006.

Aslan, Reza. *No god but God. The Origins, Evolution, and Future of Islam*. New York: Random House, 2006.

Dardess, George. *Meeting Islam: A Guide for Christians*. Brewster, Mass. Paraclete, 2005.

Firestone, Reuven, *Children of Abraham: An Introduction to Judaism for Muslims*. Jersey City, N.J.: KTAV, 2001.

Frager, Robert. *Heart, Self, & Soul: The Sufi Psychology of Growth, Balance, and Harmony*. Wheaton, Ill.: Quest Books, 1999.

Harvey, Andrew. *Light upon Light: Inspirations from Rumi*. Berkeley: North Atlantic Books, 1996.

Helminski, Kabir. *The Knowing Heart: A Sufi Path of Transformation*. Boston: Shambhala, 1999.

Ibn 'Arabi. *Divine Sayings: 101 Hadith Qudsi*. Oxford: Anqa, 2008.

Lawrence, Bruce. *The Qur'an: A Biography*. New York: Atlantic Monthly, 2006.

Nasr, Seyyed Hossein. *The Garden of Truth: The Vision and Promise of Sufism, Islam's Mystical Tradition*. New York: HarperOne, 2007.

Rahman, Jamal. *The Fragrance of Faith: The Enlightened Heart of Islam*. Bath, U.K.: Book Foundation, 2004.

Suhrawardy, Abdullah. *The Wisdom of Muhammad*. New York: Citadel, 2001.

From Judaism

Elkins, Dov Peretz. *The Wisdom of Judaism: An Introduction to the Values of the Talmud*. Woodstock, Vt.: Jewish Lights, 2007.

Morinis, Alan. *Everyday Holiness: The Jewish Spiritual Path of Mussar*. Boston: Trumpeter Books, 2007.

Ochs, Carol. *Our Lives as Torah: Finding God in Our Own Stories*. San Francisco: Jossey-Bass Inc., 2001.

Sasso, Sandy Eisenberg. *God's Echo: Exploring Scripture with Midrash*. Brewster, Mass.: Paraclete, 2007.

Schachter-Shalomi, Zalman, with Joel Segel. *Jewish with Feeling: A Guide to Meaningful Jewish Practice*. New York: Riverhead Books, 2005.

Shapiro, Rami M. *The Sacred Art of Lovingkindness: Preparing to Practice*. Woodstock, Vt.: Skylight Paths, 2006.

Slater, Jonathan P. *Mindful Jewish Living: Compassionate Practice.* New York: Aviv, 2004.

Steinberg, Milton. *Basic Judaism.* New York: Harcourt, 1947.

From Christianity

Bloom, Anthony. *Beginning to Pray.* New York: Paulist, 1970.

Borg, Marcus J. *The Heart of Christianity. Rediscovering a Life of Faith.* San Francisco: Harper, 2003.

Butler Bass, Diana. *A People's History of Christianity: The Other Side of the Story.* San Francisco: HarperOne, 2009.

Smith, Martin L. *The Word is Very Near You: A Guide to Praying with Scripture.* Cambridge, Mass.: Cowley, 1989.

Thurman, Howard. *Meditations of the Heart.* Boston: Beacon, 1981.

Walsh, James, translator. *The Revelations of Divine Love of Julian of Norwich.* St. Meinrad, Ind.: Abbey, 1975.

Weems, Renita J. *Just a Sister Away: Understanding the Timeless Connection Between Women of Today and Women of the Bible.* New York: Warner, 2005.

APPENDIX II
Quranic Verses and Hadith for Meditation

Verses of comfort and reassurance

Truly in the remembrance of God do hearts find rest (13:28).

Is it not enough that your Sustainer is a witness? (41:53).

I am closer to you than your jugular vein (50:16).

I have prepared you for Myself (20:41).

Everywhere you turn is the Face of Allah (2:115).

All that dwells upon the earth is perishing, yet still abides the Face of thy Sustainer, majestic, splendid (55:26–27).

For the sincere is an appointed nourishment: fruits and honor and dignity in gardens of felicity (37:40–43).

For men and women who surrender themselves to God . . . and for men and women who remember God unceasingly, for them God has readied forgiveness and a supreme recompense (33:35).

God has promised to believers, men and women, gardens under which rivers flow, to dwell therein, and beautiful mansions in gardens of everlasting bliss. But the greatest bliss is the good pleasure of God: that is the supreme felicity (9:72).

God is with you, and will never put you in loss for your good deeds (47:35).

As for those who have attained faith in Allah and hold fast to Him, He will cause them to enter into His Compassion and His Abundant Blessing and guide them to Himself by a straight way (4:175).

After the difficulty is the easing. After the difficulty is the easing. So when you are finished, strive again and in your Lord aspire (94:5–8).

Any who is grateful does so to the profit of his own soul (31:12).

I listen to the prayer of every supplicant when he calls on Me; let them also, with a will, listen to My call, and believe in Me (2:186).

O my servants who have transgressed against your own souls! Despair not of the Mercy of God: for God forgives all sins: for God is oft-forgiving, most merciful (39:53).

O serene soul, return to your Sustainer, pleased and pleasing in His sight. Join my righteous servants and enter my paradise (89:27–28).

Of everything We have created opposites that you might bear in mind that God alone is one (51:49).

Of knowledge We have given you but a little (17:85).

Remember you implored the assistance of your Sustainer and your God answered you: "I will assist you with a thousand of the angels, rank on ranks" (8:9).

Don't you see that God has made in service to you all that is in the Heavens and on earth and has made His Bounties flow to you in abundant measure, seen and unseen? (31:20).

Allah it is Who makes the night as a robe for you and sleep as repose, and makes every day a resurrection (25:47).

A goodly Word is firmly rooted like a good tree, its branches reaching toward the sky, yielding its fruit at all times by the permission of its Sustainer (14:24–25).

So I call to witness the rosy glow of sunset, the night and its progression and the moon as it grows into fullness: surely you shall travel from stage to stage (84:16–19).

The blessing from the Presence of God is better than any amusement or bargain! (62:11).

To God we belong and to God we are returning (2:156).

Verses of humility, inspiration, and personal responsibility

Assuredly the creation of the heavens and the earth is a greater matter than the creation of humanity, yet most people understand not (40:57).

Truly, you can never rend the earth asunder nor can you rival the mountains in stature (17:37).

The human being can have nothing but that for which he strives (53:39).

Be just; this is closest to God consciousness (5:8).

Do what is beautiful. God loves those who do what is beautiful (2:195).

Enjoy the beautiful things of this life, but do not transgress the bounds of what is right (5:87).

Good deeds, the fruit of which endures forever, are best in the sight of your Sustainer and yield the best return (19:76).

Truly those who have faith and do righteous deeds will the Most Gracious endow with love (19:96–97).

Strive with one another in doing good. Your goal is God (5:48).

The likeness of those who spend their substance, seeking to please God and to strengthen their souls, is as a garden, high and fertile (2:265).

Truly, human beings are in loss except those who have faith and do righteous deeds and encourage each other in the teaching of truth and of patient
perseverance (103:1–3).

Truly, the most highly regarded of you in the sight of God is the one who
does the most good (49:13).

Wealth and children are adornments of the present world: but the abiding
things, the deeds of righteousness, are better with God in reward and better in hope (18:46).

Who is it that will loan to God a beautiful loan? For God will increase it
manifold to his credit, and he will have besides a liberal reward (57:11).

It is better to blush in this world than in the next (hadith).

When you were born, everyone was laughing but you were crying. Live your
life so that when you die, everyone is crying, but you are laughing (hadith).

Bedouin: Should I tether my camel or trust in God alone? Muhammad:
First tether your camel, then trust in God (hadith).

Even if the religious judge advises you about worldly affairs, first consult
your heart (hadith).

Your body has a right over you, your soul has a right over you, and your
family and wife have a right over you. So give everyone the right it has over
you (hadith).

Do good deeds according to your capacity. God does not grow tired of giving rewards unless you tire of doing good. The good deeds most loved by
God are those that are done regularly, even if they are small (hadith).

Verses about divine beauty and compassion

To God belong the most beautiful names (59:24).

Whatever is in the heavens and on earth extols the limitless glory of God
(62:1).

Are you not aware that it is God Whose limitless glory all creatures in the heavens and on earth praise, even the birds as they outspread their wings? (24:41–42).

Even if all the trees on earth were pens, and the oceans ink, backed up by seven more oceans, the Words of God would not be exhausted (31:27).

Allah has spread out the earth as a carpet for you so you may walk therein on spacious paths (20:53).

Adore your Sustainer . . . who has made the earth your couch, and the heavens your canopy; and sent down rain from the heavens, and brought forth therewith fruits for your sustenance (2:21–22).

To you have We bestowed the Source of Abundance. Therefore turn to your Sustainer in Prayer and Sacrifice (108:1–2).

Allah is the Lord of Grace unbounded (2:105).

My mercy encompasses all things (7:156).

For men and women who surrender themselves to God . . . and for men and women who remember God unceasingly, for them God has readied forgiveness and a supreme recompense (33:35).

As for those who have attained faith in Allah and hold fast to Him, He will cause them to enter into His Compassion and His Abundant Blessing and guide them to Himself by a straight way (4:173).

O my servants who have transgressed against your own souls! Despair not of the Mercy of God: for God forgives all sins: for God is oft-forgiving, most merciful (39:53).

I listen to the prayer of every supplicant when he calls on Me; let them also, with a will, listen to My call, and believe in Me (2:186).

I was a secret Treasure and I longed to be known. So I created the worlds visible and invisible (hadith).

Verses about opening the heart and spiritual surrender

Bow in adoration and draw closer (96:19).

Celebrate the praises of God, and do this often; and glorify God morning and evening (33:42).

O my Sustainer! Open for me my heart! (20:25).

O my Sustainer, increase me in knowledge! (20:114).

Seeking only the Face of Thy Sustainer most High, that one will know peace of mind (92:20–21).

Do not sell your bond with God for so paltry a price (16:95).

God does not change the condition of a people unless they change what is in their hearts (13:11).

God draws to Himself those who are willing and guides to Himself everyone who turns to Him (42:13).

If one desires the rewards of this world, let him remember that with God are the rewards of both this world and the life to come (4:134).

Indeed, those who submit themselves to Allah, while doing good, will have their reward with Allah (2:112).

For men and women who surrender themselves to God . . . and for men and women who remember God unceasingly, for them God has readied forgiveness and a supreme recompense (33:35).

Die before you die (hadith).

Fountains of knowledge in the heart will gush out of the tongue of that person who dedicates himself wholly to God for forty days (hadith).

I am He and He is I, except that I am I and He is He (hadith).

I cannot be contained in the space of the earth, I cannot be contained in the space of the heavens, but I can be contained in the space of the pure loving heart of my servant (hadith qudsi).

Keep your tongue forever moistened with the name of Allah (hadith).

Move from knowledge of the tongue to knowledge of the heart (hadith).

O God, make me see things as they really are (hadith).

O God, O Turner of Hearts, turn our hearts towards Thee (hadith).

Take one step towards God, and God takes seven steps toward you; walk to God, and God comes running to you (hadith qudsi).

The freshness of my eyes is given to me in prayer (hadith).

The heart of the believer is between two fingers of the Merciful, Who turns it wherever He desires (hadith).

The oil is already in the lamp; the teacher kindles the light (hadith).

Worship as if you can see God, and if you cannot see God, know that God sees you (hadith).

Verses about human relationships and social responsibility

O mankind! We created you from a single pair of a male and female, and made you into nations and tribes, that you may know each other (49:13).

Make room for one another in your collective life; do make room; God makes room for you (58:11).

It is God Who has created you from one soul and out of it brought into being a mate, so that man might incline with love towards woman (7:189).

Repel the evil deed with the one that is better. Then lo! He with whom you shared enmity will become as though he was a bosom friend (41:34).

The servants of God most Gracious are those who walk on the earth in humility, and when the ignorant address them, they say, "Peace!" (25:63).

We believe in God and what has been sent down to us, what has been revealed to Abraham and Ismael and Isaac and Jacob and their offspring and what was given to Moses and Jesus and all other Prophets by the Creator, and we make no distinction between them (2:136).

We have made some of you as a trial for others: will you have patience? (25:20).

There is no animal on the earth, nor a bird that flies with its two wings, but they are communities like your own (6:38).

The character of a *wali* (a friend of God) is based upon nothing more than graciousness and generosity (hadith).

Have compassion on yourself and on others, and infinite compassion will be given to you (hadith).

I remember every devotee who remembers Me, but I remember even better when devotees remember Me in a group (hadith qudsi).

If a man gives up quarrelling when he is in the wrong, a house will be built for him in Paradise. But if a man gives up a conflict even when he is in the right, a house will be built for him in the loftiest realm of Paradise (hadith).

When a man gazes at his wife and she gazes at him, God looks at them both with a gaze that is compassion and mercy (hadith).

Paradise lies at the feet of your mother (hadith).

When an orphan cries, the throne of God shakes (hadith).

Your body has a right over you, your soul has a right over you, and your family and wife have a right over you. So give everyone the right it has over you (hadith).

When one of My servants is ill, you will find Me with him. When you offer him food and drink, you are offering them to Me (hadith qudsi).

Whosoever of you sees an evil action, let him change it with his hands; and if he is not able to do so, then with his tongue; and if he is not able to do that, then with his heart—and that is the weakest of faith (hadith).

APPENDIX III
The Ninety-Nine Beautiful Names of Allah[1]

Ar-Rahman—the All Merciful

Ar-Rahim—the All Beneficent

Al-Malik—Absolute Ruler, Sovereign of the Universe

Al-Quddus—the Holy One; the Pure One

As-Salaam—the Source of Peace

Al-Mu'min—Inspirer and Guardian of Faith

Al-Muhaymin—the Protector

Al-'Aziz—the Victorious, the Unconquerable

Al-Jabbar—the Compeller, the One who repairs and completes

Al-Mutakabbir—the Greatest, the Majestic

Al-Khaliq—the Creator

Al-Bari'—the One who creates all things in proportion

Al-Musawwir—the Fashioner, the One who designs all things

Al-Ghaffar—the Forgiver, the One who accepts repentance

Al-Qahhar—the Subduer

Al-Wahhab—the Bestower, the Giver of all

Ar-Razzaq—the Sustainer, the Provider

---

[1] Sources: Tosun Bayrak, *The Most Beautiful Names*; Shems Friedlander, *Ninety-Nine Names of Allah*; and Neil Douglas-Klotz, *The Sufi Book of Life*.

Al-Fattah—the Opener, the One who solves all problems and eliminates all obstacles

Al-'Alim—the All-Knowing

Al-Qabid—the Constrictor, the One who restrains excesses

Al-Basit—the Expander, the One who grants abundance and ease

Al-Khafid—the Abaser, the One who teaches humility

Ar-Rafi—the Exalter, the One who uplifts

Al-Mu'izz—the Bestower of Honors

Al-Mudhill (Al-Muzill)—the Humbler

As-Sami—the All-Hearing

Al-Basir—the All-Seeing

Al-Hakam—the Judge

Al-'Adl—the Just One

Al-Latif—the Subtle One, the One who knows the delicate meaning of everything

Al-Khabir—the All-Aware, the One who knows every secret

Al-Halim—the All-Forbearing, slow to punish

Al-'Azim—the Magnificent

Al-Ghafur—the All-Forgiving and Hider of Faults

Ash-Shakur—the Rewarder of Thankfulness

Al-'Ali—the Most High

Al-Kabir—the Greatest

Al-Hafiz—the Preserver

Al-Muqit—the Nourisher

Al-Hasib—the Reckoner, the Accounter

Al-Jalil—the Mighty, the Sublime One

Al-Karim—the Generous One

Ar-Raqib—the Watchful One

Al-Mujib—the One Who Responds to Prayer

Al-Wasi—the All-Encompassing, the All-Comprehending

Al-Hakim—the Wise

Al-Wadud—the Loving

Al-Majid—the Most Majestic and Glorious

Al-Ba'ith—the Resurrector, the One who raises from the dead

Ash-Shahid—the Witness

Al-Haqq—the Ultimate Truth, the One whose existence never changes

Al-Wakil—the Trustee, the One who solves all problems and completes all work

Al-Qawi—the Strongest, the Inexhaustible

Al-Matin—the Forceful One, perfect in strength and firmness

Al-Wali—the Friend and Protector

Al-Hamid—the Most Praiseworthy

Al-Muhsi—the Appraiser, the possessor of all quantitative knowledge

Al-Mubdi—the Originator of all that is

Al-Mu'id—the Restorer

Al-Muhyi—the Giver of Life

Al-Mumit—the Taker of Life, the Creator of Death

Al-Hayy—the Perfectly Alive Eternal One

Al-Qayyum—the Ever Self-Existing One

Al-Wajid—the Finder

Al-Majid—the Noble, the Most Glorious

Al-Wahid—the Unique, the Only One

Al-Ahad—the One, the Unity in Whom all else is united

As-Sammad—the Satisfier of All Needs

Al-Qadir—the All-Powerful

Al-Muqtadir—the Creator of All Power

Al-Muqqadim—the Expediter, the One who causes success and advancement

Al-Mu'akhkhir—the Delayer, the One who postpones success

Al-Awwal—the First

Al-Akhir—the Last

Az-Zahir—the Manifest One

Al-Batin—the Hidden One

Al-Waali—the Governor of Creation

Al-Muta'ali—the Supreme One

Al-Barr—the Doer of Good

At-Tawwab—the Guide to Repentance

Al-Muntaqim—the Great Avenger

Al-'Afu—the Forgiver, the Eliminator of sins

Ar-Ra'uf—the All-Clement

Malik Al-Mulk—the Owner of all

Dhul-Jalali Wal-Ikram—the God of Majesty and Bounty

Al-Muqsit—the Equitable One

Al-Jami'—the Gatherer, the One who brings together all that is dispersed

Al-Ghani—the Rich One, the Self-Sufficient

Al-Mughni—the Enricher

Al-Mani'—the Preventer of Harm

Ad-Darr—Creator of Evil

An-Nafi'—Creator of Good

An-Nur—the Light

Al-Hadi—the Guide

Al-Badi'—the Originator of creation

Al-Baqi—the Everlasting One

Al-Warith—the Inheritor of All

Ar-Rashid—the Righteous Teacher

As-Sabur—the Most Patient One

Bibliography

Aland, Kurt. *The Greek New Testament.* Stuttgart: UBS, 2007.

Ali, Abdullah Yusuf. *The Holy Qur'an: Text, Translation, and Commentary.* Elmhurst, N.Y.: Tahrike Tarsile Qur'an, Inc., 2002.

Asad, Muhammad. *The Message of the Qur'an.* Gibraltar: Dar Al-Andalus, 1980, 1984.

Attar, Farid ud-Din. *The Conference of the Birds.* (Translated by Afkham Darbandi and Dick Davis.) New York: Penguin, 1984.

Barks, Coleman with John Moyne. *The Essential Rumi.* Edison, N.J.: Castle Books, 1997.

Bayrak, Tosun. *The Most Beautiful Names.* Putney, Vt.: Threshold, 1985.

Bernard of Clairvaux. *On the Love of God.* In John A. Hardon, *The Treasury of Catholic Wisdom.* San Francisco: Ignatius, 1995.

Bialik, Hayim Hahman and Yehoshua Hana Ravnitzky (editors). *The Book of Legends (Sefer Ha-Aggadah): Legends from the Talmud and Midrash.* New York: Schocken, 1992.

Cordovero, Moses. *Tomer Deborah (The Palm Tree of Deborah).* In: Raphael Ben Zion, *Anthology of Jewish Mysticism.* New York: Judaica, 1981.

Cowan, James. *Rumi's Divan of Shems of Tabriz.* Dorset, U.K.: Element Books Ltd., 1997.

Crossan, John Dominic. *In Parables: The Challenge of the Historical Jesus.* New York: Harper and Row, 1973.

Division of Christian Education of the National Council of the Churches of Christ in the United States of America. *New Revised Standard Version Bible*, Anglicized Edition. Oxford: Oxford University Press, 1995.

Douglas-Klotz, Neil. *The Sufi Book of Life*. New York: Penguin, 2005.

Eliach, Yaffa. *Hasidic Tales of the Holocaust*. New York: Oxford University Press, 1982.

Eskenazi, Tamara Cohn and Andrea L. Weiss (editors). *The Torah: A Women's Commentary*. New York: URJ Press, 2008.

Esposito, John L. and Dalia Mogahed. *Who Speaks for Islam? What a Billion Muslims Really Think*. New York: Gallup, 2008.

Fishbane, Michael. *Sacred Attunement: A Jewish Theology*. Chicago: University of Chicago Press, 2008.

Friedlander, Shems. *Ninety-Nine Names of Allah*. Singapore: Graham Brash, 1980.

Friedman, Richard Elliott. *Commentary on the Torah*. New York: Harper-Collins, 2003.

Gallagher, Nora. *Practicing Resurrection: A Memoir of Work, Doubt, Discernment, and Moments of Grace*. New York: Knopf, 2003.

Griffin, Emilie. *Turning: Reflections on the Experience of Conversion*. Garden City, N.J.: Doubleday, 1980.

Helminski, Camille Adams. *The Light of Dawn: A Daybook of Verses from the Holy Quran*. Brattleboro, Vt.: Threshold, 1998.

Helminski, Kabir. *The Book of Revelations*. Watsonville, Calif.: The Book Foundation, 2005.

Helminski, Kabir (editor). *The Rumi Collection*. Boston: Shambhala, 1999.

Heschel, Abraham Joshua. *I Asked for Wonder*. New York: Crossroad, 1986.

Hoffman, Edward. *The Wisdom of Maimonides*. Boston: Shambhala, 2008.

Johnson, James W. and J. Rosamund. *The Books of the American Negro Spirituals*. New York: DaCapo, 2002.

Johnson, James Weldon. *God's Trombones*. New York: Penguin, 1990.

Jewish Publication Society. *Hebrew-English Tanakh*. Philadelphia: JPS, 1999.

Kravitz, Leonard and Kerry M. Olitzky (editors). *Pirke Avot: A Modern Commentary on Jewish Ethics*. New York: UAHC Press, 1993.

Kushner, Rabbi Lawrence. *The River of Light: Jewish Mystical Awareness*. Woodstock, Vt.: Jewish Lights, 2000.

Ladinsky, Daniel. *The Gift: Poems by Hafiz*. New York: Penguin/Arkakna, 1999.

Ladinsky, Daniel. *The Subject Tonight is Love: 60 Wild and Sweet Poems of Hafiz*. New York: Penguin, 1996.

Lewis, C. S. *The Last Battle*. New York: Harper Collins, 1994.

Merrill, Nan. *Psalms for Praying*. New York: Continuum, 2002.

Nasr, Seyyed Hossein. *Islamic Spirituality* Vol. I, *World Spirituality*. New York: Herder & Herder, 1991.

Nurbakhsh, Javad. *Traditions of the Prophet*. London: Khanigahi Nimatullahi, 1981.

Orwell, George. *Animal Farm*. New York: Signet, 1990.

Plaut, W. Gunther (editor). *The Torah: A Modern Commentary*. New York: Union for Reform Judaism, 2006.

Rabbinical Assembly, the United Synagogue of Conservative Judaism. *Etz Hayim: Torah and Commentary*. New York: Jewish Publication Society, 2001.

Schwartz, Howard. *Gates to the New City: A Treasury of Modern Jewish Tales*. New York: Jason Aronson, 1991.

Smith, Martin L. *Reconciliation: Preparing for Confession in the Episcopal Church*. Cambridge, Mass., 1985.

Tagore, Rabindranath. *Fireflies*. New York: Macmillan, 1955.

The Book of Common Prayer. New York: Oxford, 1990.

Walsh, James (translator). *The Revelations of Divine Love of Julian of Norwich*. St. Meinrad, Ind.: Abbey, 1975.

Wiesel, Elie. *Messengers of God*. New York: Summit, 1976.

Winston, Kimberly. *Bead One, Pray Too: A Guide to Making and Using Prayer Beads*. Harrisburg, Penn.: Morehouse, 2008.